Original text by Sally Roy and Josephine Quintero
Revised and updated by Lucy Ratcliffe

Edited, designed and produced by AA Publishing, a trading name
of AA Media Limited, whose registered office is Fanum House,
Basing View, Basingstoke, Hampshire RG21 4EA. Registered
number 06112600.

Published in the United States by AAA Publishing,
1000 AAA Drive, Heathrow, Florida 32746.
Published in the United Kingdom by AA Publishing.

ISBN 978-1-59508-436-1

Cover design and binding style by permission of AA Publishing
Color separation by AA Digital Department
Printed and bound in China by Leo Paper Products

A04413
Maps in this title produced from mapping © MAIRDUMONT/
Falk Verlag 2011
Transport map © Communicarta Ltd, UK

SPIRALGUIDE

Travel With Someone You Trust®

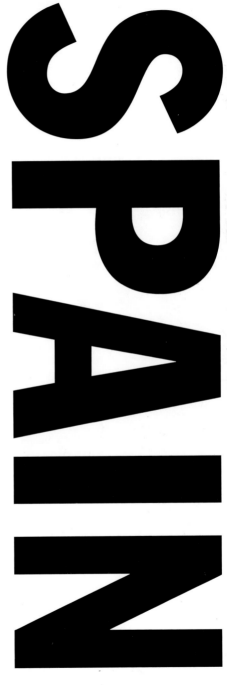

SPAIN

Contents

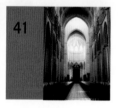

The Magazine

A great holiday is more than just lying on a beach or shopping till you drop – to really get the most from your trip you need to know what makes the place tick. The Magazine provides an entertaining overview to some of the social, cultural and natural elements that make up the unique character of this engaging country.

SPANISH REGIONALISM:
PARTS OF A WHOLE

Spaniards rarely see themselves as Spanish: they're from Madrid, or they're Catalan, or Andalusian, or Galician, or Basque... This regionalism is a fundamental part of the Spanish psyche and essential for an understanding of the county.

Spain is a huge nation covering 195,000sq km (75,290sq miles), with vast, sparsely populated plains, high mountain ranges and coasts lapped by different seas. The northeast of the country is attached to southern Europe while the southern coast is only a few kilometres from Africa. No wonder then that the regional divides are strong.

¿SE HABLA ESPAÑOL?

Autonomy has hugely encouraged the importance of the country's regional languages and the number of people that speak them.

Basque One of the world's most obscure languages, Basque has no apparent linguistic links with any other tongue. Signs and notices throughout the Basque country are in Basque, and it's worth checking up on place names in particular if you're touring. Remembering that Castilian "ch" becomes "tx","k" replaces "c", "y" is "i" and "v" is "b" may help.

Catalan Catalan is perhaps the most radically promoted of the country's regional languages. Schoolchildren learn almost entirely in Catalan. All menus, street signs, tourist information and public notices by law must be in Catalan; the obligatory Castilian translation is often nowhere to be seen. Descended from Latin, Catalan is closer to French and Italian than Castilian.

Galician Galician *(Gallego)* is widely spoken in Galicia, with some small communities speaking nothing else, and is used on road signs, notices and museum information. It sounds like a fusion of Portuguese and Castilian, and has its own body of literature. There are lots of Xs, pronounced "sh", instead of Castilian Gs, Js and Ss; "l" becomes "r", "la" is "a" and "el" is "o".

Valencian This is used throughout València for street signs and general information. To outsiders, Valencian has many similarities with Catalan, though the Valencians would disagree.

GALICIA

Regional Identity

There's a vast gulf between a fiery, fine-boned Andalusian, all passion and *joie de vivre*, and a sombre, hard-working Galician, moulded by grey skies and wet weather. Catalans see themselves as more European than Spanish whilst Castilians are proud of their role at the physical and historical centre of the country.

Shaped by History

And it is history that has probably had the strongest influence on the regional divides. Arabic influences are strongest in the south, where the Moorish occupation lasted longest. The north was more directly affected by the sporadic wars with France and the Low Countries that lasted for over 200 years. Catalonia and the Basque Country benefited most from the industrial revolution at the turn of the 20th century.

However, it is the legacy of General Franco's 40 years of dictatorship that has had the strongest effect on Spanish regionalism. To strengthen his regime's central control, Franco banned local languages and all representations of regional pride, including folk celebrations, were outlawed. After his death, with the creation of the *autonomías* (▶ panel, below) the pride, rediscovery and celebration of regional identity and language have flowered, albeit at the expense of a national identity.

THE AUTONOMÍAS

Under the Spanish Constitution of 1978, 17 autonomous regions were granted a large degree of self-rule – their own presidents, parliaments and civil administrations. Established partly as a backlash against Franco's repressive centralization, the *autonomías* have proved a bit of a mixed blessing. While undoubtedly helping to contain the more aggressive forms of nationalism, autonomy has given Catalonia (Catalunya) and the Basque region considerable clout in Madrid, where they held the balance of political power for much of the last two decades at the expense of central government.

SPANISH HISTORY: INVASION, REVOLUTION AND PRIDE

A bridge between Europe and Africa, between Europe and the Americas, Spain has a complicated history of invading and being invaded. From the Arabic names you'll find throughout the peninsula to obstinate regional pride, a little background will help put Spain's extraordinary heritage into context.

Early Beginnings

Native Iberian peoples are some of the earliest European settlements recorded dating from 800,000BC. Invasions from Phoenicians, Carthaginians and Greeks setting up trading posts were followed by Romans in the first century AD, who in turn were ousted around the sixth century by the Visigoths coming over the Pyrenees.

The Moors and the Reconquista

In 711, Moors swept through Spain via North Africa, the start of an era that was to last in places for more than 700 years. Córdoba rose to pre-eminence and became the capital of the Western Islamic Empire. This independent Arab state, or caliphate, enjoyed widespread unity from the 10th to mid-11th centuries, a period considered to be the great age of Moorish Spain. The occupation was largely peaceful, with tolerance and assimilation on both sides. From the 1040s onwards the power of the Cordoban caliphate disintegrated into smaller independent states, called *taifas*. Their internal struggles were instrumental in helping the Reconquista, the Catholic re-conquest of the country. From the ninth century the Moors were gradually driven south and in 1492, the last stronghold, Granada, fell to the Catholic Monarchs Ferdinand and Isabella. In the same year, Christopher Columbus, sponsored by the Spanish crown, discovered the New World and its seemingly infinite riches.

The Golden Age

During the 16th century, Spain was united under the rule of Habsburg monarchs. In 1519, Charles I became Holy Roman Emperor, taking the title of Charles V and bringing immense power and wealth to Spain from all over Europe and South America. In 1561, Philip II made the geographical centre of the country, Madrid, the capital too. The era saw a great flourishing in Spanish art and literature. But it was set against a background of economic unrest and ruinous wars across Europe.

Invasion and More Wars

In 1700, Habsburg king Charles II died without an heir. The Spanish crown passed to Philip of Anjou, a member of the Bourbon dynasty – but not without a fight. Europe became embroiled in the Wars of Spanish Succession (1701–14). Spain went on to lose many of its territories abroad and fell under French influence being drawn into the Napoleonic Wars in the early 19th century. The War of Independence or the Peninsular War (1808–14) was a struggle against French domination and typified the century's opposition to, and revolts against, the monarchy.

Civil War, Dictatorship and Democracy

Neutral in World War I, Spain spent the first decades of the 20th century struggling with political unrest and crippling strikes before succumbing to Civil War in 1936. Fought between well-equipped fascist Nationalists (with military support from Mussolini and Hitler) and Republicans (in an uneasy alliance with national and international Communists and Anarchists), the three-year war was one of the bloodiest and most bitter in modern history.

It was followed by 40 years of repressive dictatorship under General Franco and isolation from the rest of Europe. His death in 1975 saw the beginning of democratic peace for Spain with King Juan Carlos I declared a constitutional monarch. The establishment of the *autonomías* (► 7) gave a voice and real power to the regions.

Modern Spain

Reintegration into European and indeed world politics has followed. Spain joined the European Union in 1986 and adopted the Euro as its currency in 2001. Tragically, the bombing of Madrid commuter trains by Islamic fundamentalists in 2004 confirmed its place on the world stage.

Top left: The historic meeting between Christopher Columbus and Queen Isabella

Fiesta!

WHERE AND WHEN

Local tourist offices and websites have details of what's on when in their areas. For major festivals, you'll need to reserve accommodation well in advance. The biggest ones are:

- **Carnival** Everywhere in Spain stages pre-Lenten festivities, with those in Cádiz and Sitges being the best known, February–March.
- **Fallas de San José** València, March.
- **Semana Santa** Celebrated everywhere, but best in Seville, Málaga, Córdoba, Granada and throughout Castile, March–April.
- **Feria Seville**, April.
- **San Isidro Madrid**, mid-May.
- **Romería del Roció Huelva**, Whit week.
- **Fiesta de San Fermín**, Pamplona (Iruñea), July.
- **Fiesta de Santiago**, Santiago de Compostela, July.
- **Mysteri d'Elx**, Elx (Elche), August.
- **La Mercè**, Barcelona, September.

No matter how big or small, every Spanish community devotes at least one day a year to staging the biggest, noisiest, best fiesta it can afford. These festivals are the perfect antidote to cultural overdose and a great way to get an inkling of what makes Spaniards tick.

Religious Celebrations

Every festival is different, but there are some common strands underlying the celebrations. Most of the biggest fiestas have their origins in the key points of the Christian year – Lent and Easter, or individual feast days dedicated to the Virgin or an important saint. Fiestas are mainly focused around processions or parades, which can be a highly charged religious experience or a riotously uproarious display with giant carnival figures, bands and fireworks. Apart from the pre-Easter processions of Semana Santa (Holy Week), all festivals are imbued with an atmosphere of communal rejoicing – helped along by music, dance, food and drink.

Regional Pride

These are occasions for people to celebrate their identities and re-affirm their local cultures – so you'll see regional flags and traditional costume, while the music, food, drink and activities are equally specific to the area. Fiestas are celebrations of being part of a community and sharing a common history and culture. They are for the Spanish, but everyone's welcome, outsiders being swept along and caught up in the experience.

Respect and Revelry

The form of celebration depends on where you are and what's being celebrated. The whole of Spain is out on the streets for Carnival, when there are parades with giant figures and sumptuous floats, a massive splurge before Lent. The gloom deepens during the Easter Week processions, parades of heavy religious tableaux carried by hooded penitents atoning for their sins. This is followed by the celebrations marking Corpus Christi, a religious feast celebrating the Sacred Host. From now on it's a joyous litany of fun throughout spring and summer, as communities all over the country celebrate in their different ways. Some regions celebrate with week-long festivities and folk music, others concentrate on local produce; you could celebrate the rice crop at a paella competition or the tomato glut in a messy tomato-throwing parade.

Wherever you are, ask around to identify the big events – the memory of an entire town feasting in the main plaza, the scream and thumps of spectacular fireworks and the staccato rhythms of guitar, drums and bagpipes may be among the best memories you'll take home from Spain.

Let the festivities begin: the opening ceremony of Pamplona's annual San Fermín fiesta

A Taste of Spain

In a global food market, Spanish cooking manages to stay true to its own local and seasonal produce. This means that like all things in Spain, food is highly regional. At its best, Spanish food is a marriage of fresh local ingredients and perfectly timed, simple cooking.

Basque cooking concentrates on rich fish dishes, such as *shangurro* (stuffed king crab) and squid in ink sauce but is perhaps even more famous for its *pintxos* – bite-sized tapas skewered with a cocktail stick and chosen from the bar in front of you. Due east, Catalonia is known for mixing *mar i muntanya* (surf and turf) ingredients and for adding dried fruits like raisins and apricots to create many unusual combinations.

In the interior of Spain, in Madrid, Castile and La Mancha you find the best roast meats, in particular *cochinillo* (suckling pig); as well as *migas*, a poor man's mainstay of breadcrumbs cooked in dripping and served with grapes, and *cocido*, a filling chickpea and sausage stew.

In València eating rice is a way of life. This is the home of paella, with dozens of variations, including meat, fish, snails or vegetables; *fideuá* is a similar dish made with short noodles instead of rice. Further south, cooling gazpacho and fried fish and seafood are native to Andalucía.

Jamón and Tortilla

Several dishes are found throughout the country, most notably Spain's famous *jamón* (dried ham) – at its best in *jamón de bellota* from acorn-fed free-range pigs. Chorizo (spicy sausage) and *morcilla* (blood sausage), too, make the most of the nation's prized pig community. Deliciously thick *tortilla de patatas* (Spanish omelette) is usually ordered by the slice (*un pincho*). Pulses are also popular everywhere especially chickpeas served in salads or with seafood or lentils, which are frequently cooked with diced ham.

Salads and Vegetables

Fresh vegetables are relatively side-lined in Spain but you will find red and green peppers, spinach and beans offered in various guises. Mixed salads

Fresh fruit and vegetables piled high at Barcelona's La Boqueria market. The market is renowned for the quality of its produce and many chefs source ingredients here

tend to include everything under the sun. If you're vegetarian or vegan, outside the main cities, you may need to be prescriptive with your orders requesting "*sin jamón, carne, pescado, huevos o productos lácteos*" (without ham, meat, fish, eggs or milk products).

Desserts

If you're looking for a culinary symbol of the country's unity, however, you'll find *flan* (crème caramel) and *arroz con leche* (cold rice pudding) on dessert menus the length and breadth of the country.

BEST FOOD MARKETS

The local market is still a very important part of food shopping for many Spaniards. The central markets in several of the country's cities are experiences in their own right. Wonderful for a stroll simply to take in the sights and smells, they are also great for buying produce to take home or to put together a picnic for a nearby park or beach.

■ Mercado Antón Martín (► 63), Mercado de San Miguel (► 63), Madrid
■ Mercat de la Boqueria, Barcelona (► 117)
■ Mercado Central, València (► 145)
■ Mercado Central, Alicant (Alicante) (► 150)
■ Mercado de Abastos, Santiago de Compostela (► 92–94)

Architecture IN SPAIN

The fabric of towns and cities throughout the country bear witness to Spain's turbulent history. Some cities' architectural riches date neatly from one epoch, other places have a glorious and heady mix.

Roman

Roman architectural style (first century BC to fifth century AD) was similar all over the Empire, and was typified by solid stonework and classic proportions. Monumental public constructions such as aqueducts, theatres and arches are some of the best remaining examples.

Romanesque

The harmonious rounded arches and solid forms that epitomize Romanesque architecture (eighth to 13th centuries) came from Italy to Catalonia, and from France over the Pyrenees and along the pilgrim route to Santiago de Compostela (➤ 26–27).

Moorish

The legacy of Moorish rule in Spain (eighth to 15th centuries) is an architectural highlight of the country. The three main surviving building types are mosques, *alcázares* (palaces) and *alcazabas* (fortified castles) with their unmistakeable horseshoe arches, intricate plasterwork, and red-and-white brick and stonework. Moorish architects also incorporated water into their designs, either for Islamic ritual washing in mosques, or as a cooling architectural element in courtyards and gardens.

Gaudí's ceramic-clad Casa Batlló, a masterpiece of Modernista architecture, is one of three buildings that make up the Manzana de la Discordia in Barcelona

Gothic

Spain's most impressive cathedrals are Gothic (12th to 16th centuries), huge structures with no transept, a single nave and pointed stone arches. In time, they became bigger and lavish stone decoration became a feature, a style known as Isabelline. Mudejar is the name given to work carried out by Moors in the Christian-occupied parts of the country after the Reconquest.

Renaissance and Plateresque

Early Spanish Renaissance architecture (16th century) is called plateresque, because its ornate stone decoration is reminiscent of silverwork. The style drew on the harmonious proportions of Italian architecture but gave it a distinctly Spanish twist.

Baroque

In the 17th and 18th centuries, architects began looking for ways to soften the austerity of the classical lines, adopting sweeping lines and forms and adding increasingly lavish decoration known as baroque. This reached its apogee in the Churrigueresque style with its twisted columns and extravagant stonework.

Modernism

Modernism emerged in Catalonia towards the end of the 19th century, a home-grown, ebullient art nouveau style that used a mixture of modern materials and organic forms, with hardly a straight line to be seen. One of the main exponents was Antoni Gaudí, whose work has become synonymous with the city of Barcelona.

Contemporary Architecture

The latter part of the 20th century saw an extraordinary flowering in Spanish contemporary architecture with a particular stylish approach to marrying the old with the new. There is quality contemporary architecture in small villages and large cities throughout the country but it is the striking signature buildings that really draw the crowds.

WHERE TO SEE THE BEST

- **Roman** Mérida (➤ 148), Tarragona (➤ 130), Segovia (➤ 72–73).
- **Romanesque** Along the Camino de Santiago (➤ 26–28), Santiago de Compostela (➤ 92–94), Salamanca (➤ 74–77).
- **Moorish and Mudejar** Córdoba (➤ 164–165), Seville (➤ 160–163), Granada (➤ 166–168).
- **Gothic and Isabelline** León (➤ 78–79), Burgos (➤ 70–71), Toledo (➤ 140–142), Seville (➤ 160–163), Segovia (➤ 72–73), Salamanca (➤ 74–77).
- **Renaissance and plateresque** Salamanca (➤ 74–77), Burgos (➤ 70–71), Toledo (➤ 140–142), Granada (➤ 166–168), El Escorial (➤ 58).
- **Baroque** Salamanca (➤ 74–77), Madrid (➤ 41–57), Santiago de Compostela (➤ 92–94).
- **Modernism** Barcelona (➤ 108–130)
- **Contemporary** Ciutat de les Arts i les Ciències, València (➤ 145–146), Museo Guggenheim Bilbao (➤ 99–100), Madrid's art galleries, La Rioja (➤ 80).

Art's SUPERSTARS

Although on the periphery of European culture for centuries, Spain has produced an enviable collection of artists. Many of those from the 20th century in particular have become household names throughout the world. In the major cities, spectacular art galleries attract visitors throughout the year.

Artistic Influences

Unlike some countries, Spanish painting developed in fits and starts, producing peaks rather than a smooth progression of stylistic growth. Catalonia was dominant in Gothic art, its painters relying heavily on Flanders and the International Gothic school. Other painters such as the Berruguete father and son studied abroad and borrowed stylistically from both Italy and the north. However, it took a foreigner working in Toledo, Domenicos Theotocopoulos (1541–1614), better known as El Greco, to forge one of the first quintessentially Spanish styles epitomized in his highly personal, spiritual canvases.

The Old Masters

Next in line, Diego Velázquez (1599–1660) is one of the giants of Spanish art, whose piercingly searching court portraits are some of the finest ever painted. Contemporaneously, Francisco de Zurbarán (1598–1664) was brilliantly illustrating monastic life, while his fellow-Sevillian Bartolomé Esteban Murillo (1618–82) painted sweet Madonnas and street children, popular all over Europe. The second half of the 18th century through to

the 1820s was overshadowed by the work of Francisco Goya (1746–1828), a prolific genius whose paintings covered a wide range of subjects and style bearing witness to both the nation's and his own personal struggles at one of the harshest times in Spain's history.

El Greco's masterful painting *The Holy Family wih St Anne and the Young St John the Baptist*

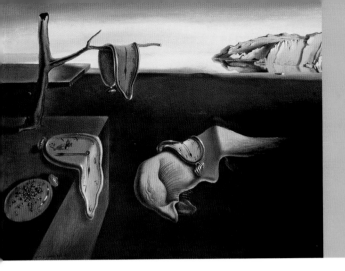

Surrealist painter Salvador Dalí's 1931 work *The Persistence of Memory*

Modern Superstars

Pablo Picasso (1881–1973), co-founder of the Cubist movement, is among the 20th-century Spanish artists to have acquired international superstar status. Born in Malaga, he grew up in Galicia and Barcelona although he lived much of his adult life in self-imposed exile in France. In the popular psyche he is closely followed by the Surrealist painter Salvador Dalí (1904–1989), whose eccentricity became as renowned as his paintings. Another Catalan, whose work revolutionized the international art scene was the painter and sculptor Joan Miró (1893–1983).

More recent names that are worth looking out for include Antonio Saura (1930–1998) and Antoni Tàpies (1923), whilst works by the very different sculptors Eduardo Chillida (1924–2002) and Juan Muñoz (1953–2001) have pride of place in public spaces and galleries around the country – indeed, the world.

GREAT GALLERIES

Spain's art galleries are unmissable. Housed in stunning new or converted buildings they hold fascinating collections to appeal to all tastes:
- Museo del Prado, Madrid (► 50–53)
- Museo Thyssen-Bornemisza, Madrid (► 48–49)
- Museo Nacional Centro de Arte Reina Sofía, Madrid (► 54)
- Museo Guggenheim, Bilbao (► 99)
- Museu Picasso, Barcelona (► 118–119) and Málaga (► 170)
- Fundació Joan Miró, Barcelona (► 123)
- Museu Nacional d'Art de Catalunya, Barcelona (► 123)
- Museo de Arte Abstracto Español, Cuenca (► 144)
- Museo de Bellas Artes, València (► 146)
- Museo de Bellas Artes, Seville (► 162–163)

The big outdoors

Spain's big outdoors is big. Travelling through the country, you'll be surprised at the scale, grandeur and emptiness of the landscape, and impressed by its diversity.

Looking for proper mountains? Try the Pyrenees and the Sierra Nevada. Woods and forests? Discover the oak and beech, pine and fir of northern Spain, the cork and conifers of Andalucía. Glorious coast? Head for the north Atlantic shore, the fjord-like *rías* (inlets) of Galicia, and the wetlands of the eastern coastlines. Whether you want to use it or admire it, Spain's countryside will add a new dimension to your trip.

Back to Nature – Hiking, Walking and Climbing

After Switzerland, Spain is the most mountainous country in Europe. The high grounds are stunning and attract thousands of serious hikers and climbers throughout the summer. The Pyrenees in Catalonia and Aragón, the Cordillera Cantábrica, which runs parallel with the northern coast and includes the Picos de Europa, and the Sierra Nevada in

The magnificent view from Fuente Dé, in the heart of the Picos de Europa, Asturias

the south are the main draws, areas where you can disappear for days, hiking the high trails and sleeping in mountain refuges. All have small towns that act as jump-off points in their foothills, where you can rent equipment, buy excellent maps and guidebooks and plan your route with expert help. Paths and trails are well-marked; the GRs (Grandes Routes, the cross-European walking trails), with their red-and-white markers, guide walkers along the extensive and taxing Pyrenean routes. Serious mountaineers use these to access the demanding climbs of the high tops. These are the areas, also, where you're most likely to see Spain's showiest wild animals – chamois, ibex, red and roe deer, wild boar, even wolves and brown bear, though these last two are adept at keeping themselves hidden.

See it in Comfort

If you'd prefer, there's plenty of superb landscape to admire from the comfort of a vehicle. Roads run well into the Pyrenees, the Picos and the Sierra Nevada, so you can explore some of the high country and dramatic gorges with the minimum of effort. Another great plus in Spain's empty landscape is that even the most humdrum journey will traverse some splendid country, where you can stop to stretch your legs and sniff the clean air as the fancy takes you. Coastal pottering, beach strolls, picnics beside some of the huge inland reservoirs and woodland walks all add a further dimension, and even the longest cross-country drive is enhanced by the frequent sightings of great birds of prey.

IN SEARCH OF WILD FLOWERS

- **Andalucía** Late winter, spring and early summer are the best months for seeing wild flowers, though the Sierra Nevada is at its peak through to July. Winter-flowering iris, squill and coastal and maritime flora can be found along the Atlantic coast, and daffodils, gentians, tulips, peonies, aquilegia in the mountains. There is excellent *matorral* (maquis) vegetation and large cork and pine forests.
- **Pyrenees** Superb upland and alpine flora cloaks the Pyrenees throughout the summer months. Meadows and slopes have huge spreads of spring flowers, including narcissi, pasque-flowers, gentians, lilies, fritillaries; edelweiss and mountain saxifrage can be found at high altitude. There is a wide range of orchid species. Autumn bulbs include cyclamen and crocus.
- **Asturias and Cantabria** Swathes of oak and beech forest are interspersed with meadowland in this area. There are stunning displays of meadow flowers, spring bulbs, peonies, tulips and purple monkshood as well as myriad different orchid species. Late spring is the best time for the mountains, but coastal flowers start earlier in the year.

GREAT PLACES FOR TWITCHERS

■ **The Ebro Delta, Catalonia** The lagoon and wetlands of the Parque Natural del Delta de l'Ebre, with woodlands and rice paddies, are best during the spring and autumn migration seasons. You can see wildfowl such as coot, teal and grebe, plus resident egret, flamingo, avocet and purple heron. Visiting birds include the lapwing, oystercatcher and tern.

■ **Picos de Europa, Asturias** This prime site for mountain birds is best from May to October. Head here for the golden eagle, Bonelli's eagle, griffon vulture and rare mountain species such as chough, snow finch and citril.

■ **Monfragüe Natural Park, Extremadura** To see a wide range of raptors and migrant visitors the best time to visit these wooded hills and gorges is during the summer. Large raptors including the kite, griffon and black vulture; golden, Spanish imperial and Bonelli's eagle; golden oriole, shrike, hoopoe, bee-eater and roller.

■ **Ordesa y Monte Perdido National Park, Aragón** Access to high-altitude birds in the Pyrenees is easiest during the summer months. Ptarmigan, snow finch, chough, eagle owl, vulture, eagle and breeding lammergeier can all be seen here.

Meadow flowers near Brozas, Extremadura. Its diverse terrain and climate mean that many different species of plants flourish in Spain

Costas
UNCOVERED

Whether you fancy taking your bucket and spade, a wetsuit and board, or just a towel, the Spanish coastline has it all. Sun-bleached sands, craggy cliffs and windswept dunes offer an experience far beyond the Costas' reputation of old.

A Grand Plan

In the 1960s, Franco decided to exploit Spain's coastline to attract much-needed foreign income. A few pretty fishing villages, including Benidorm and Lloret de Mar on the Costa Brava and Torremolinos on the Costa del Sol, were chosen. Hotels were built, foreign tourists came and these famous coastlines became synonymous with Spain. But while these resorts continue to provide sun and carefree indulgence to many foreigners, the Spaniards have kept the best for themselves.

Beating the Development

The Costa de la Luz on the southwestern shore of the country is just a hop across the straits from Morocco. Here the sweeping sands of the western

---

BEST OF THE COSTAS

■ **Coasts with good family resorts** Costa Brava (➤ 128), Costa Blanca (➤ 150), Costa del Sol (➤ 170). Or follow the Spanish and try Costa Verde (➤ 95–96), the Rías Baixas (➤ 101) and the Costa de la Luz (➤ 171).

■ **Unspoiled coastlines** Explore the off-the-beaten-track stretches of the Costa Verde (➤ 95–96), Costa da Morte (➤ 101) and Costa de la Luz (➤ 171).

■ **Dance all night** Beyond the Costa Blanca's Benidorm (➤ 150) and Benalmádena on the Costa del Sol (➤ 170), València, (➤ 147), Barcelona (➤ 126) and Gijón (➤ 96) will keep you up till dawn.

■ **Great beaches** Huge sandy expanses along the Costa Blanca (➤ 150), the Costa Vasca and the Costa de la Luz (➤ 171); cliffs and coves on the Costa Brava (➤ 128) and the Costa Verde (➤ 95–96).

■ **Activities** Play golf on the Costa del Sol (➤ 170) and the Costa Blanca (➤ 150); head for the Costa Blanca (➤ 150) and Costa Brava (➤ 128) for water sports and sailing; try the Costa Verde (➤ 95–96) and Costa de la Luz (➤ 171) for some of Europe's best surfing and wind- and kitesurfing.

Clear waters and unspoiled sandy beaches at Galicia's Rías Baixas (Rías Bajas)

end are favoured by Spanish families in the summer months, while the sand-dune beaches around Tarifa are recognized as some of the top spots in the world for wind- and kitesurfing. There are more water sports on offer to the northeast of the country, off the rugged coastline of Costa Brava. The waters here provide fine scuba diving and kayaking. Further south lie the resorts of the Costa Blanca. Although they are overdeveloped, these resorts have infinitely better beaches than the Costa del Sol, good sailing and several nature reserves nearby with lagoons and salt pans, which are ideal for birdwatchers (➤ 21).

Whereas the southern and eastern coasts are lapped by the Mediterranean, the north and northwestern coasts face on to the mighty Atlantic Ocean with its crashing waves and chillier waters. Here the weather is not as reliably warm and dry but in return you get the run of great swathes of white sands, delightful rocky coves and lush, green estuaries. There are working fishing communities, elegant small towns and resorts attracting mainly Spanish and French families. The northern coast is famed too for its surfing while the coastal walks on the windswept headlines of the northwest are unbeatable.

Urban Beaches

Another Spanish speciality is the urban beach. A facelift in preparation for the 1992 Olympics completely refocused Barcelona reclaiming the beaches from light industry, and a similar operation regenerated València for the Americas' Cup in 2007. Cities such as Donostia (San Sebastián), A Coruña (La Coruña), Santander, as well as other smaller beach towns have a longer history of making the most of their location. They all proudly offer combed beaches, clean waters and a vibrant focus for summer nightlife and weekend seafood munching.

Flamenco
and beyond

Flamenco – passionate, sensuous, heart-stopping – is Spain's greatest musical heritage. But it's not the only folk music to be heard, and guitars and castanets by no means epitomize Spanish musical traditions. Spain embraces different peoples, languages and cultures, and their diversity is nowhere better shown than in their music and dance.

Flamenco

Flamenco evolved from the sounds and rhythms of Eastern cultures fusing with Arab and Jewish elements in southern Spain. Its most famous exponents were often gypsies, a people who perhaps more than others could understand the heart-rending mix of pain and joy which is expressed in the most sublime flamenco. It is played, sung and danced, often heard at its best when it occurs spontaneously, late at night in some smoke-filled bar. Its ultimate expression is song, particularly the pain-racked *cante jondo* (deep song), where the singer passionately pours out his soul, inspired and encouraged by the guitars' rhythm and the shouts of the listeners. The lighter side of flamenco is expressed in dance – tangos,

WHERE TO HEAR IT

- **Flamenco** Head for the flamenco clubs or bars, the *tablaos* or *peñas* in Andalucía and Madrid, where you'll hear flamenco properly performed – avoid the tourist-trap "flamenco shows".
- **Catalan music** Catalan pipes and drums accompany all local festivals. There are summer festivals devoted to the South American-influenced *habanero* on the Costa Brava and the Costa Blanca.
- **Galician music** Track it down at live music clubs and summer fiestas. Santiago hosts an annual folklore festival in July.
- **Basque music** For live Basque music, try clubs in Bilbao and throughout the region at festivals – in Asturias there's the Oviedo Folk Festival, where you'll hear the best of Basque and Galician rhythms.

fandangos and *sevillanas* – where the graceful, sinuous body movements contrast with the furious, staccato footwork. Colour and movement, rhythm and sound, and, above all, passion, are flamenco's hallmarks.

An Expression of Identity

Catalan folk music and song was a major force in helping to keep alive the region's culture and spirit during the Franco years. The *sardana*, the Catalan national dance, came to represent a free Catalonia, and still plays an important role in all festivities. Catalan orchestras have their own style, playing traditional dance music with more than a touch of salsa to it – you can hear Spanish America too, in the Cuban-inspired *habanera* songs.

Celtic Pipes and Drums

Folk music is alive and thriving in Galicia, but don't expect guitars; listen instead for pipes and drums and the steady drawl of the bagpipes. Galicians are Celts, and their music has much in common with that of Scotland and Ireland. The *jotas* (folksongs) are foot-tapping and robust, while the melancholy yearning held in common by all Celts manifests itself in the traditional love songs.

Euskadi

At the eastern end of Spain's north coast lies the Basque country, with an equally strong indigenous musical tradition. Here, there's a growing fusion of the traditional wild accordion music, *trikitrixa* (the name means devil's bellows), with Celtic and rock elements – fantastic stuff.

Renowned flamenco guitarist Paco de Lucía

LEGENDS IN THEIR TIME

Flamenco Music
- El Camarón de la Isla
- Paco de Lucía
- Tomatito
- Paco Peña
- La Chanca
- Cristina Hoyos

Catalan Music
- Els Setge Jutges
- Lluís Llach
- Joan Manuel Serrat
- Raímon

Galician Music
- Milladoiro
- Carlos Nuñez
- Palla Mallada
- Matto Congrio
- Xorima

Basque Music
- Josepa Tapia
- Kepa Junkera
- Ruper Ordorika
- Benito Lertxundi

The Camino de Santiago

Look at a Spanish tourist map and you'll see a clearly marked route, stretching through the countryside across the top of northern Spain from the Pyrenees to the city of Santiago de Compostela near the western Atlantic coast. This footpath, one of the oldest in Europe, is known as the Camino de Santiago, the Way of St James.

St James or Santiago

To medieval Europeans, a pilgrimage was a means of earning extra grace and thus attaining heaven faster; it also meant travel, excitement and fun. Pilgrimages were made to many holy places, but the great goals were Jerusalem, Rome and Santiago de Compostela, the burial place and shrine of the apostle St James, Santiago in Spanish. According to legend, he had preached in Spain before returning to martyrdom in Judaea. His disciples brought his body back to northern Spain where it lay hidden until 813, when a hermit was drawn to a particular hillside by starry visions – hence the name Compostela, *campus stellae*, the "field of stars". The King of Asturias, the only part of the peninsula not under Moorish domination, came to pray here and St James, was adopted as the champion of Christian Spain against the Infidel. In 844 he inspired a Christian victory at Clavijo, gaining himself the title of *Matamoros*, the Moorslayer, and a role as patron saint of Spain.

> "a pilgrimage was a means of earning extra grace…it also meant travel and excitement"

The Way of St James

By the mid-12th century between 500,000 and 2 million people annually were travelling from all over Europe to pray at St James's tomb, a vast number in terms of contemporary population sizes. Roads to Spain threaded their way across the continent, but once across the Pyrenees they joined to follow a well-organized route across the north of Spain, the Camino Francés. Administered by a special religious military order, the Camino was policed and waymarked along its length, with hostels, inns and churches offering practical and spiritual sustenance. Towns grew up around the stopping points, with their own churches, hospitals and hospices. Pilgrims were distinguishable by the scallop shells they wore, an emblem of the saint, that also served as a scoop for drinking water. There was even a guidebook, written by the French monk Aymery Picaud, which gave routes and useful tips about what the pilgrim might encounter en route. On arrival in Santiago, the custom was to enter the cathedral and kiss the golden effigy of the saint placed above his tomb, while giving alms and thanks in gratitude for the safe completion of the pilgrimage, an act which would guarantee remission of half the pilgrim's time in purgatory.

The Camino Today

The custom of walking the Camino died out during the reforming 16th century, to be revived around 1880, though it's really the last

The bronze statue at O Cebreiro greets pilgrims on one of the highest parts of the route

20 years that have seen a phenomenal increase in pilgrim numbers. It's a stunning route combining the best of northern Spain's rural countryside with Romanesque and Gothic masterpieces. Less than half the people undertaking the Camino today are Roman Catholic; most are there to enjoy a different pace of life, experience the communal atmosphere and realize the personal challenge that the route presents. The governments of the regions along the Camino have invested heavily in upgrading the paths, building hostels and restoring some of the historic churches and buildings along the way.

A Pilgrim's Passport

Most pilgrims start their journey in the Spanish Pyrenees, from where the distance to Santiago is around 760km (471 miles). You can do the Camino on foot, by bicycle or on horseback, all recognized as means of gaining the *compostela*, the certificate issued by the cathedral authorities in Santiago which confirms the completion of the pilgrimage. The *credencial*, the pilgrim's passport, a small, multi-page folder is stamped by the ecclesiastical and civil authorities at the towns along the Camino to prevent any cheating. This precious document also entitles the pilgrim to stay for a pittance at the hostels along the way, making the pilgrimage as accessible to everyone today as it was in the Middle Ages.

The cockle shell, emblem of the Camino de Santiago pilgrimage, on the Calle Mayor in Santiago de Compostela

TO FIND OUT MORE

If you'd like to know more, contact the Confraternity of St James, a non-denominational charity dedicated to helping English-speaking pilgrims and promoting the Camino (27 Blackfriars Road, London SE1 8NY, (tel: 020 7928 9988, www.csj.org.uk) or consult two other useful resources www.caminolinks.co.uk and www.mundicamino.com

Finding Your Feet

First Two Hours

Spain has international gateways in all areas of the country, with Madrid, Barcelona, Málaga, Alacant (Alicante), València and Bilbao (Bilbo) being the busiest tourist entry points. Transport into these cities from their airports is by bus, train, metro or taxi. Travellers arriving from the UK by sea will dock at Santander or Bilbao, both on the north coast, while long-distance and local trains go round the Pyrenees from France.

Arriving in Madrid

- International flights arrive at the **Aeropuerto de Barajas** (tel: 902 404 704, www.aena.es), 13km (8 miles) north-east of the city. Most international flights arrive at the new Terminal 4, which has doubled the airport's capacity. Facilities include a Tourist Information Office (tel: 915 881 636, daily 9–8), a 24-hour currency exchange, a RENFE office for booking train tickets, car hire offices, post office and hotel reservations desk.
- **Taxis**, which leave from outside all the terminals, are the easiest way to get into central Madrid. The journey costs up to €25, depending on traffic.
- The next best option, after a taxi, is the **metro link** (daily 6am–2am; metro ticket plus €2 supplement). Take Line 8 and change on to Line 4 at Mar de Cristal.
- **Shuttle buses** run every 10–15 minutes from 4:45am–2am from outside each terminal into Plaza de Colón, where you can connect with the metro system at Serrano. The journey takes between 30 and 50 minutes, depending on traffic and costs under €3.

Tourist Offices

⊠ Plaza Mayor 27

☎ 915 881 636
Ⓓ Mon–Sat 10–8, Sun 10–3

⊠ Calle del Duque de Medinaceli 2
☎ 914 294 951
Ⓓ Mon–Fri 9–7, Sat 9–3

⊠ Atocha Station, Plaza Emperador Carlos V, s/n
☎ 915 284 630
Ⓓ Mon–Fri 8–8, Sat 9–3

⊠ Estación de Chamartín
☎ 913 159 976
Ⓓ Mon–Fri 8–8, Sat 9–3

- The general telephone number for Madrid tourist offices is 902 100 007; for information in English dial 010.
- Useful websites include: www.esmadrid.com www.munimadrid.es www.madrid.org/turismo www.madrid.es
- In case of crime against tourists tel: 902 102 112

Arriving in Barcelona

- Barcelona is served by the **Aeroport El Prat de Llobregat** (tel: 932 983 838, www.aena.es), 13km (8 miles) southwest of the city. International flights arrive at all three terminals. Each terminal has Tourist Information Offices (open daily 9–9), car rental offices and exchange facilities.
- The **taxi trip** into the centre takes around 30 minutes and costs around €25; taxis leave from outside all terminals.
- **Trains** run every 30 minutes to Estació-Sants from 6:15am–11:30pm and cost under €3. The journey time is approximately 30 minutes.
- The **airport bus**, the easiest option if you are using public transport, departs every 10 minutes from outside each terminal from 6am–midnight, and costs under €4. The journey time is 30–40 minutes to the city centre,

where the bus stops at Plaça d'Espanya, Plaça de la Universitat and Plaça de Catalunya.

- If you're arriving in Barcelona **by train** from another Spanish destination, the main station is Estació-Sants, where you can pick up metro Line 3 or take a taxi from outside the station. There are also stations at Estació de França, Plaça de Catalunya, Arc de Triomf, Plaça d'Espanya and Passeig de Gràcia. All connect with the metro system.

Tourist Offices

⊠ Plaça de Catalunya
☎ 932 853 834
🕔 Daily 9–9

⊠ Estació-Sants
🕔 Apr–Sep daily 8–8; Oct–Mar Mon–Fri 8–8, Sat–Sun 8–2

⊠ Ajuntament, Plaça de Sant Jaume
☎ 906 301 282
🕔 Mon–Fri 9–8, Sat 10–8, Sun 10–2

Useful websites include:
www.barcelonaturisme.com
www.bcn.es www.gencat.net/probert

Arriving in Málaga

- **Aeropuerto de Málaga** (tel: 952 048 484) is 10km (6 miles) southwest of the centre. Facilities at the airport include an exchange bureau and car rental offices.
- The easiest way to reach the city centre is by train, which runs every 30 minutes from 7am–11:45pm, costs under €2, and takes about 10 minutes. Reach the station by going up to the Salidas (Departure) hall and follow the Ferrocarril signs across the pedestrian overpass. Use the platform furthest away from you for Málaga trains and stay on the train to Centro-Alameda.
- **Taxis** cost around €15 and leave from outside the terminal with a journey time into the centre of around 20–30 minutes.
- The **airport bus** runs from outside the terminal every 30 minutes from 7am–midnight, with a journey time of 20 minutes, and costs €1.
- **Trains** arrive from other Spanish cities at the RENFE station, a short distance from the centre of town.

Tourist Office

⊠ Plaza Marina 11
☎ 952 122 020; www.malagaturismo.com
🕔 Mon–Fri 9–7, Sat–Sun 10–7 (closes at 6pm Nov–Mar)

Arriving in Alacant (Alicante)

- **Alicante Aeropuerto El Altet** (tel: 966 919 000) is 12km (7.5 miles) southwest of the centre, with exchange facilities, a post office and car hire offices.
- You can pick up a **taxi** outside the terminal; the journey time to the centre is around 20 minutes and costs around €15.
- **Airport buses** leave every 40 minutes from 7am–11pm, take around 30 minutes to reach the centre and cost under €2.
- The main **train station** is the Estación de Madrid, Avenida Salamanca; if you're **connecting** to one of the Costa Blanca resorts, coastal services leave on the FGV tram line from Playa de Postiguet.

Tourist Office

⊠ Avenida Rambla de Méndez Núñez, 23
☎ 965 200 000; www.alicanteturismo.com
🕔 Mon–Fri 9–8, Sat 10–2, 3–8

Arriving in València

- The **Aeropuerto de Manises** (tel: 961 598 500) is 8km (5 miles) west of València; there are exchange facilities, a Tourist Information Office and car hire offices.
- **Airport buses** run every 20 minutes from outside the terminal (from about 6:30am–midnight) to the city centre; the journey takes around 45 minutes and costs under €3.
- **Metro line 5** connects the airport with central València and the port. The journey costs €1.70 and takes around 25 minutes.
- **Taxis**, which cost around €15–20, leave from outside the terminal, with a journey time of about 30 minutes.
- **Trains arrive** from other Spanish destinations at the Estación del Nord, close to the city centre.

Tourist Offices

⊠ Plaza de la Reina 19
☎ 963 153 931;
www.turisvalencia.es
◉ Mon–Sat 9–7, Sun 10–2

⊠ Plaza del Ayuntamiento
☎ 963 524 908
◉ Mon–Sat 9–7, Sun 10–2

Arriving in Bilbao (Bilbo)

- The **Aeropuerto de Bilbao** (tel: 944 869 300) is 12km (7.5 miles) north of the city centre; it has a currency exchange, a Tourist Information kiosk and car rental offices.
- Bilbao centre is around a 30-minute **taxi** ride away. The journey costs around €20; taxis leave from outside the terminal.
- **Airport buses** leave from outside the terminal every 30 minutes between 6:15am and midnight for the 40-minute trip to town. Tickets cost under €2 each way.
- The **main train station** is the Estación de Abando where you'll arrive from other regions of Spain. If you're **moving on along the coast**, use either the Estación Atxuri, or, for FEVE services to Santander and León, the Estación de la Concordia.
- **Ferries from the UK** (Portsmouth) dock at Santurtzi on the river mouth to the north of the centre. Buses and trains run from the docks to the city centre; if you're **driving** you can join the A8 *autopista* (motorway) from the docks.

Tourist Offices

⊠ Plaza Ensanche 11
☎ 944 795 760
◉ Jul, Aug Tue–Sat 10–7, Sun 10–6;
Sep–Jun Tue–Fri 11–6, Sat 11–7,
Sun 11–3

⊠ Museo Guggenheim Bilbao
◉ Jul–Aug Mon–Sat 10–7,
Sun 10–6; Sep–Jun Tue–Fri
11–6, Sat 11–7, Sun 11–2

Arriving in Santander

Ferries from the UK (Plymouth) arrive at the Estación Maritima de Ferries at the Puerto Grande. You'll have to follow the signs for Oviedo or Bilbao and negotiate the city to join the main coastal highway, the N634.

Tourist Office

⊠ Jardines de Pereda s/n
☎ 942 203 000; www.santanderciudadviva.com
◉ Jun–Sep daily 9–9; Oct–May Mon–Fri 9:30–1:30, 4–7,
Sat–Sun 9:30–1:30

Getting Around

Spain is a big country, and if you're planning an extensive trip, it's worth considering using internal flights. The slower option, the national rail network, supplemented by some private lines, covers the whole country, as does the bus system. In terms of speed and cost, there is often little to choose between trains and buses, remoter places being served only by buses.

Domestic Air Travel

■ Spain's national carrier, Iberia (tel: 902 400 500, www.iberia.com) offers **internal flights** throughout the country, as does Air Europa (tel: 902 401 501, www.air-europa.com), Vueling (tel: 902 104 269, www.vueling.com) and indeed Ryanair (www.ryanair.com). Each region of Spain has at least one airport.

Trains

■ RENFE (www.renfe.es), the Spanish rail company, operates three main types of **train services**. *Cercanías* are local commuter trains, which operate in and around the main cities; *regionales* connect cities, and *largo recorrido* express trains cover the long-distance routes. Spain has a multiplicity of high-speed trains, including the Intercity, Estrella and Talgo, all with many variations. At the top of the range is the AVE, which runs from Madrid to Seville and Málaga in one direction, and Zaragoza and Barcelona in the other. The Euromed runs from Barcelona to Alacant (Alicante). All these services have greatly reduced travelling times through Spain. FEVE is a private rail line which runs along the north coast from Donostia (San Sebastián) to Ferrol; it connects at various places along its route with RENFE trains. FGC and FGV operate services in Catalonia and València respectively.

■ **Advance reservations** are essential on the *largo recorrido* trains; this can be done at the window marked *venta anticipada* at main stations or at any travel agent displaying the RENFE sign. Many large towns have their own RENFE office or you can reserve via the website (www.renfe.es). Be aware that different **timetables** are issued for different train categories, so there may be more services to a destination than you think at first glance.

■ **Prices** vary considerably depending on the category of train; fares on the faster *largo recorridos* cost more than double those on the slower *regionales* services.

■ **Discounts** are available on return fares and also for children, senior citizens and travellers with disabilities. RENFE accepts InterRail and Eurail **passes**, and has its own pass, the Tarjeta Explorerail for passengers aged under 26. FlexiPass, available only to visitors resident outside Europe, gives 3–10 days unlimited first- or second-class travel within a 2-month period (current prices start at US$175 for 3 days second-class travel, plus US$30 for each subsequent day). Children (aged 4–11) travel for half-fare. Before you buy a rail pass, consider how much train travel you are likely to do, remembering that remoter areas are often served only by buses, to see whether it is worth the investment. Note that supplements may be payable on the faster services.

Buses

■ Spanish **buses** are reliable, air-conditioned and comfortable. There are dozens of companies, most of which operate from the various provincial capitals. Ask at the tourist offices for more information. **Sunday and holiday services** are few and far between.

Finding Your Feet

Taxis

- Taxi services in both rural and urban areas are inexpensive and reliable. Either go to taxi ranks or call in advance; outside Madrid and Barcelona it is not usual to hail a taxi on the street. Supplements are payable for extra passengers and luggage and late-night trips. Tipping is discretionary, but a few euros will suffice.

Driving

- **Drivers** in Spain must hold an **EU driving licence**; US and Canadian licences are also accepted. For peace of mind, North American visitors might want to invest in an **International Driving Licence**. UK visitors whose licences do not comply with the EU format should carry photo ID with them or obtain an International Driving Licence. These are obtainable through the AA and RAC in the UK and similar driving organizations in other countries. Carry your licence with you at all times when driving. Drivers must be 18 or over.
- **Third-party insurance** is compulsory in Spain. If you're bringing your own car, you will need a **green card** from your insurers; a **bail bond** is recommended. Take your **vehicle registration document** with you.
- **Spanish major roads** are generally good, though remote roads in rural areas can have bad surfaces and, in mountainous regions, precipitous drops. Tolls (*peajes*) are levied on some motorways (*autopistas*).
- City traffic can be hectic; it's a good idea to negotiate the approaches to a strange city during siesta time, when the streets are quiet.
- **Check** regulations before you travel – www.theAA.com has comprehensive European driving information.

Driving Know-how

- Drive on the **right-hand side** of the road.
- **Seat belts** are compulsory in the front of the car and rear seat belts, if fitted, must be worn; **children under 12** are not meant to sit in the front unless the seat has a special belt.
- The blood **alcohol** limit is 0.05 per cent (0.03 per cent for new drivers).
- **Yield** to vehicles coming from the right.
- **Speed limits** are 50kph (31mph) on urban roads, 90kph (56mph) outside built-up areas, 120kph (75mph) on motorways; police speed traps are common.
- On-the-spot **fines** are levied for all traffic offences. Obtain a receipt.
- **Vehicle crime** is widespread: never leave anything visible in the car, remove the radio and use hotel parking to avoid leaving your car on the streets, especially if you have foreign number plates.
- Make sure you know what the **breakdown procedures** offered by your own insurer or car rental company are before you start your trip. The Spanish Motoring Club (*Real Automovil Club d'España*) has reciprocal agreements with the AA, US AAA, Australian AAA, CAA and NZAA.

Renting a Car

- Cars can be rented by **drivers over 21** who have held a licence for at least a year on presentation of a **full driving licence**.
- The **cheapest deals** are to be had by booking in advance with rental firms, or as part of a **fly-drive package**. It's worth shopping around on the **internet** to compare rates and find local companies.
- You will usually have to pay a **deposit**; this is normally charged on your credit card and refunded when you return the car.
- All the **major rental companies** have offices at airports as well as in city centres and main railway stations.

Urban Transport

You can walk around the main sights in most of the Spanish cities; historic centres are small and many are pedestrian-only. Madrid, Barcelona, València and Bilbao (Bilbo) have metro systems, all towns have efficient bus services, and taxis everywhere are plentiful and relatively inexpensive.

Madrid

- The **metro** runs daily from 6am–2am, serves most of the places you'll want to get to, and is clean and efficient. The **flat-fare tickets** are also valid on buses; a 10-trip ticket (*bono de diez viajes*) will save you money. There are 13 colour-coded lines, the direction of travel shown by the name of the terminus station. You can pick up a free **map of the system** at any station.

- Madrid's **bus system** is comprehensive, but more complicated to understand than the metro. Buses run from 6am–11:30pm, with services on more than 20 routes throughout the night. **Flat fare and 10-trip tickets** are interchangeable with metro tickets. Pick up a **plan** at the information offices in the Plaza de la Cibeles and the Plaza Puerta del Sol. Tickets must be validated by punching them in the machine on board the bus.

- **Taxis** are white with a red stripe and show a green light on top when they are available. **Supplements** are charged for luggage, train, bus station and airport trips, and journeys outside the city limits. You can hail a taxi in the street, from a taxi rank or phone a taxi company (tel: 914 055 500 or 914 475 500).

- Madrid Vísion runs hop-on, hop-off **tourist buses** around the main sights (Calle San Bernardo 23, tel: 917 791 888, www.madridvision.es).

Barcelona

- Barcelona's excellent **metro system** runs Sun–Thu 5am–midnight (Fri–Sat 5am–2am) on six lines. You can buy single or multiple (*targeta T1/T10*) **tickets,** which must be validated before you board. Tickets are interchangeable with bus tickets. You can also buy **travel passes** lasting up to five days.

- **Bus routes** are numbered and marked at bus stops as well as on the transport map; **ticketing** is the same as for the metro system. The daytime system, which runs from 6am–10:30pm, is supplemented on the main routes by a night bus service from 10pm–4am.

- Barcelona also has a **commuter train line**, the FGC, with stations at Plaça de Catalunya and Plaça d'Espanya. To get up Montjuïc, there's the option of the **funicular railway** and **cable car** (▶ Inside Info, page 124).

- **Taxis** are black and yellow and show a green roof light when they are available for hire. Hail them in the street, find a taxi stand or phone a taxi company (tel: 933 577 755, tel: 933 001 100 or tel: 933 033 033).

- The *bus turistic* (www.barcelonabusturistic.cat), a hop-on, hop-off service starting in the Plaça de Catalunya, links all the main sights. Red buses head south, and blue north. The ticket price includes the funicular and cable car, and discounts to some attractions.

- Many companies rent **bicycles** by the hour or day. Child seats, children's bikes and even trikes with front boxes for carrying children are also available. Many of the companies also arrange sightseeing **cycle tours**.

Admission Charges

The cost of admission for museums and places of interest mentioned in the text is indicated by the following price categories:

Inexpensive under €4   **Moderate** €4–€10   **Expensive** over €10

Accommodation

Spain has an excellent cross-section of competitively priced accommodation, ranging from small family-run *hostales* (modest hotels) to Paradors (the state-owned chain of luxurious hotels). Away from the more popular tourist destinations, you can usually find a room at short notice, particularly at a *hostal* or *pensión* (boarding house). During the summer, however, it is always wise to reserve ahead, even if you are heading for somewhere off the beaten track.

Types of Accommodation

■ If you can afford it, Paradors are wonderful places to stay. Many are converted castles, palaces and monasteries, which have successfully retained the historical character of the building, while incorporating all the amenities you would expect from a luxury hotel. There are about 90 Paradors throughout Spain. Advance reservations are recommended. Some agencies offer good rates: in the UK, try Keytel International (tel: 020 7616 0300, www.keytel.co.uk) or in the US, California-based Petrabax Tours (tel: 1/800 634-1188, www.petrabax.com). Alternatively, book online at www.parador.es, or contact Central de Reservas, Calle Requena 3, 28013, Madrid (tel: 902 54 79 79, www.parador.es).

■ Spanish **hotels** are regionally classified with one to five stars (*estrellas*) depending on the amenities. A 5-star hotel is truly luxurious, with prices and facilities to match. A 4-star hotel is only slightly less deluxe and still offers first-class accommodation. A 3-star hotel is considerably lower in price but the rooms are perfectly adequate and will include TV and air-conditioning, while a 1- or 2-star hotel is more basic and relatively inexpensive. Online hotel booking facilities are available on the following websites: http://interhotel.com/spain/es, www.sleepinspain.com and the global (but including Spain) www.all-hotels.com and www.travelweb.com.

■ Small, family-run *hostales* often provide better accommodation and value than inexpensive hotels. *Hostales* are also categorized from 1 to 3 stars. A *hostal* with 3 stars is the equivalent of a 2-star hotel.

■ A *pensión* is more like a boarding house. Rooms are clean but spartan, and you often have to share a bathroom. Often a *pensión* will require you to take either full-board (three meals) or half-board (breakfast, plus lunch or dinner). Check when booking what is included in the price.

■ *Camas/habitaciones* are the closest equivalent to a bed-and-breakfast, usually advertised in the windows of private houses and above bars and *ventas* (rural restaurants), perhaps with the phrase *camas y comidas* (bed and meals). Don't expect an en-suite bathroom.

■ A *fonda* is a small inn offering basic no-frills accommodation.

■ All Spanish **campsites** are routinely inspected and approved by the Spanish tourist authority and classified under four categories according to their amenities. The Guía de Campings provides a comprehensive list of campsites in Spain. Camping is forbidden on beaches and at tourist resorts. Always check with the local tourist office before you start hammering in the pegs or you may be subject to a fine.

■ **Apartment rental** is becoming an increasingly popular choice for families and small groups, both in Spanish cities and on the coast. Many apartments are purposely refurbished and set in atmospheric, narrow lanes. Before signing up, check what is included and beware of all-night noise from bars and clubs. Rental companies include:
Friendly Rentals tel: 932 688 051, www.friendlyrentals.com
Get Ready Rentals tel: 931 845 886, www.getreadyrentals.com
Rent4days tel: 933 684 700, www.rent4days.com

Finding a Room

■ If you haven't reserved ahead, visit the local tourist office as it will have a list of accommodation with prices. In towns or villages where there is no tourist office, head for the main plaza or centre of town where you're likely to find the greatest concentration of hotels and *hostales*.

■ You will be asked to show your passport when you check in; this will be used to complete a registration form. Ask to see the room first, especially in cheaper accommodation.

■ Check-out is normally at noon, although at some *hostales* and *pensiones* it is 11am. Always find out in advance, to avoid paying an extra day. If you plan to leave early in the morning, advise the front desk and if necessary, pay in advance, otherwise there may be no one around to settle the bill.

■ Hotels will normally store your luggage until the end of the day. *Hostales* are not always as accommodating, however, due to lack of lobby space.

Seasonal Rates

In popular summer resorts, July and August are the high season (*temporada alta*) when room rates can increase by 25 per cent. In winter resorts, like the Sierra Nevada (Granada), high season is logically over the winter period. During national holidays and local fiestas (such as the April *feria* in Seville), accommodation can cost as much as three times more. Out of season, many hotels offer lower rates, and some will have reduced prices at weekends.

Accommodation Prices

Expect to pay for a double room per night:

€ up to €100   €€ €101–€180   €€€ €181–€240   €€€€ over €240

Food and Drink

While eating habits and hours are more or less uniform throughout Spain, there is no national cuisine, as such, aside from a few dishes such as *paella* (rice, saffron, chicken and/or seafood), *tortilla española* (potato omelette) and *gazpacho* (chilled tomato, pepper and garlic soup), which are popular nationwide. Indeed, each Spanish region guards its culinary traditions as jealously as its regional dialects and languages. See pages 12–13 for more information on Spanish cuisine.

Meal Timetable

■ Breakfast (*desayuno*) is usually coffee with toast (*tostada*), which locals prefer topped with olive oil instead of butter. Other toppings include pork lard (*manteca*), coloured a lurid orange by the addition of paprika, and crushed tomato with olive oil (*tomate y aceite*), often served with a garlic clove on the side. *Churros* (strips of deep-fried dough) and hot chocolate are another popular choice. Most Spaniards drink coffee in the morning, either strong and black (*café solo*), with hot milk (*café con leche*), or black with a dash of milk (*café cortado*). If you find the coffee too strong, you may prefer the more diluted *americano*.

■ Lunch (*almuerzo*), usually served between 2pm and 4pm, is the most important meal of the day. It is typically three courses accompanied by a bottle of wine. Most restaurants and bars serve a *menú del día* (set menu), which is usually good value for money. It includes a starter, main dish and choice of dessert or coffee, and often a drink too. Opting for the *menú del día* is an inexpensive way to try local cuisine and an affordable way to enjoy a meal in the country's top restaurants.

■ Dinner (*cena*) is eaten any time from 9:30pm onwards and is generally a lighter meal than lunch. Few restaurants offer their cut-price menu in the evening. Instead, you can choose *à la carte*.

Tapas and Snacks

Tapas are an integral part of the national culinary tradition. They range from a few olives or some crisps given free with an alcoholic drink to a plateful of local sausage, fried fish or freshly cooked *tortilla* (omelette). Tapas are usually available throughout the day, although the choice will be restricted to cold options outside kitchen hours. If you want a larger plateful to share, ask for a *racion*. The northern version of tapas are *pintxos* (also *pinchos*), usually served on a small piece of bread. These are laid out across the bar for you to help yourself; you are charged per cocktail stick.

Bocadillos are baguette-style sandwiches stuffed with your chosen hot or cold filling. They are available from bars and bakers throughout the day, usually freshly made to order.

What to Drink

■ **Beer** (*cerveza*) is extremely popular and many Spaniards prefer it to wine. A *cervecería* is a bar that specializes in beer and usually has several brands on tap, plus a wide range of bottled and imported beers.

■ **Wine** (*vino*) is enjoyed throughout Spain: ask for *tinto* (red) or *blanco* (white). Rioja is world-famous, but there are 40 other wine denominations in Spain. You may want to try a house wine (*vino de la casa*) or, for a refreshing alternative, a *tinto de verano* of red wine with lemonade (*gaseosa*). Another popular way to drink wine in Spain is in a glass of *sangría*, where red or white wine is mixed with pieces of fruit, fruit juice and perhaps a drop of rum.

■ **Sherry** is produced in the Jerez region of Andalucía. *Fino* and *manzanilla* are dry, straw-coloured sherries; *amontillado* is medium dry, and *oloroso* is sweet and dark.

■ The northern coast of Spain, especially Asturias, is famed for its **cider** (*sidre*), traditionally poured into a glass from a height to make it fizzier.

■ **Spirits** are much cheaper in Spain than in many other countries and the measures are generous. Spanish spirits cost far less than international brands and there is little difference in quality. However, Spanish whisky is better avoided!

■ The usual choice of **non-alcoholic drinks** is available, including brands such as Pepsi, Coca-Cola and Seven-Up, as well as fruit juice (*zumo*). For something different, try *Bitter Kas*, which is similar in flavour to Campari, or ice-cold *horchata*, a nutty milk-like beverage made from tiger nuts (*chufas*), available at most cafés.

Tipping

The Spanish tip an average of five per cent but there is rarely any arithmetic involved. It's more a matter of just leaving spare change. IVA (value added tax) is normally included in the price of meals, usually stated on the menu.

Restaurant Prices

Expect to pay per person for a meal, including wine and service:
€ up to €12   €€ €12–€35   €€€ over €35

Shopping

Since Spain joined the European Union, the country's shopping scene has been transformed with the opening of numerous shopping malls and hypermarkets. Despite this, there is a fierce loyalty among the Spanish to support the small family-run *tiendas* (shops), which consequently still seem to flourish, particularly in the *pueblos* (small towns).

Opening Hours

Shopping hours in Spain can vary depending on the region, city or town and the type of shop. There are no statutory closing days or hours for retail outlets, except in Catalonia where shops must close by 9pm. Small shops throughout the country still tend to close from 1 or 2pm to 4 or 5pm for the afternoon siesta, although some shops in the larger cities, such as Madrid and Barcelona, as well as supermarkets, souvenir shops and department stores stay open all day.

What to Buy

- Among the best buys in Spain are the local handicrafts. These are wonderfully diverse and include ceramics, embroidery, fans, glassware, ironwork, damascene (decorative metalwork), jewellery, lace, paintings, porcelain, rugs and carved woodwork. Most of the handicrafts reflect a regional variation, with many products found close to where they are made.
- Leather goods are not as cheap as they once were but the quality is dependably high. You can also save a little on fashionable Spanish exports such as Camper shoes when you buy in Spain.
- Spanish fashion at its best is audacious, colourful and stylish, as exemplified by Ágatha Ruiz de la Prada's designs. Home-grown Zara is the world's third largest clothing retailer and has nationwide boutiques, selling stylish, yet affordable clothing, while the equally ubiquitous Mango also offers a range of smart and stylish fashion for men and women. Two of the more popular menswear chains are Massimo Dutti and the slicker, more expensive, Adolof Domínguez.

Department Stores

El Corte Inglés is a nationwide Spanish institution and Europe's second-largest department store chain. The stores are huge and stock a wide selection of Spanish and international products. Most outlets also have an excellent but expensive supermarket.

Markets

Virtually every village and town will have a daily market selling seasonal produce. Weekly street markets, particularly in the tourist resorts, can be a good place to pick up inexpensive pottery and household goods. The city flea markets such as Madrid's Rastro (▶ 63) sell everything from jewellery and ornaments to second-hand clothes.

Payment

The Spanish generally pay cash when shopping. Credit and debit cards are widely accepted but must always be accompanied by a passport or photo ID. Personal cheques, even local ones, are rarely accepted. Avoid carrying your money around too conspicuously and watch your handbag in crowded shopping streets, especially Madrid, Barcelona and Seville, all of which are notorious for bag snatching.

Entertainment

You don't necessarily have to dig too deep into your pocket to enjoy yourself in Spain. Time a visit to coincide with one of the country's more than 3,000 festivals and appreciate first hand the *alegría* (joy) that is an integral part of the Spanish character for little more than the price of a drink.

Music

- Spain has a wealth of traditional folk music and dance, particularly flamenco and classical guitar made famous by, among others, Andrés Segovia and Carlos Montoya.
- Contemporary music festivals include **Benicássim** near València in mid-July (www.fiberfib.com), **Sónar** in Barcelona in mid-June (www.sonar.es), **WOMAD** at Cáceres in early May (www.womad.org), **Festimad** in Madrid at the end of April (www.festimad.es), **Azkena Rock Festival** at Vitoria-Gasteiz at the end June (www.azkenarockfestival.com) and **Creamfields Andalucia** in mid-August (www.creamfields-andalucia.com).
- There are annual jazz festivals in many cities, including Barcelona and Santander. Madrid, Barcelona and València all stage classical music seasons in winter. Granada hosts a summer International Festival of Music and Dance, and the Autumn festival in Madrid includes concerts, opera, drama and ballet.

Advance Tickets

Advance tickets for concerts, theatre and other events can be bought through various online, ATM and telesales operations, including those run by the banks **La Caixa** (www.servicaixa.com) and **Caixa Catalunya** (tel: 902 101 212, www.caixacatalunya.com). Branches of El Corte Inglés and Fnac usually have desks where you can book tickets in person.

Nightlife

Spain is famous for its nightlife, especially in the major cities and resort areas. Most clubs don't warm up until after midnight and some actually open at daybreak. A few have early evening sessions for teenagers. *Bares de copas* (night-time bars specializing in cocktails and long drinks), are a good place to start a night out with cocktails and dancing, before moving on to a nightclub in the early hours. Admission to many of these bars is free.

Sports and Outdoor Activities

- Spain is the second most mountainous country in Europe and has more than 30 **ski resorts**, including the Pyrenees and spectacular Sierra Nevada. In warmer weather, climbing and walking are popular activities, with well-organized routes and equipment widely available.
- **Golfers** are similarly well catered for with more than 200 courses. The majority are along the western Costa del Sol from Málaga to Cádiz, an area dubbed the Costa del Golf (www.golf-andalucia.com is useful).
- **Water-sports** enthusiasts have plenty of scope for wind- and kitesurfing, water-skiing, jet-skiing, surfing and sailing (▶ 176).
- **Football** is a national passion, with big-name La Liga teams including FC Barcelona and Real Madrid. Stadium atmospheres are usually welcoming. For details of games, contact clubs directly or tourist offices.
- **Bull fighting** is still a popular sport in Andalucía and Madrid although it has been banned in Catalonia and is very marginal in the Basque country. The season runs from March to October and tourist offices can provide details of *corridas*, although the big ones sell out quickly.

Madrid

Getting Your Bearings

Spaniards themselves – as long as they come from neither place – would agree it's debatable whether Madrid or Barcelona is bigger, better or livelier. Whatever you think, since 1561, when Philip II decreed it, Madrid has been the capital of Spain, giving it an automatic edge over its Catalonian rival.

Madrid is noisy, vibrant and chaotic, a city where great wealth exists side by side with grinding poverty. Since Franco's death in 1975 *Madrileños* have embraced the values and ideals of the late 20th and early 21st century with enthusiasm. The result is an exuberant and fast-moving city, with still enough of the old-style way of life to provide a sharp, if elusive, contrast.

Puerta del Sol is the hub of the city, surrounded by the tangled lanes of the old town. Madrid de los Austrias is the name given to the district west of here, an area where you will find the Palacio Real and the grand squares designed by the 17th-century monarchs who made Madrid their capital. To the east of the Puerta del Sol, the sweeping avenues of 18th-century Bourbon Madrid lead past the city's top art galleries and over to Parque del Retiro. Exploring all this gives a wonderful sense of contrast.

The city is divided into *barrios*, best described as neighbourhoods, each completely individual, with its own characteristics and charm. *Madrileños* associate the different *barrios* with different activities and atmosphere, and are fiercely loyal to their own *barrio*, though opinions frequently differ about where one ends and the next starts. *Barrios* are both distinct and elusive, and even a short visit to Madrid can result in an attachment to a particular one. Each has its own shops stuffed with the best of its own particular Spanish style, there are literary and artistic associations everywhere, and the entire city seems sports mad. Above all, it's the nightlife that amazes first-time visitors – Madrid really does party all night, with things hotting up well after midnight and traffic jams at 4am.

Map labels: Palacio del Senado, Santo Domingo, Jardines de Sabatini, Callao, Monasterio de las Descalzas Reales **5**, Palacio Real, Plaza de Oriente, Opera, Calle de Arrieta, Plaza de la Armería, Madrid de los Austrias **1**, Calle Arenal, Catedral de la Almudena, Plaza de la Villa, Calle Mayor, Plaza Mayor, Calle de Sacramento, Palacio de San Cruz, Calle de Toledo, Colegiata de San Isidro, Pla de Tirso de Molin, La Latina, Calle de Embajadores, BAILEN, CALLE DE

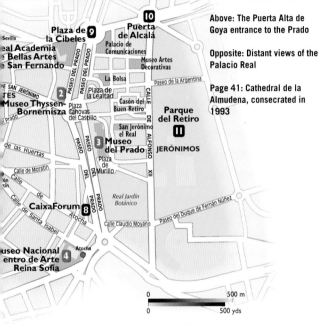

Above: The Puerta Alta de Goya entrance to the Prado

Opposite: Distant views of the Palacio Real

Page 41: Cathedral de la Almudena, consecrated in 1993

In Four Days

If you are not quite sure where to begin your travels, this itinerary recommends four practical and enjoyable days in Madrid, taking in some of the best places to see using the Getting Your Bearings map on the previous page. For more information see the main entries.

Day 1

Morning
Take the metro to the **6 Puerta del Sol** (➤ 55) and walk west to the **Plaza Mayor** (➤ 46), where you can visit the tourist office to pick up maps and information. Head west on the Calle Mayor, pausing to admire the **Plaza de la Villa** (➤ 46). Turn right up Calle de Bailén to head to the splendid **Palacio Real** (➤ 46–47). Have lunch at the Café de Oriente on the **Plaza de Oriente** (➤ 47), one of Madrid's loveliest open spaces.

Afternoon
Head east from the Plaza de Oriente to the **5 Monasterio de las Descalzas Reales** (➤ 55) before a stroll down the monumental Gran Vía, Madrid's commercial heart, lined with fine early 20th-century buildings and thronged with shoppers. Cross over to the Chueca district for trendy independent shops or head down to Plaza Puerta del Sol for the city's main department stores.

Day 2

Morning
Head for the superb collections at the **3 Museo del Prado** (➤ 50–53), one of the world's great art galleries. If Old Masters aren't your thing, take the metro to Atocha and concentrate on the modern masterpieces at the **4 Museo Nacional Centro de Arte Reina Sofía** (➤ 54). Stop for a bite to eat at one of the museum cafés.

Afternoon
When you have finished at the galleries, walk the few blocks to **11 Parque del Retiro** (above, ➤ 57) for a stroll in the park and to look at the **10 Puerta de Alcalá** (➤ 56). The park frequently has entertainment on offer, particularly at the weekend.

Day 3

Morning
Start the day off once again on the Paseo del Prado, this time enjoying the collection at the **2 Museo Thyssen-Bornemisza** (➤ 48–49).

Afternoon
Take the metro or a taxi to Serrano, to have a late lunch in the Barrio de Salamanca, Madrid's designer shopping district, with plenty of chances for window-shopping and people watching afterwards.

Evening
Head back over to the old town for drinks and evening tapas in the La Latina neighbourhood around Cava Baja.

Day 4

Morning
Take an early train from Estación de Atocha for the 50km (31-mile) journey to San Lorenzo de El Escorial, from where a local bus runs regularly up the hill to the monastery of **12 El Escorial** (above, ➤ 58). Built by Philip II, it is the largest Spanish building of the Renaissance. Spend the morning there before heading back to San Lorenzo for lunch.

Afternoon
Catch the direct bus from El Escorial to **Valle de los Caídos** (➤ panel, page 58), Franco's monument to the dead of the Civil War. Head back via San Lorenzo de El Escorial to Madrid in time to arrive for the *paseo*, the early-evening promenade, and stroll with the locals.

Evening
Spend time exploring some of the bars and *tascas* (taverns) in the Santa Ana and Huerta *barrio* between Puerta del Sol and Museo del Prado (➤ 61–62).

❶ Madrid de los Austrias

Madrid de los Austrias is the name given to the bustling central area of Madrid, which stretches from Puerta del Sol to the Palacio Real and encompasses Plaza Mayor, Plaza de la Villa and Plaza de Oriente.

Plaza Mayor

Calle Mayor runs west from Puerta del Sol. Off here you'll find the Plaza Mayor, its harmonious brick facades punctuated with elegant stonework, the ground-floor arcades designed for shelter. Planned by Philip II, it was built in the early 1600s by Philip III as a focus for the new capital, and was used for state occasions throughout the 17th and 18th centuries. The oldest building is the **Casa de la Panadería** (Bakers' Guild) on the north side; recognize it by its frescoed facade. It is now the main tourist office. The square is lined with pavement cafés and holds a stamp and coin fair on Sunday mornings.

Plaza de la Villa

Further west and just off the Calle Mayor, you'll find Plaza de la Villa, the city's oldest square. The plaza's oldest structure is the **Torre de los Lujanes**, built in the 15th century, with a fine, though much-restored, Mudejar tower. This is balanced by the 1537 **Casa de Cisneros**, now the mayor's office, richly ornamented in the plateresque style. On the west side of the plaza stands the **Casa de la Villa**, finished in 1693 to house the city council, a function it still fulfils. The statue in the centre is the 16th-century naval hero, the Marquis of Santa Cruz.

Palacio Real

The grandiose Palacio Real (Royal Palace) stands just off the end of the Calle Mayor. Although no longer the home of the royal family, it is still used for state entertaining. The palace became the royal residence when the court moved to Madrid in 1561, remaining so until a fire destroyed it in 1734. The rebuilding process was completed in 1764 under Charles III.

Cross **Plaza de la Armería** to the entrance, taking in the colonnaded south front and the gardens of the Campo del Moro. The opulent main staircase leads to the **Salón de los Alabarderos** (Halbardiers' Room), with a wonderful ceiling by Tiepolo, and the tapestried **Salón de las Columnas** (Columned Hall). The next highlight is the **Salón del Trono** (Throne Room), which still preserves its original 18th-century Bourbon décor. High above the red velvet-swagged walls and gilded furniture, Tiepolo's mighty 1764 ceiling illustrates *The Grandeur of the Spanish Monarchy*. The next three rooms were **Charles III's private apartments**; look out for the two pairs

Casa de la Panadería, one of the elegant buildings lining the Plaza Mayor

of fine Goya royal portraits. The **Sala de Porcelana** (Porcelain Room) follows, with displays of 18th-century porcelain from the Buen Retiro factory. Then follows the **Comedor del Gala** (State Dining Room), still used for banquets, the **Capilla Real** (Royal Chapel), and outside the main building, the **Armería Real** (Royal Armoury) and **Farmacia** (Pharmacy).

To the west of the palace stands the **Plaza de Oriente**. Once a focus for Franco's public addresses, it is now one of Madrid's most pleasant squares with the inviting Café de Oriente (➤ 61).

TAKING A BREAK

Immediately north of the palace lie the shady **Jardines de Sabatini** and to west the **Campo del Moro**. Both parks offer welcome green spaces and shaded benches.

Palacio Real
➕ 198 A3 ✉ Calle de Bailén ☎ 914 548 800 🕐 Apr–Sep Mon–Sat 9–6, Sun 9–3; Oct–Mar Mon–Sat 9:30–5, Sun 9–2 💷 Expensive; free on Wed for EU citizens 🚇 Opera

Plaza de Oriente
➕ 198 A3 🚇 Opera

Plaza de Mayor
➕ 198 B2 🚇 Sol

Plaza de la Villa
➕ 198 B2 🚇 Sol, La Latina, Opera

MADRID DE LOS AUSTRIAS: INSIDE INFO

Top tip Many key sights are closed on Mondays, so plan your visit accordingly.

One to miss Skip the guided tour at the Palacio Real. It is better to wander at your own speed along the fixed route, though bear in mind that labelling throughout the palace is poor.

2 Museo Thyssen-Bornemisza

The Museo Thyssen-Bornemisza has to be one of the world's greatest private art collections, a stunning array of works amassed over 80 years by the German-Hungarian father-and-son industrial magnates, Heinrich and Hans Heinrich Thyssen-Bornemisza. This highly personal collection, covering nearly every major artist and movement, is brilliantly exhibited in beautifully remodelled 18th-century buildings opposite the Prado.

Seeking a new home for his paintings in the early 1990s, Baron Thyssen was influenced by his Spanish wife, Tita. The site, opposite the Prado, also played a part, and in 1993, fighting off competition from Prince Charles, the Getty Foundation and others, the Spanish state successfully secured the collection at a knock-down price of US$350 million.

Works Reunited

The core of the 14th–18th century collection was purchased during the 1920s and 1930s by the present Baron's father; pictures, sculpture, and objets d'art. On his death in 1947 the collection was split between his heirs. The present Baron bought back some works and began buying on his own account. He started with **old masters**, but from the 1960s concentrated on **German Expressionism, Cubism, Futurism and 19th-century American art**. The reunited, stellar collection of **European old masters** includes four Renaissance portraits by Raphael and Hans Holbein. There are

The museum's collection of 20th-century works is exhibited on the ground floor

The museum's galleries are light and airy

Dürers and Cranachs, their linear northern style the perfect contrast to the acidic Mannerism of the El Grecos and the voluptuous colourwork of Titian, Tintoretto and Canaletto.

Visiting the Collection

Moving down from the second floor the museum changes gear, with rooms devoted to cool **Dutch** interiors, **neoclassical** painting and **European Romanticism**. The Impressionists are very well represented, including an important collection of works by Gaugin. Don't miss Monet's *Thaw at Vétheuil* and Degas's *Race Horses in a Landscape*. Here too you'll find the finest collection of 19th-century **American paintings** outside the US, displayed in rooms 29 and 30. Romantic landscapes by Thomas Cole typify the American dream of the virgin land, while Frederick Remington's taut action pictures pay homage to the native people. There's a charming portrait by Gilbert Stuart, sea and river scenes by Winslow Homer and society portraits by John Singer Sargent.

On the ground floor you'll find **20th-century art** up to the 1970s, with the accent on Cubism – look out for Picasso and Braque. There are pictures too by such luminaries as Jackson Pollock, Francis Bacon and Roy Lichtenstein, one of the few places in Spain where you can see their challenging work.

TAKING A BREAK

The ground floor bar-café serves light refreshments and there are tables outside in summer.

✚ 199 D2 ✉ Paseo del Prado 8 ☎ 913 690 151; www.museothyssen.org
🕐 Tue–Sun 10–7 💶 Moderate; reduced entrance fee with the Paseo del Arte
▶ Top Tips, page 53 🚇 Banco de España

❸ Museo del Prado

The Museo del Prado, Madrid's most-visited attraction, is one of the world's great museums and a showcase for the finest collection of Spanish paintings, as well as outstanding works by every major European artist. You may find your visit overwhelming, mind-blowing or frustratingly crowded, but you won't forget it. Pace yourself, be selective, and remember you can always come back.

The Prado's Collection

More than most national museums, the Prado represents the personal taste of the monarchs through the centuries and is thus immensely strong in some areas, less so in others, with a noticeable emphasis on religious and courtly paintings. It's particularly focused on Spanish painting, and very rich in Italian High Renaissance and Flemish art – reflecting the aesthetics of the royal family, whose paintings form the nucleus of the collection.

    The Prado's main neoclassical building, designed by Juan de Villanueva in 1785, was finally opened in 1819, when Ferdinand VII moved the royal painting collection here. Amid this vast treasure-house, the Spanish works shine brightest, culminating in *Las Meninas* (*The Maids in Waiting*) by Velázquez, often described as "the finest painting in the world". Goya's work occupies many rooms, as do Italian pictures by Fra Angelico, Botticelli, Titian and Tintoretto. The surreal work of the Flemish painters Hieronymous Bosch and Peter Brueghel the Elder, are also among the collection's highlights, and there are fine 17th-century French pictures by Poussin and Lorraine.

Right:
Velázquez's masterful painting *Las Meninas* (1656), one of the Prado's treasures

Below:
Galleries in the museum's original neoclassical building

LAS MENINAS

Las Meninas (above), one of the world's most famous, and certainly greatest pictures, was painted in 1656 by Diego Velázquez, Philip IV's court painter. No other picture so perfectly traps a single moment in time, capturing a transient scene with such precision that you feel you're part of it, standing in Velázquez's own studio in Philip IV's palace. He's possibly painting a portrait of Their Highnesses, who are standing directly in front of you – their reflections can be seen in the mirror on the back wall. Beside the artist stands the royal couple's little daughter, the Infanta Margarita, heir to the throne, surrounded by her maids, the much-loved court dwarfs and a manservant. A favourite dog lies quietly settled. Just outside the room a courtier surveys the scene – or is he about to disturb it? It is this sense of fleeting time that makes *Las Meninas* such a great picture. Reams have been written about the handling of perspective, light, colour and space, the superlative, loose brush work – well worth close inspection, but what you'll remember is the moment. The great Impressionist artist Manet probably summed it up best when he saw the painting and commented "After this I don't know why the rest of us paint".

Tackling the Prado

This is a huge gallery with an immense collection and even with only a fraction on display at any one time you'll still need to pick and choose to get the best out of your visit. Years of refurbishment finally finished in 2007 and the new extension, including the adjacent convent of San Jerónimo el Real, adds refreshing new spaces for temporary exhibitions plus good visitor facilities. There is no set route around the museum but, if given the option by the security guards outside who control the flow of visitors entering the museum, enter up the steps through the Puerta Alta de Goya, the main entrance, to feel the grandeur of the building and launch straight into the collection's star exhibits. Each room is clearly marked with a Roman numeral above the door – though the eye-level signs on the door frames are perhaps easier to spot.

Execution of the Defenders of Madrid (1814), part of the museum's extensive collection of works by Goya

FRANCISCO DE GOYA

The Prado's collection of works by Francisco de Goya (1746–1828) is the largest in the world – around 140 paintings and more than 500 drawings and engravings. They cover every aspect of Bourbon Spain's greatest artist's output, from the light-hearted, sunny tapestry cartoons to the apocalyptic pessimism of the *pinturas negras*, the dark pictures. Born in Fuendetodos, Zaragoza, Goya studied in Italy, returning to Spain to work at the Royal Tapestry Workshops before becoming court painter to Charles IV in 1789. Deaf from 1792, his style became increasingly intense and troubled as he became isolated from the world around him. He moved to France in 1824, where he died four years later.

STAR PAINTINGS

The Tapestry Paintings – *Spring, Summer, Autumn, Winter*; *The Clothed Maja*; *The Naked Maja*; *The Family of Charles IV*; *Self-portrait*; *The Third of May 1808*; *Saturn Devouring One of his Sons*

PICK OF THE PRADO

- *Nobleman with his Hand on his Chest* – El Greco (Domenicos Theotocopoulos)
- *Las Meninas* – Diego Velázquez
- *The Immaculate Conception* – Bartolomé Esteban Murillo
- *The Clothed Maja* – Francisco de Goya
- *The Naked Maja* – Francisco de Goya
- *The Third of May 1808* – Francisco de Goya
- *The Annunciation* – Fra Angelico
- *Madonna with a Fish* – Raphael
- *Ecce Homo* – Titian
- *Christ Washing the Disciples' Feet* – Tintoretto
- *The Garden of Delights* – Hieronymous Bosch
- *The Triumph of Death* – Peter Brueghel the Elder
- *The Three Graces* – Peter Paul Rubens
- *Artemesia* – Rembrandt
- *Self-portrait* – Albrecht Dürer

Pictures are frequently moved around, or lent to other museums, but the big stars are normally on view; though some pictures, particularly those by Velázquez and Goya, attract big crowds and you may have to wait to see them. Information is poor throughout the museum so it makes sense to buy a guide before you tackle the galleries. As a general guide, the first floor is home to European Renaissance paintings and the pick of the Spanish stars – head here for the Velázquez and Goya rooms. There are more works by Goya on the second floor, while the ground floor is devoted to earlier masterpieces.

TAKING A BREAK

The refurbishment has created a very pleasant café/restaurant near the gift shop in the adjacent Los Jerónimos building. In peak periods, however, you might do better to head to one of the tapas bars along Calle Medinaceli.

🚩 199 D2 ⊠ Paseo del Prado ☎ 902 107 077; www.museodelprado.es 🕙 Tue–Sun 9–8 💶 Moderate; free Mon–Sat 6pm–8pm, Sun 5pm–8pm; included in the Paseo del Arte and Madrid Card (► below) 🚇 Banco de España/Atocha

---

MUSEO DEL PRADO: INSIDE INFO

Top tips There are three main entrances: the Puerta Alta de Goya – the most imposing – on Calle de Felipe IV, up the steps above the ticket offices; Los Jerónimos entrance in the new extension, and the Puerta de Velázquez on the Paseo del Prado for Madrid Card holders (► below). The Puerta de Murillo entrance by the Real Jardín Botánico is reserved for groups.

- Arrive as early as you can to escape the worst of the crowds caused by guided tours, and be prepared to wait to get near the star draws. Lunchtimes (from 1pm–3pm) often see a reduction in crowds, too.
- Pictures are frequently moved around or lent to other museums, so pick up an up-to-date floorplan on your way in.
- The illustrated guidebook is both informative and well-produced.
- If you intend visiting the Prado, Museo Nacional Centro de Arte Reina Sofía (► 54) and Museo Thyssen-Bornemisza (► 48–49), the **Paseo del Arte** ticket, on sale at all three, gives a small discount on entry price. The **Madrid Card** can also be a good deal. Available for one, two and three days, passes give prioritized access to the Prado, the Palacio Real, the Thyssen-Bornemisza and the Reina Sofía, plus free admission to 40 other museums and attractions, and discounts in many shops and restaurants.

One to miss Unless you're hooked on 19th-century painting, don't bother with the pictures in the Casón del Buen Retiro, a separate building to the east.

④ Museo Nacional Centro de Arte Reina Sofía

The light, airy galleries at the Museo Nacional Centro de Arte Reina Sofía create the perfect backdrop for the many large-scale works that form the backbone of the collection. Here hang works by the greatest Spanish exponents of the different movements of 20th-century art, with pride of place going to Picasso's *Guernica*. A sleek extension by French architect Jean Nouvel, completed in 2005, has added to the exhibition space.

The main body of the museum complex was created in the 1980s to provide a stunning setting for works by luminaries such as **Solana**, **Dalí** and **Miró**. The development of 20th-century art is traced from the Spanish perspective, with enough key works from other countries to put it in international context. The first, second

and fourth floors of the original museum building house the **permanent collection**, which also extends into the new building on the ground floor. The other spaces are devoted to **changing exhibitions** of contemporary art and design.

Guernica, Picasso's powerful indictment of war, takes pride of place in the museum

Guernica

Most visitors come here to see Picasso's huge *Guernica* (second floor), one of the 20th century's greatest paintings. Painted in 1937 during the Civil War, *Guernica* was inspired by the bombardment of the defenceless town of Guernica by Nationalist and German forces. Packed with symbolism, it is a stunning indictment of the futility of war.

TAKING A BREAK

There's a café, bar and restaurant in the new extension but for something a little more lively head to El Brillante tapas bar (Glorieta del Emperador Carlos V 8), a Madrid institution.

✚ 199 D1 ✉ Calle de Santa Isabel 52 ☎ 917 741 000; www.museoreinasofia. es 🕐 Mon and Wed–Sat 10–9; Sun 10–2:30 💷 Moderate; free Sat pm and Sun; reduced entrance fee with the Paseo del Arte, ► Top tips, page 53 Ⓜ Atocha

At Your Leisure

5 Monasterio de las Descalzas Reales

The Monasterio de las Descalzas Reales (Monastery of the Barefoot Royal Ladies) is one of the city's great hidden treasures. It was founded in 1564 by Juana de Austria, Philip II's sister, as a convent for aristocratic ladies seeking, or being forced into, the religious life. The wealthy entrants brought a dowry and the convent became one of the wealthiest in Europe, with relics and 33 specially commissioned chapels, each more opulent than the last. The two levels of the cloister, each lined with chapels, are connected by a magnificent staircase. The monastery is still home to sisters of the barefoot Franciscan order.

🞧 198 B3 ✉ Plaza Descalzas Reales 3 ☎ 914 548 800 🕙 Tue–Thu and Sat 10:30–12:45, 4–5:45, Fri 10:30–12:45, Sun 11–1:45; guided tours only, some in English 💶 Moderate; free on Wed for EU citizens 🚇 Callao, Sol

6 Puerta del Sol

Puerta del Sol is the geographical heart of Spain, Kilometre Zero, from where all distances throughout the country are measured; there's a plaque in front of the neoclassical Casa de Correos (1768) to prove it. During the Franco years it housed the headquarters of the feared security police; today, it's the seat of the Madrid regional government. The square's clock officially ushers in New Year, when *Madrileños* try to eat a grape on each stroke to ensure 12 lucky months. Sol's two other landmarks are the equestrian statue of Charles III and the other statue of the city's emblem, a bear and *madroño* (arbutus) tree.

🞧 198 C3 ✉ Puerta del Sol 🚇 Sol

7 Real Academia de Bellas Artes de San Fernando

Philip V instituted the Real Academia de Bellas Artes de San Fernando (Royal Academy of Fine Arts), which has occupied the same building since 1773. For those not sated with the treasures of the Prado (► 50–53) and Thyssen-Bornemisza (► 48–49), this is a treat – one of Spain's most important galleries, crammed with painting and sculpture. The stars here are Spanish, with Velázquez, Murillo, Goya and Picasso well represented, but there are also works by French and Italian artists.

Goya's self-portraits deserve close scrutiny, as does *Spring* by the Italian artist Arcimboldo – the sitter's features are entirely composed of fruit and vegetables.

🞧 198 C3 ✉ Calle de Alcalá 13 ☎ 915 240 864 🕙 Tue–Sat 9–5, Sun 9–2:30 💶 Moderate; free on Wed 🚇 Sevilla

The restoration museum of the Real Academia de Bellas Artes de San Fernando

8 CaixaForum

CaixaForum, right on the Paseo del Prado, is a stunning addition to Madrid's art galleries. Architects Herzog & de Meuron transformed an old industrial building, creating a sculptural space in which to stage diverse, but always excellent, free exhibitions. The attractive spaces, which include a relaxed top-floor café and restaurant and a good book and gift shop, are a great place to stop for a calming break. The building appears to float over the small plaza on which it stands, its design enticing visitors to enter the museum, and is marked by a vertical garden making a natural carpet on the adjacent building.

🚩 199 D1 ✉ Paseo del Prado 36 ☎ 913 307 300 🕙 Mon–Sun 10–8 💶 Free 🚇 Atocha

9 Plaza de la Cibeles

Glistening buildings on an epic scale surround the Plaza de la Cibeles; prosaically, the one most resembling a wedding cake is home to the main post office, while the others are the Army HQ, the Banco de España and the Casa de América (Palacio de Linares), a showcase for Latin American visual arts. For many *Madrileños*, the plaza's ebullient architecture is a real symbol of the city, with the central fountain, a popular bathing spot for victorious Real Madrid fans, taking star billing. The fountain, whose central sculpture depicts the goddess Cibeles in her chariot, was completed in 1792 for Charles III.

🚩 199 D3 🚇 Banco de España

10 Puerta de Alcalá

Surrounded by roaring traffic, the Puerta de Alcalá (Alcalá Gate) is a symbol of Madrid, a fine example of neoclassical architecture, and one of the first things to catch the eye on the way in to the city. Standing on the site of the old city walls, the gateway was completed in 1778 for Charles III as the main entrance to Madrid. It's on a monumental scale, with five grandiose arches topped by lion heads, cherubim and coats of arms.

🚩 199 E3 ✉ Plaza de la Independencia 🚇 Retiro

The neoclassical central fountain in iconic Plaza de la Cibeles

The 1920s Monument a Alfonso XII presides over the lake in the Parque del Retiro

⑩ Parque del Retiro

The Parque del Retiro (Retreat Park) was laid out in the 1630s as part of an immense French-style pleasure gardens, complete with palace and lake, designed as a royal playground. The palace's ballroom, the Casón del Buen Retiro still survives, and houses the Prado's 19th-century collection; most of the rest was destroyed during the Napoleonic Wars. Since 1868, when the Retiro became municipal property, it has been Madrid's favourite park, bright with flowers, scattered with statues and fountains, and a favoured place for the Sunday *paseo*. Many people head straight for the lake, dominated by an ornate statue of Alfonso XII, but there's plenty more, including the Palacio de Cristal, a wonderful 19th-century glass palace, an 18th-century parterre, the world's only statue of Lucifer, *El Angel Caído*, and drifts of roses. There's always a good programme of concerts and exhibitions, a children's puppet show on weekends and often folk dancing on Sunday.

➕ 199 F2 ✉ Calle de Alcalá, Calle de Alfonso XII, Avenida de Menéndez y Pelayo, Paseo Reina Cristina 🎟 Free Ⓜ Retiro, Atocha

FOR KIDS

- There is plenty to keep children occupied in the **Parque del Retiro** (► above), with the advantage that it's right in the middle of town, a couple of blocks east of the museums. You can rent a boat, sample the playgrounds, or enjoy watching street entertainers or a puppet show on weekends.
- For younger children there are plenty of other squares in town in which to let off steam. In **Plaza Santa Ana**, just south of Plaza del Sol, the gated children's areas are conveniently located next to some pavement cafés.
- The Teleférico cable-car ride (Paseo del Pintor Rosales, tel: 915 417 450, www.teleferico.com/madrid, summer daily noon–dusk, winter Sat–Sun noon–dusk, inexpensive, metro: Argüelles), which gives great views of the city, takes you into the huge parkland of the **Casa de Campo**, to the west of the Palacio Real (A194 off A4, metro: Batán). Here there is a boating lake and the permanent fairground, the Parque de Atracciones (tel: 914 632 900, www.parquedeatracciones.es, open Apr–Sep daily noon–dusk, Oct–Mar Sat–Sun noon–dusk, check website for precise schedule). It is moderate without rides, expensive with unlimited access to rides. Older children will love La Lanzadera, a vertical drop, and the white-water raft ride, Los Rápidos. There's an open-air auditorium and plenty of parades take place. The park is also home to the Zoo-Aquarium (tel: 915 123 770, open summer daily from 10:30–8, winter from 11–5:30, expensive).

Further Afield

⑮ El Escorial

The massive religious complex known as El Escorial, 50km (31 miles) from Madrid, is one of the most impressive monuments in Spain, giving a true insight into the extraordinary wealth and power of the 16th-century Spanish monarchy.

In 1557 Spanish forces defeated the French at St Quentin. In thanksgiving, Philip II, a deeply religious man, conceived the idea of building a monastery dedicated to San Lorenzo (St Lawrence), which would also serve as a royal palace and burial place. Between 1563 and 1584 some 1,500 builders worked on the vast structure designed by Juan Bautista de Toledo and Juan de Herrera.

Externally, **El Escorial** is rectangular, but its ground plan is patterned on a grid, said to recall the gridiron on which St Lawrence was martyred.

The **Patio de los Reyes** (Courtyard of the Kings) fronts the huge basilica, with its 40 side altars and Philip's collection of holy relics. Below the monumental church lies the **Panteón de los Reyes** (Royal Pantheon), where the majority of Spanish kings from Charles V onwards are buried.

The **Salones Reales** (Royal Apartments) were extended by the Bourbon monarchs; their sumptuous interiors are a marked contrast to the simplicity of Philip II's private apartments.

A mind-bogglingly ornate ceiling is the highlight of the second-floor **Biblioteca** (Library) while the **picture museum** numbers works by Rubens, Titian, Tintoretto, Roger van der Weyden and El Greco among its treasures.

🚩 211 F4 ✉ Calle Juan de Bourbón y Battemberg s/n, San Lorenzo de El Escorial ☎ 918 905 902 🕐 Apr–Sep Tue–Sun 10–6; Oct–Mar 10–5 💰 Expensive; free on Wed to EU citizens 🚊 From Atocha 🚌 Autocares Herranz (tel: 918 969 028); buses leave from Moncloa bus station

GETTING THERE

■ Regular trains (from Estación de Atocha) and buses (from Intercambiador de Moncloa) run the hour-long trip to El Escorial. Otherwise several companies run guided tours from Madrid – try Juliatour (Gran Vía 68, tel: 915 599 605); Pullmantour (Plaza de Oriente 8, tel: 915 411 805) or Trapsatur (Calle San Bernardo 5/7, tel: 915 416 321).

■ If you've got your own transport, it's worth driving 7km (4.3 miles) along the Ávila road to the lookout point at Silla de Felipe II. This rocky outcrop is supposedly the point from which Philip watched the construction of his monastery and there's a little café with splendid views of the buildings and surrounding countryside.

VALLE DE LOS CAÍDOS

The basilica complex at Valle de los Caídos (Valley of the Fallen), ostensibly a memorial to the Civil War dead, was built by the enforced labour of survivors of the Republican army between 1940–58 and is aimed clearly at the glorification of Franco's regime. The dictator is buried behind the high altar. A huge cross stands on the mountain above the basilica – take the funicular up to enjoy the superb views.

🚩 211 F4 ✉ Carretera de Guadarrama, Valle de Cuelgamuros 🕐 Apr–Sep Tue–Sun 10–6; Oct–Mar 10–5:30 💰 Moderate; free on Wed to EU citizens; combined ticket with El Escorial 🚊 From El Escorial Tue–Sun at 3:15

Where to...
Stay

Prices
Expect to pay for a double room per night:
€ up to €100   €€ €101–€180   €€€ €181–€240   €€€€ over €240

Hostal Lido €
A great-value *hostal*, the Lido is on one of Madrid's most happening streets, close to the city's major galleries. There are ten rooms with a choice of shared or en suite bathroom. Heating fans and fridges are included in the price. Singles are a real bargain costing around €35 a night.
🚪 198 C2 ⊠ Calle de Echegaray 5, 2º Izqda ☎ 913 694 643; www.hostallido.com 🚇 Sevilla, Antón Martín

Hotel de las Letras €€€–€€€€
The good-sized rooms at this stylish boutique hotel in the heart of town are bright and elegantly colourful. Service is friendly and professional and the excellent facilities include a spa, library, restaurant and hip rooftop bar.
🚪 198 C3 ⊠ Gran Vía 11 ☎ 915 237 980; www.hoteldelasletras.com 🚇 Gran Vía, Sevilla

Hostal Persal €€
The functional en-suite rooms are decent if slightly anonymous in this large, landmark hotel in an imposing building on Plaza del Ángel. The Persal enjoys an excellent position on a pedestrian plaza between buzzy Plaza Santa Anna, renowned for its nightlife, and stately Plaza Mayor. Ask for one of the brighter rooms higher up in the building.
🚪 198 C2 ⊠ Plaza del Ángel 12 ☎ 913 694 643; www.hostalpersal.com 🚇 Sol, Antón Martín

Hotel Wellington €€€€
The luxurious Hotel Wellington is a grand, old-style hotel with comfortable, classic furnishings and attentive, professional staff. Facilities include an open-air swimming pool in summer, a spa and a gymnasium. The hotel is set away from the hustle and bustle of central Madrid, in the smart shopping neighbourhood of Salamanca, a short walk from the Retiro park.
🚪 199 F4 ⊠ Calle Velázquez 8 ☎ 915 754 400; www.hotel-wellington.com 🚇 Retiro, Velázquez

La Macarena €€
This elegant cream-and-white building sits on one of the city's most charming old streets across from several famous 18th-century *tascas* (bars), just west of the Plaza Mayor. All of La Macarena's 23 rooms have satellite TV and cheery yellow paintwork. Try to request a room with a balcony, particularly recommended is number 303 for its extra size. There's a lively café downstairs where you can join the locals for breakfast.
🚪 198 B3 ⊠ Calle Cava de San Miguel 8 ☎ 913 659 221; www.silserranos.com 🚇 Sol, Opera

Las Meninas €€
In a side street near the Palacio Real, the mid-range Las Meninas is slick and stylish without being over-designed. The hotel offers a range of bright, tastefully decorated rooms, including some fabulous attic suites. There is also a small gym with wonderful views over the rooftops.
🚪 198 B3 ⊠ Calle Campomanes 7 ☎ 915 412 805; www.hotelmeninas.com 🚇 Opera

Petit Palace Alcalá Torre €€

This large hotel is conveniently located halfway between Sol and the Paseo del Castellano. Contemporary styling and touches like WiFi and family rooms with bunk beds make this a good option. The emblematic 12-storey building includes a rooftop restaurant with wonderful views across the heart of the city.

🚇 198 C3 ⊠ Calle Virgen de los Peligros 2 ☎ 915 321 901; www.hthoteles.com ⓜ Sevilla

Radisson Blu, Madrid Prado €€€

A small, new boutique hotel, the Radisson Blu occupies a beautifully converted neoclassical building on a pretty plaza set back from the Paseo del Prado, with easy access to the city's major art galleries and its vibrant nightlife. The hotel's 54 rooms are smart and comfortable, the service friendly and professional. Facilities include an indoor pool, a spa and well-equipped gym, as well as a good restaurant and bar.

🚇 199 D2 ⊠ Calle Moratín 52 ☎ 915 242 626; www.radissonblu.com ⓜ Antón Martín

Room-mate Óscar €€

Part of a small chain, the Óscar is one of four well-located, funky Room-mate hotels in central Madrid. The rooms are bright and stylish, the staff friendly and the city's key sights are just a short walk away. The delicious breakfast buffets are available until midday – perfect after a late night out. The delightful rooftop pool is a real bonus.

🚇 198 C3 ⊠ Plaza de Vázquez de Mella 12 ☎ 917 011 173; www.room-matehotels.com ⓜ Gran Vía

Posada Real Valencia €

Sitting plump on the Plaza de Oriente, in the heart of the city, this old-style pensión on the third floor of an apartment block, is decorated in pretty pastel colours. Its seven comfortable rooms are all en suite. The discreet, friendly service and the excellent location make it a very popular option, so make reservations well in advance to avoid disappointment.

🚇 198 A3 ⊠ Plaza de Oriente 2, 3 izqa. ☎ 915 598 450; www.posadarealvalencia.com ⓜ Opera

Tijcal €

In one of the quieter streets, only steps from the Plaza Mayor, this good-value hostal offers helpful service and bright, decent quality accommodation. The air-conditioned rooms are en suite with WiFi included and guests are even greeted with a complimentary drink on arrival.

🚇 198 B2 ⊠ Calle Zaragoza, 6, 3º ☎ 913 655 910; www.hostaltijcal.com ⓜ Sol

Urban €€€€

The centrally situated Urban is Madrid at its most chic. The hotel provides the ultimate in contemporary luxury and even has its own private collection of ancient Egyptian and ethnic art. Top-flight facilities include a rooftop plunge pool, a well-equipped gym and an oyster bar.

🚇 198 C3 ⊠ Carrera de San Jerónimo 34 ☎ 917 877 770; www.derbyhotels.com ⓜ Sevilla

Westin Palace €€€€

The classic grande dame of Spanish hotels, dates from 1912 and is now part of Starwood Hotels. The hotel décor is fittingly palatial, with prices to match. The entrance lobby and surrounds are wonderfully sumptuous – particularly eye-catching is the stained-glass domed ceiling in the entrance salon where you can sit and sip a sherry even if you can't afford to stay. The hotel covers an entire city block with more than 400 rooms, plus a panelled library, restaurants, bars and a modern fitness centre.

🚇 199 D2 ⊠ Plaza de las Cortés 7 ☎ 913 608 000; www.palacemadrid.com ⓜ Sevilla, Banco de España

Where to...
Eat and Drink

Prices
Expect to pay per person for a meal, including wine and service

€ up to €12   €€ €12–€35   €€€ over €35

Al-Jayma €€

Cushions and low lighting help recreate a Moroccan atmosphere in this good-value restaurant. Choose either to sit on floor cushions or at wooden tables to enjoy the tasty dips, tagines and healthy portions of couscous. Advance reservations are required.

🕇 199 D3 ⊠ Calle Barbieri 1 ☎ 915 231 142 🕐 Daily 1:30–4, 9:30–midnight 🚇 Chueca, Gran Vía

La Barraca €€

La Barraca is the place to head for an authentic Valencian paella. There are nine different paellas from which to choose and the restaurant is also renowned for its *buñuelos de bacalao* (battered cod balls). Inside, whitewashed walls and ceramics lend a traditional Valencian air.

🕇 198 C3 ⊠ Calle de la Reina 29 ☎ 915 327 154; www.labarraca.es 🕐 Daily 1:30–4:30, 8:30–midnight 🚇 Gran Vía

El Bocaíto €€

A timeless classic, this tile-lined establishment has some tables towards the back for more relaxed dining but the real atmosphere is in the two bars, whose walls are adorned with bullfighting pictures and reproductions of masterpieces by Goya. Classic tapas include *pescaíto frito* (fried whitebait), excellent *croquetas* (croquettes) and tasty *embutidos* (cured hams).

🕇 199 D3 ⊠ Calle Libertad 4–6 ☎ 915 321 218; www.bocaito.com 🕐 Mon–Fri 1–4, 8:30–midnight, Sat 8:30pm–midnight. Closed August 🚇 Chueca

El Botín €€–€€€

Botín is one of the city's original old taverns, complete with smoke-blackened brick walls, wood-fired oven and low ceilings. The speciality is suckling pig and roast meats of every description. You can expect to pay a minimum of €30 a head for a memorable gastronomic experience.

🕇 198 B2 ⊠ Calle Cuchilleros 17 ☎ 913 664 217; www.botin.es 🕐 Daily 1–4, 8–12 🚇 Sol/Tirso de Molina

Café de Oriente €€

In a wonderful location on the Plaza de Oriente, this belle époque-style café has outside tables with views across the plaza to the Palacio Real. Drinks outside are understandably pricey but the lunchtime menu is good value. The café is also a popular choice for breakfast.

🕇 198 A3 ⊠ Plaza de Oriente ☎ 915 413 974; www.cafedeoriente.es 🕐 Mon–Thu 8:30am–1:30pm, Fri–Sun 9am–1:30am 🚇 Ópera

La Casa del Abuelo €–€€

One of the many traditional tapas bars in the rowdy streets, La Casa del Abuelo excels in prawn dishes like *gambas al ajillo* (prawns in garlic). Find a corner, grab a drink and enjoy the very *Madrileño* bustle.

🕇 198 C2 ⊠ Calle de la Victoria 1 ☎ 915 212 319; www.lacasadelabuelo.es 🕐 Tue–Sun 12–12 🚇 Sol, Sevilla

Casa Ciriaco €€

This traditional Castilian taverna near the Royal Palace offers a range of unpretentious fare such as *gallina en pepitoria* (chicken in egg and saffron), *cocido madrileño* (a hearty stew made with chorizo sausage) and *perdriz con judiones* (partridge with broad beans). There is a good wine list too.

+ 198 B2 ⊠ Calle Mayor 84 ☎ 915 480 620 ⊙ Thu–Tue 1–4.30, 8–12.30. Closed Aug ⓠ Opera

El Estragón €–€€

Expect generous helpings at this vegetarian restaurant. Dishes include risotto verde, and some have an Eastern tang. The restaurant stands on one of Madrid's most attractive and ancient squares, and is now a fashionable meeting place for the younger set. There's an inexpensive *menu del dia* during the week, and two sittings for dinner. The imaginative desserts are well worth trying.

+ 198 A2 ⊠ Plaza de la Paja 10 ☎ 913 658 982 ⓞ Daily 1:30–5, 8–midnight ⓠ La Latina

La Finca de Susana €–€€

This is the perfect spot to celebrate an occasion without breaking the bank. Elegant furnishings, slick service and a good range of well-

considered dishes at unbeatable prices ensure the restaurant's popularity. Arrive early, as you can't make advance reservations and lines form before the place opens.

+ 198 C3 ⊠ Calle de Arlabán 4 ☎ 913 693 557; www.lafinca-restaurant.com ⓞ Daily 1–3.45, 8:30–11.45 ⓠ Sevilla, Sol

José Luis €

This *cervecería* and tapas bar is a city institution. Stop for a pick-me-up and a bite to eat when you're in the well-heeled Salamanca district checking out the designer shops. Old-time professionals serve traditional canapés with *boquerones* (anchovies in vinegar), smoked salmon or grilled chorizo.

+ 198 E5 ⊠ Calle de Serrano 89 ☎ 915 630 958; www.joseluis.es ⓞ Mon–Sat 12:30–4, 6–midnight ⓠ Serrano

Naïa €€

This modern restaurant is situated on Plaza de la Paja, one of Madrid's prettiest squares, with tables in the shade of the church on warmer

days. The creative cooking blends fresh ingredients and unusual tastes – try the tuna with leek tempura or baked risotto. There is a downstairs chill-out lounge where you can relax afterwards.

+ 198 A2 ⊠ Plaza de la Paja 3 ☎ 913 662 783; www.naiarestaurante.com ⓞ Tue–Sat 1:30–4.30, 8:30–midnight, Sun 1:30–4:30 ⓠ La Latina

Ribeira do Miño €€–€€€

A delight for lovers of seafood, this simple Galician restaurant serves a wonderful range of finger-licking dishes washed down with a chilled cup of Albariño. Alternatively, enjoy drinks and nibbles at the bar. Reservations are advisable at weekends.

+ 198 C4 ⊠ Calle Santa Brígida 1 ☎ 915 219 854; www.marisqueriaribeira.aliste.info ⓞ Tue–Sun 1–5, 8–12 ⓠ Tribunal, Gran Via

La Terraza del Casino €€€

Superstar Catalan chef Ferran Adrià has chosen the unlikely setting of this old-school gentlemen's club as

his Madrid base. With a chemistry set of liquid nitrogen, foams and gels he recreates the essence of Spanish classics like *croquetas del jamón* (ham croquettes) and *tortilla en tres pisos* (Spanish omelette). Trust in the *menú de degustación* (€110) to give you a taste of the restaurant's award-winning cuisine. It is obligatory for men to wear a jacket and tie.

+ 198 C3 ⊠ Calle de Alcalá 15 ☎ 915 321 275; www.casinodemadrid.es ⓞ Mon–Fri 1:30–4, 9–11.45, Sat 9pm–11.45pm. Closed Aug ⓠ Sol, Sevilla

El Tempranillo €€

The wooden tables in this lively bar, in a street lined with legendary restaurants and bars, are a great spot to settle down with a glass of wine and a plate of *embutidos* (mixed cold cuts) or *tostas* (toast toppings). Grab what space you can at the bar if the tables are full.

+ 198 B2 ⊠ Calle Cava Baja 38 ☎ 913 641 532 ⓠ La Latina ⓞ Daily 1–4, 8–midnight

Where to... Shop

One of the delights of shopping in Madrid is exploring the idiosyncratic small shops. Many have remained in the same family for several generations and are a nostalgic reminder of the days before bland high street chains.

At the centre is Plaza Mayor where, amongst the inevitable souvenir bazaars, are located such gems as **Casa Yustas** (tel: 913 665 084, www.casayustas.com, metro: Sol), an extraordinary hat emporium founded in 1894. A short walk away, **Casa Hernanz** (Calle de Toledo 18, tel: 913 665 450, metro: Sol) is famous for its espadrilles, while **Gonzapur** (Calle de Esparteros 18, tel: 915 222 796, metro: Sol) is one of the best places for Spanish shawls, fans, hair combs and the lace mantillas traditionally worn at Mass. **Capas Sesena** (Calle de la Cruz 23, tel: 915 316 840, www.sesena.com, metro: Sevilla) is equally famous for its wool capes, while **Loewe** (Gran Via 8, tel: 915 226 814, www.loewe.com, metro: Gran Via) is easily Spain's most elegant leather store.

In the same class, the well-heeled Salamanca district is home to Spanish classics including **Purificación García** (Calle de Serrano 28, tel: 914 358 013, www.purificaciongarcia.com, metro: Serrano), with its elegant women's collection. **Agatha Ruiz de la Prada** (Calle de Serrano 27, tel: 913 190 501, www.agatharuizdelaprada.com, metro: Serrano) and **Sybilla** (Calle de Jorge Juan 12, tel: 915 781 322, www.sybilla.es, metro: Serrano) are colourful design giants who made their names during the Movida Madrileña counterculture of the late 1970s and 1980s. Up-and-coming designers hustle around Calle Fuencarral in the trendy Chueca district, with contemporary international names rubbing shoulders with independent shops.

Popular mid-range stores cluster around Plaza Puerta del Sol, Gran Via, Calle del Carmen and Calle Preciados in the very heart of town, including outlets from Spain's home-grown Zara empire as well as Mango and other well-known international names.

DEPARTMENT STORES

The city's biggest one-stop shop is **El Corte Inglés** (www.elcorteingles.es), providing all the goods and services you expect in a department store. There are several branches throughout the city, the most central being at Calle de Preciados 1–4 (tel: 913 798 000, metro: Sol).

MARKETS

The famous Sunday flea market at El Rastro (Calle de la Ribera de Curtidores, metro: La Latina), open from dawn to approximately 2pm, sells everything from glorified junk to genuine antiques (▶ 178–179).

The fruit and vegetable markets are also worth visiting. Try **Mercado de San Miguel** (Plaza de San Miguel, www.mercadodesanmiguel. es, metro: Sol) or **Mercado Antón Martín** (Calle de Santa Isabel 5, metro: Antón Martín), with its old-style tiled frontage and mouth-watering produce displays.

CAKES AND PASTRIES

Casa Mira (Carrera de San Jerónimo 30, metro: Sevilla) dates from 1842 and still prepares turrón (nougat) and other delicious sweets, while **La Mallorquina** (Plaza Puerta del Sol 8, metro: Sol) has a café upstairs, where you can enjoy cakes and pastries made on the premises.

Where to...
Be Entertained

Pick up *In Madrid*, a free, monthly English-language magazine, to see what's going on in the city, or buy the glossy monthly magazine, *The Broadsheet*, which has a useful classified section. There is also the weekly Spanish language *Guía del Ocio* (www.guiadelocio.com/Madrid) magazine with entertainment, cinema and restaurant listings.

NIGHTLIFE

Dusk-to-dawn partying is the norm in Madrid, Europe's nocturnal capital. Start your evening with drinks and music, often played by live DJs, at one of the *bares de copas* (▶ 40). Good areas for bar hopping are around Calle de las Huertas and Plaza Santa Ana or, cooler still, around Chueca. Particularly good in summer, Plaza de la Paja in La Latina has some fun places, including the now legendary **El Viajero** (Plaza de la Cebada, metro: La Latina).

Jazz enthusiasts go to **Café Central** (Plaza Angel 10, tel: 913 694 143, www.cafecentralmadrid.com, metro: Antón Martín) with nightly concerts at 10, and **Café Popolart** (Calle Huertas 22, tel: 914 298 407, www.populart.es, metro: Antón Martín); open from 6pm, music from 11pm.

After 3am people head on to clubs and discobars. There is often an admission fee for these, which usually includes a drink. Disco diehards have seven floors to choose from at **Kapital** (Calle de Atocha 125, tel: 914 202 906, www.grupo-kapital.com, metro: Atocha). **Palacio Gaviria** (Calle del Arenal 9, tel: 915 266 069, www.palaciogaviria.com, metro: Opera) provides a fabulous baroque setting and varied choice of music.

CLASSICAL MUSIC AND THEATRE

The **Teatro Real** (tel: 915 160 600, www.teatro-real.es, metro: Opera) on Plaza de Oriente is the city's principal opera house.

The city is also the home of *zarzuela*, a more spirited version of the Viennese operetta and best enjoyed at the **Teatro de la Zarzuela** (Calle Jovellanos 4, tel: 915 245 400, http://teatrodelazarzuela.mcu.es/, metro: Banco de España).

Classical music buffs can check out the programme at the **Teatro Monumental** (Calle de Atocha 65, tel: 914 292 181, metro: Antón Martín), which is also open to the public on Thursday mornings at rehearsal time. Serious theatre (as well as music and dance) can be seen at several venues in Madrid, with the greatest variety available during the **Festival de Otoño** (Autumn festival, Oct–Nov).

FLAMENCO

There are several flamenco *tablaos* (shows) in town. Among the best and priciest is at **Café de Chinitas** (Calle de Torija 7, tel: 915 471 502, www.chinitas.com, metro: Santo Domingo), where some of Spain's top dancers perform.

For an Andalucian atmosphere, head for **Al Andalus** (Calle del Capitán Haya 19, tel: 915 561 439, metro: Cuzco). After the show the mainly Spanish audience dances *sevillanas* until dawn. If you want to practise first, try **Almonte** (Calle de Juan Bravo 35, tel: 915 632 504, www.almontesalarociera.com, metro: Núñez de Balboa). There's no live show, but plenty of foot-stomping on the dance floor.

Castilla, León and La Rioja

Getting Your Bearings

If your vision of Spain has been shaped by the sun 'n' sand Costa image, you'll find no greater antithesis than Castilla (Castile), León and La Rioja. Here there's nothing but mile after mile of rolling, empty countryside beneath immense skies, outcrops of isolated mountains and thread-like rivers, the plains and valleys dotted with a few remote towns. From this lonely landscape rise the great cities of Spain's central plateau – Burgos, Segovia, Salamanca and León, rich monuments to a great past.

In European terms, distances here are big, and often seem greater because of the emptiness of the land. But the long drives between the cities give a real sense of what oases they are – entering a beautiful, historic place after hours on the road gives a real buzz. If you're not up for a lot of driving, aim to concentrate on the square formed by the main cities of Burgos, Segovia, Salamanca and León. This way you'll see the best in terms of cathedrals and monuments and also get a taste of Spain's upland interior.

Just to the east of this historial region lies the rolling countryside of La Rioja, famed for its vineyards. Elegant provincial towns and sleepy villages intersperse with fascinating *bodegas* (wineries), some housed in stunning buildings designed by world-renowned architects.

Away from the major centres, Castilla and León have picturesque villages too, like Covarrubias, and once-major cities, such as sleepy walled Ávila, make a civilized contrast to the scenic delights of the Sierra de Guadarrama, Madrid's outdoor playground. Travelling around is easy: roads are, on the whole, excellent and uncrowded, and the entire area is relatively undiscovered by foreign tourists. Your main problem may be trying to decide what to miss, or not having as much time as you'd like in each place.

0   50 km

0   50 miles

r de Campoo
☐ Oña

Burgos **1**

A:P1

Santo Domingo
de la Calzada
☐ Belorado

BURGOS

La Rioja 5   Arnedo ☐   **AP68**

Covarrubias **6**

Lerma ☐

☐ Villar
del Río

Hontoria
del Pinar

Aranda ☐   San Esteban   El Burgo   Soria   Almenar
e Duero   de Gormaz   de Osma   ☐   de Soria

☐ ☐   SORIA   **N234**

Ayllón ☐   *Duero*   ☐ Almazán

EOS

VA
ra de
rama **7**

govia

Above: Detail of the ornate Gothic
cathedral, Burgos

Previous page: The forested hills
of the Sierra de Guadarrama

Above: The towering granite arches of Segovia's first-century AD Roman aqueduct

In Seven Days

If you are not quite sure where to begin your travels, this itinerary recommends seven practical and enjoyable days in Castilla, León and La Rioja, taking in some of the best places to see using the Getting Your Bearings map on the previous page. For more information see the main entries.

Day 1

Spend the morning exploring the historic centre of **❶ Burgos** (➤ 70–71), visiting the **cathedral** before having lunch at one of the restaurants along Calle de la Paloma, perhaps La Taberna de Quico (➤ 71).

Head across the river to visit the **Real Monasterio de las Huelgas** (➤ 71), returning to the centre in time for some shopping before joining the strolling evening crowds along the **Paseo de Espolón**. Have a pre-dinner drink at one of the bars on **Plaza Rey San Fernando** near the cathedral before sampling a local restaurant, such as Casa Ojeda (➤ 84).

If you do not intend on returning to Burgos at the end of your holiday, spend a few days exploring the Rioja region (➤ 80–81) before continuing to Segovia.

Day 2

Take the A1 south **towards Segovia**, detouring perhaps on to the N234 to visit **❻ Covarrubias** (below, ➤ 82) and **Santo Domingo de Silos** (➤ 82), where you could have lunch. In the afternoon, continue south on the A1, then turn southwest on the N110 to **❷ Segovia** (➤ 72–73). Get your bearings by strolling around the city and viewing the **aqueduct** before visiting the **cathedral** and the **Alcázar**. A drink at one of the outdoor cafés on the **Plaza Mayor** makes a good start to the evening; follow it up with dinner and a late-night stroll.

Day 3

Leave Segovia via **Iglesia de la Vera Cruz** (➤ 73), then head southwest to **8 Ávila** (➤ 82), where you could have lunch before walking a section of the walls. In the afternoon, take the N501 northwest to **3 Salamanca** (➤ 74–75) arriving in time to walk to the **Plaza Mayor** as the shops open and the city starts to gear up for the evening.

Day 4

Spend the morning tackling Salamanca's big sights, the cathedral and the university, before relaxing over lunch in the Plaza Mayor. After lunch, you'll have time to take in some of the city's churches and monasteries before heading north on the N630 to arrive in **4 León** (➤ 78–79) in time for a typically late Spanish dinner.

Day 5

Get up early to see the morning light on the **cathedral** before exploring the interior. Then it's time to visit **San Isidoro** (➤ 78) and the **Panteón** (➤ 78) before lunch at Boccalino (➤ 85) on the plaza outside.

Spend the afternoon in modern León window-shopping before ambling through the riverside gardens to treat yourself to a drink at the bar in the Parador at **San Marcos** (➤ 78–79). Spend the evening back in the historic centre, dining and experiencing the atmosphere in the bars around **Plaza San Martín** (➤ 79).

Day 6

After visiting the big cities, return to **5 La Rioja** (➤ 80–81) for a relaxed end to your holiday. Make an early start and take the A231 towards Burgos and then switch on to the slower but very attractive N120 which takes you through to **Logroño** (➤ 80) and the heart of the Rioja Alta. Perhaps stop for lunch on the way in the old pilgrim town of Santo Domingo de la Calzada.

Explore the ancient stone streets and porticoed squares of Logroño. The attractive cathedral and impressive churches have served pilgrims on the Camino de Santiago (➤ 26–28) for centuries. In the evening head to the renowned tapas bars on Calle Laurel and Calle de San Juan, each specializing in a different dish, after 9pm when things get going. Note that many are closed on Sunday and Monday nights.

Day 7

Join one of the wine-tasting tours (information is available at the tourist office ➤ 81) so that you can forget about driving. If you're set on exploring under you own steam, head over the river to the famous *bodegas* of the Rioja Alavesa (➤ 80).

In the evening, head back into Logroño and down to the river for a stroll or a break on the grassy banks before heading back to try the tapas you couldn't manage the night before.

▯ Burgos

Rising from the plains of Castile, historic Burgos and its
great cathedral are inextricably linked with the glory days
of the Reconquista and the pilgrim path to Santiago. Thriving
modern Burgos pulsates with civic pride, its historic buildings
and riverside setting forming the perfect backdrop to the
pleasures of a prosperous provincial capital.

Burgos was the capital of Castile from 1037–1492; from here,
Ferdinand III recaptured Murcia, Córdoba and Seville from
the Moors, and it was he who commenced the building of
the cathedral. Get your bearings by wandering around the
pedestrianized centre to the arcaded **Plaza Mayor**, keeping an
eye out for the sweeping glass-galleried frontages of so many
of the buildings, typical of this part of Castile.

The City Centre

Two historic bridges cross the River Arlanzón. The **Puente
de San Pablo** is lined with stone figures, dominated by a
dramatic equestrian statue at its far end of the legendary
11th-century hero El Cid, who was born near
Burgos. From here, the tree-lined Paseo de
Espolón, scene of Burgos' evening promenade,
leads down beside the river to the **Puente de
Santa María** bridge and the great white **Arco
de Santa María**. This gateway was once part
of the town walls and was castellated and
decorated with statues in the 16th century –
you'll be able to spot El Cid here as well.

The Arco leads to the lovely plazas
surrounding the **cathedral** – a nice place to
pause at a café table. From here, you'll get
your first close-up of the astounding forest
of spires, pinnacles, stone carving and statuary adorning this
masterpiece of Gothic art. Founded in 1221 by Ferdinand
III, the cathedral is Spain's third largest, and, architecturally,
covers the evolution of the Gothic style from the 13th to
the 15th centuries. Inside, northern elements are fused with
Hispano-Moorish features in a mind-boggling profusion of
doorways, chapels, vaulting and sculpture. Burgos impresses
with its complexity, not as a unified whole. So concentrate
on the individual highlights, the simple **tombstone of El
Cid** beneath the transept crossing, the superb **star-vaulting**
– a Moorish borrowing – and, above all, the chapels, large
enough to be churches in their own right. Best of these is the
octagonal **Capilla del Condestable** behind the high altar,
founded in 1482 and largely the work of Simon of Cologne,
a second-generation Hispano-German architect. Nearby, you
can admire the splendid **Escalera Dorada** (Golden Staircase),
a double stairway in the north transept. The **Capilla del
Santo Cristo**, just off the southeastern corner of the nave,

The equestrian
statue of El
Cid in the city
centre

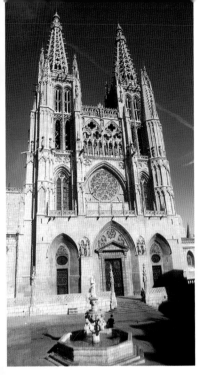

though far plainer, contains a much-venerated image of the crucified Christ, a 14th-century figure endowed with human hair and covered with buffalo hide to resemble human skin.

Real Monasterio de las Huelgas

The Real Monasterio de las Huelgas, set in a tranquil backwater across the river, was founded in 1187 as the resting place for Alfonso VIII and his English wife Eleanor of Aquitaine, daughter of Henry II. This lovely monastery was one of the most powerful in Spain and the burial place of many Castilian monarchs. It is renowned for its **Mudejar craftmanship**, which you'll see on the ceiling of the main Gothic cloister – look out for the typical star patterns and

The city's superb Gothic cathedral, an architectural tour de force

peacock designs (a bird revered by the Moors). Its museum contains fine medieval textiles and jewellery, the church is splendid and there's a cult statue of St James with an articulated right arm for dubbing knights.

TAKING A BREAK

Near the cathedral you'll find stylish **La Taberna de Quico** (Calle La Paloma, tel: 947 271 973), where you can enjoy sophisticated tapas, *bocadillos*, and salads.

BURGOS: INSIDE INFO

Top tips Use the English-language audioguide to get the most out of your visit to the cathedral.
- If you're visiting Las Huelgas, ask at the ticket desk if your guide on the tour speaks English; if not, it may be worth waiting for the next one.
- Climb up behind the cathedral for wide city views from the Mirador del Castillo.

Hidden gems Pause to admire the planting along the river where wildflowers, trees, shrubs and grass provide one of the most tranquil city-centre elements you'll ever see.

🖪 205 E3

Tourist Information Office
✉ Plaza Alonso Martínez 7
☎ 947 203 125; www.aytoburgos.es ⏰ Mon–Fri 9–2, 5–7, Sat–Sun 10–2, 5–8

Cathedral
✉ Plaza Santa María
☎ 947 204 712 ⏰ Mon–Sat 9:30–1, 4–7, Sun 9:30–11:45, 4–7
🎫 Inexpensive

Real Monasterio de las Huelgas
✉ Compases ☎ 947 201 630
⏰ Tue–Sat 10–1, 3:45–5:30, Sun 10–2 🎫 Moderate, guided tours mainly in Spanish; free Wed

2 Segovia

Beautiful Segovia, crammed with mellow stone monuments, churches, mansions and squares, spreads along a rocky ridge against the stunning backdrop of the Sierra de Guadarrama. Retaken from the Moors in the 11th century, it was here that Isabel the Catholic was proclaimed Queen of Castile in 1474; the finest buildings date from these centuries. Intimate yet sophisticated, grand but cosy, Segovia is rightly one of the top choices for anyone exploring Castile and León.

The Roman Aqueduct

The great Roman *acueducto* (aqueduct) constructed in the first century AD brought water from over 15km (9 miles) away. Towering above the Plaza de Azoguejo in Segovia's lower town, the 166 granite arches of this remarkable structure, 800m (875 yards) long and around 30m (98ft) high, have stood firm with no cement or mortar, though traffic and pollution are taking their toll.

The Cathedral

In 1525, centuries after the aqueduct was built, work started by the order of Charles V on the cathedral. It was the last important Gothic building constructed in Spain, built over more than 200 years. Outside, pinnacles, domes and flying buttresses soar skywards; inside, the space is filled with the heavy central green marble *coro* (choir). The rooms

Segovia's fairy-tale Alcázar

SEGOVIA: INSIDE INFO

Top tips You can rent an English language audio-guide at the Alcázar; there's also an informative English leaflet.

■ Make a point of walking out along the roads surrounding the city for ever-changing views of the cathedral and Alcázar. Best overall views are about 2km (1 mile) out to the north on the Cuéllar road.

■ Spend time just wandering around; you'll come across hidden corners and splendid buildings at every turn.

■ Make sure you have an outside table at one of the cafés in the Plaza Mayor – relax with a drink, soak up the atmosphere and enjoy some great people-watching.

In more depth If you're keen on Romanesque churches head for San Martín, La Trinidad, San Millán and San Justo (daily 10–2, 4–7). La Trinidad has superb capitals on the pillars of its double-arched apse; San Millán has the characteristically Segovian open portico and a *mozarabe* tower (► 15).

One to miss Unless weapons and artillery really fascinate you, skip the Royal Artillery Museum at the Alcázar.

surrounding the cloisters contain the cathedral **museum**, while to one side, looms the free-standing tower.

The Alcázar

Segovia's Alcázar, complete with pointed turrets and sloping roofs, stands at the opposite end of the ridge from the aqueduct. Originally built between the 14th and 15th centuries and once a royal residence, today's whimsical castle – used as a model for the original Disneyland castle – is largely an 1862 reconstruction, following a fire. It's well worth exploring the interior, all gilding and Mudejar-style friezes, as much for the fine views as for the pictures and furniture. You'll get even better vistas from the **top of the tower** – 141 steps up and no lift.

Iglesia de la Vera Cruz

Below the walls and outside the city stands one of Spain's most remarkable ecclesiastical buildings, the 12-sided Iglesia de la Vera Cruz (The True Cross), built for the Knights Templar in the 13th century. Modelled on the Church of the Holy Sepulchre in Jerusalem, its form is unique in Europe. Inside, there's a two-storied central temple, where Templars once kept vigil. Awe-inspiring in its antiquity, redolent with mysticism, Vera Cruz deserves to be better known.

TAKING A BREAK

Head for **La Concepción** (Plaza Mayor 15, tel: 921 460 930), affectionately known as "La Conche" locally, to taste the very best of Castilian regional cooking and imaginative tapas while you watch the world go by.

➕ 211 F5

Tourist Information Office
✉ Plaza Mayor ☎ 921 466 070; www.segoviaturismo.es 🕓 Summer daily 9–8; winter Mon–Sat 9–2, 4–7, Sun 9:30–5

Cathedral
✉ Calle Marqués de Arco ☎ 921 435 325 🕓 Apr–Oct daily 9:30–6:30; Nov–Mar 9:30–5:30 🎫 Museum: inexpensive

Alcázar
✉ Plaza de la Reina Victoria Eugenia ☎ 921 460 759; www.alcazardesegovia.com 🕓 Apr–Sep daily 10–7; Oct–Mar 10–6 🎫 Moderate; free third Tue of month to EU citizens

Iglesia de la Vera Cruz
✉ Carretera de Zamarramala ☎ 921 431 475 🕓 Summer Tue–Sun 10:30–1:30, 4–7; winter 10:30–1:30, 4–6 🎫 Inexpensive

❸ Salamanca

Salamanca's wonderful mix of graceful churches, mansions and plazas, its ancient university and tradition of scholarship all combine to make it one of Spain's most seductive cities. It is a city on a human scale, made even more alluring by the glowing honey-coloured stone of its buildings. There's plenty to see, but one of the chief pleasures is wandering the streets and absorbing the atmosphere of a city that is more than the sum of its parts.

The best place to start exploring Salamanca is the **Plaza Mayor**, built in the 18th century by Philip V, and one of the world's great squares. The symmetry of the three-storey, arcaded buildings around this harmonious space is punctuated on the north side by the grander mass of the Ayuntamiento (Town Hall). Above the arcade arches you'll notice a series of portrait medallions of Spanish monarchs and famous men – look out for El Cid and Christopher Columbus. Constantly criss-crossed by locals and tourists alike, the Plaza is the real hub of Salamanca.

The harmonious 18th-century Plaza Mayor is at the heart of city life

From the Convento de as Dueñas here are spectacular views of the cathedral

Cross the road on the south side to head down the Rúa Mayor, which leads towards many of the city's finest monuments. Halfway down, on a corner on the right, is the **Casa de las Conchas** (The House of the Shells), a mellow 15th-century building whose exterior walls are decorated with more than 400 stone cockle shells, a reminder of the pilgrims who passed through the city on their way to Santiago de Compostela (➤ 26–28). Opposite looms the church of the **Clerecía**, a 17th-century baroque building, built for the Jesuits, with an impressive cloister.

The University of Salamanca

Salamanca's **university** was founded in the 13th-century and quickly made its mark as one of Europe's intellectual powerhouses, renowned for its freedom of thought and its huge academic prowess. It thrived for more than five centuries, its influence only waning under the attack of 18th-century extreme clericalism and the depredations of the Napoleonic troops. Today, it's outshone by the universities of Madrid and Barcelona, but retains its social prestige and is very popular with foreign Spanish-language students.

The tiny **Patio de las Escuelas**, flanked by a lovely courtyard, stands opposite the university's main entrance, a good place to admire this elaborate plateresque **facade** (1534). It is covered with superb decoration, a riot of foliage, heraldic decorations and medallions – the central one shows Isabella and Ferdinand, the Reyes Católicos (Catholic Monarchs). See if you can spot the tiny carved frog – good luck comes if you find it unaided. (Cheats should concentrate halfway up on the right pilaster.)

The entrance leads into a courtyard, surrounded by the old lecture halls, still in use today, from where you can explore the rest of the complex. Pick of the bunch is the **Aula Fray Luís de León**, which still retains its 16th-century furnishings. It was to here that Fray Luís returned in 1578 after five years in the hands of the Inquisition, starting his lecture with the words *"Dicebamus hesterna die…"* (as we were saying yesterday). On the upper floor you'll find the 18th-century **library**, lined with some 40,000 incunabula (early books) and 16th–18th century books.

The Cathedrals and Beyond

There's more plateresque work on the entrances to the **Catedral Nueva** (New Cathedral), just behind the university. Started in 1513, the New Cathedral acted as both a statement of Salamanca's prestige and a buttress to the Romanesque **Catedral Vieja** (Old Cathedral), which was in danger of imminent collapse. It's the wonderful contrast between the two buildings, one ornate and flamboyant, the other simple and serene, that makes the complex so special. The New Cathedral was largely complete by the 1560s, with later baroque additions. A door in the south aisle leads into the stunning Old Cathedral, all light and lofty golden stone. Glowing behind the main altar hangs the huge 15th-century *retablo* (altarpiece) by Nicolás Florentino, with 53 panels showing scenes from the Life of Christ and the Virgin. The adjoining cloister is surrounded by chapels, many of which were used as overflow university lecture rooms. Star of the show is the **Capilla de Anaya**, with its two exquisite alabaster tombs and a quirky little organ, said to be the oldest in Europe.

The entrance to the Universidad Pontificia de Salamanca

Behind the cathedral there's a contrast in the form of the **Museo Art Nouveau y Art Deco** (Museum of Art Nouveau and Art Deco). It contains lovely glass and porcelain, lamps and furniture but it's the building itself, the Casa Lis, which takes top prize. Filled with light and colour, it was built largely of coloured glass for an enthusiast in the early 1900s.

More Churches

East from here, the **Convento de San Esteban** (Convent of St Stephen) boasts a splendid plateresque facade, a beautiful portico and fine 16th-century Gothic-Renaissance cloisters. Inside, the east end is dominated by a baroque **retablo** by José Churriguera, a riot of decorative columns, statuary and wonderfully ornate decoration.

There are more cloisters at the **Convento de las Dueñas**, perhaps the most striking in Salamanca. Climb the creaky stairs to the upper level for a fabulous view of the cathedral, framed by the irregularly shaped cloisters themselves.

To the north, the **Convento de Santa Clara** is crammed with treasures, many of which hid under whitewash for years until rediscovery in the 1980s. The most riveting find was the orginal 14th-century ceiling of the church, decorated with the castles and lions of Castile and León, which had been covered by a baroque false ceiling.

TAKING A BREAK

Choose from one of the restaurants surrounding the Plaza Mayor, all of which serve tapas. **Don Mauro** (Plaza Mayor 19, tel: 923 281 487) is one of the best.

➕ 211 D5

Tourist Information Office
✉ Plaza Mayor 32 ☎ 902 302 002; www.salamanca.es 🕐 Summer Mon–Fri 9–2, 4:30–8, Sat 10–8, Sun 10–2; winter closes at 6:30pm

Casa de las Conchas
✉ Calle Compañia ☎ 923 269 317 🕐 Mon–Fri 9–9, Sat 9–2, Sun 10–2, 5–8 🎟 Free

La Clerecía
✉ Calle Compañia ☎ 923 277 100 🕐 Tue–Fri 10:30–12:45, 5–6:30, Sat 10–1, 5–7:15, Sun 10–1 🎟 Inexpensive

Universidad
✉ Patio de Escuelas ☎ 923 294 400 🕐 Mon–Fri 9:30–1:30, 4–7, Sat 9:30–1:30, 4–6:30, Sun 10–1:30 🎟 Moderate

Catedral Nueva
✉ Plaza de Anaya ☎ 923 217 476 🕐 Daily 9–1, 4–6 🎟 Free

Catedral Vieja
✉ Plaza de Anaya ☎ 923 217 476 🕐 Daily 10–2:30, 4–5:30 🎟 Moderate

Museo Art Nouveau y Art Deco
✉ Calle Expolio 14 ☎ 923 121 425 🕐 Tue–Fri 11–2, 5–9, Sat–Sun 11–9 🎟 Moderate

Convento de las Dueñas
✉ Plaza Concilio de Trento ☎ 923 215 442 🕐 Apr–Sep Mon–Sat 10:30–12:45, 4:30–6:45, Sun 11–12:45, 4:30–6:45; Oct–Mar Sun–Fri 11:30–12:45, 4:30–5:30 🎟 Inexpensive

Convento de San Esteban
✉ Plaza Concilio de Trento ☎ 923 215 000 🕐 Daily 10–1, 4–7:15 🎟 Inexpensive; free Mon am

Convento de Santa Clara
✉ Calle Santa Clara ☎ 923 269 623 🕐 Mon–Fri 9:30–1:30, 4–6, Sat–Sun 9–2:30 🎟 Inexpensive

SALAMANCA: INSIDE INFO

Top tips If you're pushed for time concentrate on the Plaza Mayor, the cathedrals and the university. Be sure to leave an hour or so simply to wander.
- The best time for a drink in the Plaza Mayor is after dark, when the square is beautifully floodlit.
- The Convento de las Dueñas still sells delicious cakes and biscuits made by the enclosed nuns. Ring the bell beside the hatch in the entrance hall, put in your order and money and the goods will appear on the turntable.

One to miss The religious art collection at the Museo de Salamanca (Bellas Artes) is pedestrian, though the exterior of the 15th-century mansion is superb.

Hidden gems It is worth the stroll down to the Puente Romano behind the cathedral; this graceful bridge has superb views back to the old city on the hill above.

4 León

First a Roman settlement, then the capital of the northern Christian kingdom during the Reconquista, León's power reached its peak from the 11th to the 13th centuries. Its finest monuments date from this time, grouped, with one exception, in the compact huddle of the old quarter. Around this nucleus a lively modern city spreads down to the River Bernesga, with everything you would expect from a stylish provincial capital with a big university presence.

León's great buildings are graphic examples of how French Romanesque architecture crept over the Pyrenees and through northern Spain in the wake of the pilgrims following the Camino de Santiago (➤ 26–28). León was a stopping point along the route, where pilgrims worshipped in the cathedral, founded in 1255, and rested before one of the hardest sections of the route.

The Cathedral
The soaring cathedral, with its flying buttresses and great rose windows, might easily have been transported straight from France – go inside for the assault of glowing colour from Spain's finest **stained glass** and you'll be even more struck by the similarities to French Gothic cathedrals. But here, the colours are less muted, vibrant reds and yellows replacing the soft pinks and blues found in France. Outside, two towers rise above the **central doorway** with its lively scenes of the Last Judgement.

The soaring towers and rose window on the facade of León's Gothic cathedral

San Isidoro
A 10-minute walk northwest through the old city from the cathedral lies the complex of **San Isidoro**, dating from the mid-11th to 12th centuries. The church, with its Moorish arches, was built after the **Panteón** next door, constructed by Ferdinand I as a mausoleum. The vaulted roof is covered with **12th-century paintings** portraying Christ Pantocrator and the Evangelists, surrounded by biblical scenes and decoration. The rural scenes representing the months of the year are as appealing as the day they were painted.

Hostal de San Marcos
West again and well outside medieval León, stands the Hostal de San Marcos, founded in 1168 as a pilgrim hostel. The original building was replaced in the 16th century when it

became the headquarters of the Knights of Santiago – look out for St James tackling the Moors above the main entrance. Behind the extravagant **plateresque facade** there is a beautiful cloister; part of the Parador now occupying San Marcos. The monastery's church is still open to visitors, although much of the complex is currently undergoing renovation.

TAKING A BREAK

If you're near the cathedral, head for the popular **Restaurante Catedral Bar** (Calle Mariano D Berrneta 17, tel: 987 215 918) where you'll find excellent tapas at the bar and full meals served in the restaurant behind.

➕ 204 B3

Tourist Information Office
✉ Plaza de la Regla 3 ☎ 987 237 082; www.aytoleon.com
🕐 Jul–Aug Mon–Fri 9–7, Sat–Sun 10–8; Sep–Jun Mon–Fri 9–2, 5–8, Sat–Sun 10–2, 5–8

Cathedral
✉ Plaza de la Regla ☎ 987 875 770; www.catedraldeleon. org 🕐 Jul–Sep Mon–Sat 8:30–1:30, 4–8, Sun 8:30–2:30, 5–8; Oct–Jun Mon–Sat 8:30–1:30, 4–7, Sun 8:30–2:30, 5–7

Museo Diocesano
✉ Plaza de la Regla ☎ 987 875 770 🕐 Jun–Sep Mon–Fri 9:30–2, 4–7:30, Sat 9:30–2, 4–7; Oct–May Mon–Fri 9:30–1:30, 4–7, Sat 9:30–1:30 ✋ Inexpensive

Panteón y Museo de San Isidoro
✉ Plaza de San Isidoro ☎ 987 876 161 🕐 Jul–Aug Mon–Sat 9–8, Sun 9–2; Sep–Jun Mon–Sat 10–1:30, 4–6:30, Sun 10–1:30 ✋ Inexpensive; free Thu pm

Iglesia de San Marcos
✉ Plaza San Marcos ☎ 987 237 300 🕐 May–Sep Tue–Sat 10–2, 5–8:30, Sun 10–2; Oct–Apr Tue–Sat 10–2, 4–7, Sun 10–2 ✋ Inexpensive

LEÓN: INSIDE INFO

Top tips Don't miss Antonio Gaudí's Casa de Botines, opposite the 16th-century Palacio de los Guzmanes on the edge of the old town.

■ The best way to visit Hostal de San Marcos and see its lovely cloister is to stay in the Parador there – but anyone can have a drink in the bar.

■ Head for the streets around the Plaza San Martín for León's liveliest and most atmospheric bars and restaurants.

■ If you are driving, park your car by the river, which is convenient for all the major sights.

One to miss Unless you are interested by ecclesiastical museums, skip the cathedral museum, though it's worth popping in to look at the cloister.

5 La Rioja

Vineyards in the rolling landscape along the valley of the
River Ebro produce Rioja, Spain's best-known quality wine.
Wine lovers could easily spend a couple of days following the
wine trails in the area, sampling and purchasing along the
way. Alternatively you can explore the region under your own
steam – on foot, by bicycle or even on horseback.

Haro

Haro is the capital of the region, an unremarkable working
town with some attractive buildings and plenty of
opportunities for wine-tasting. Famous wine producers like
Bodegas Bilbainas, Cune and about a dozen more are within
walking distance of the town. Ask at the tourist offices for
tours or visiting times for the *bodegas*, most of which are open
to the public.

Logroño and Laguardia

Further down the valley lies Logroño, a prosperous town
with a fine cathedral, pleasant riverside gardens and fantastic
tapas. Across the river, in the Rioja Alavesa, and so technically
in the Basque country, lies tranquil Laguardia, an old fortress
town. It is only kilometres away from the striking, temple-
like Bodegas Ysios, created by Spanish architect Santiago
Calatrava, and Frank Gehry's stunning Bodegas Marqués de
Riscal. There are more examples of top-class contemporary
architecture in other *bodegas* around the region.

TAKING A BREAK

If you have any space left after indulging in the nibbles that
accompany most wine tastings, head for Calle Laurel and
Calle de San Juan in central Logroño. These streets are lined
with bars each specializing in different tapas.

Right: Vinyards
in the fertile
valley of River
Ebro produce
Rioja wines

Left: Rioja
wines are aged
in oak barrels

🔲 206 A3

Tourist Information Office, Haro
🔲 206 A4 ✉ Plaza Forentino Rodriguez ☎ 941 303 366; www.beronia.org, www.lariojaturismo.com
🕐 Mon–Sat 10–2, 4:30–7:30, Sun 10–2

Tourist Information Office, Logroño
🔲 206 B4 ✉ c/ Portales 5 ☎ 941 273 353; www.logroturismo.org
🕐 Mon–Sat 10–2, 4:30–7:30, Sun 10–2

Tourist Information Office, Laguardia
🔲 206 B4 ✉ Palacio Samaniego, Plaza de San Juan ☎ 945 600 845; www.laguardia-alava.com

Bodegas Bilbainas
🔲 206 A4 ✉ Calle Estación 3, Haro ☎ 941 310 947; www.bodegasbilbainas.com 🕐 Tours: Tue–Sat 11am, 12pm, 5pm. Sun–Mon 11am. Reservations required.

Cune
🔲 206 A4 ✉ Barrio del Estación, Haro ☎ 941 304 809; www.cvne.com
🕐 Mon, Thu–Sat 10–6:30, Sun 11–3. Reservations required.

Bodegas Ysios
🔲 206 B4 ✉ Camino de la Hoya, Laguardia ☎ 945 600 640; www.ysios.com 🕐 Tours: Mon–Fri 11am, 1pm, 6pm, Sun 11am, 1pm. Reservations required.

Bodegas Marqués de Riscal
🔲 206 B4 ✉ C/ Torrea 1, Elciego ☎ 945 180 888; www.marquesderiscal.com 🕐 Phone for times

---

LA RIOJA: INSIDE INFO

Hidden gem The vineyards disappear if you head southeast into the Rioja Baja to be replaced by an even more ancient sight. The **Centre Paleontológico** (tel: 941 396 093, www.dinasaurioslarioja.org) is the starting point for several trails following impressive fossilized dinosaur tracks. There is also good information about other sites and giant replica dinosaurs.

At Your Leisure

6 Covarrubias and Surrounding Area

Covarrubias, southeast of Burgos, is a pretty, small town, complete with an historic church and picturesque half-timbered buildings, whose flower-draped walls shelter cool arcades.

From Covarrubias you could head south again to visit the Benedictine abbey of Santo Domingo de Silos. Its great double-storeyed Romanesque cloister was built in the 11th century and is one of the loveliest in Spain. The sculptural reliefs are outstanding, as are the capitals of its columns, but what you'll chiefly remember is the atmosphere of peace and the lazy splash of water in the central fountain. The abbey's monks are famed worldwide for Gregorian chant. Sung Mass is celebrated on Sundays at noon.

✚ 205 E2

Monasterio de Santo Domingo de Silos
✉ Valle de Tabladillo ☎ 947 390 039; www.abadiadesilos.es 🕓 Tue–Sat 10–1, 4:30–6, Sun–Mon 4:30–6 💶 Moderate

7 Sierra de Guadarrama

The range of mountains known as the Sierra de Guadarrama stretches to the northwest of Madrid, a natural barrier between Madrid and Castile,

The castle at Manzanares el Real

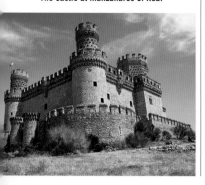

and a favourite recreational area for *Madrileños*. These beautiful hills enclose two regional parks (Peñalara and La Pedriza), which have kept large areas relatively unspoiled. You could take the little train which runs from Cercedilla to Puerto de Navacerrada, the heart of the ski area, or visit the magnificent castle at Manzanares el Real. Across the range, the highlights are the two Bourbon summer palaces of La Granja, with its spectacular fountains, and Riofrío, surrounded by a deer park.

✚ 212 A5

8 Ávila

Ávila is famous on two counts – its wonderfully preserved city walls and its home-grown saint, the mystic St Teresa. Alfonso VI's Muslim prisoners built the walls in the 1090s following the re-capture of the city from the Moors. These massive structures, still complete with their 88 watch towers, encircle the old city, and walking at least one section should be high on your list. Ávila's architectural hotchpotch of a cathedral backs on to them; started in the 11th century, the apse is actually an integral part of the walls. There are several convents and museums associated with St Teresa – she is the joint patron saint of Spain along with Santiago (St James).

✚ 211 E4

Tourist Information Office
✉ Plaza de Pedro Dávila 8 ☎ 920 211 387; www.avilaturismo.com 🕓 Jul–Sep Mon–Thu 9–8, Fri–Sat 9–9; Oct–Jun daily 9–2, 5–8

Murallas (City Walls)
✉ Puerta del Alcázar, Puerta del Rastro 🕓 Tue–Sat 10–2, 4:30–7:30, Sun 10:30–2 💶 Inexpensive

Cathedral
✉ Plaza de la Catedral ☎ 920 211 641 🕓 Mon–Sat 10–7:30, Sun 12–6:30 💶 Moderate

Where to...
Stay

Prices
Expect to pay for a double room per night:
€ up to €100   €€ €101–€180   €€€ €181–€240   €€€€ over €240

BURGOS

El Mesón Del Cid €€

In the very heart of the old city, this comfortable hotel faces the cathedral and overlooks the Plaza Santa María. The rooms are light and airy – try to get one in the main building, though those in the nearby annexe share the view and are up to a similar standard. The private parking is a real bonus; the staff are friendly and efficient and the attached restaurant is a good choice if you don't want to venture out.

➕ 205 E3 ⊠ Plaza Santa María 8 ☎ 947 208 715; www.mesondelcid.es

Norte y Londres €€

Pretty balconies and the glass-fronted galleries so typical of Burgos adorn the facade of this fine old hotel on Plaza Alonso Martínez, not far from the cathedral in the centre of town. There is a grand reception area and the 50 spacious, wood-floored rooms are simply furnished with classic, stately furniture, and there's a refined but welcoming feel throughout. A good breakfast is served in the hotel's elegant dining room.

➕ 205 E3 ⊠ Plaza Alonso Martínez 10 ☎ 947 264 125; www.norteylondreshotel.com

SEGOVIA

Infanta Isabel €€

Overlooking the Plaza Mayor and the cathedral, this traditional old hotel has wooden floors and is decorated with flowery prints. Many of the comfortable en-suite rooms have great views of town.

➕ 211 F5 ⊠ Plaza Mayor ☎ 921 461 300; www.hotelinfantaisabel.com

Los Linajes €€

This pleasant mid-range hotel in a quiet corner of the old town offers comfortable accommodation and traditional service. Some of the spacious bedrooms have private balconies and there's a large outdoor terrace with lovely views.

➕ 211 F5 ⊠ Calle Doctor Velasco 9 ☎ 921 460 475; www.loslinajes.com

SALAMANCA

Petit Palace Las Torres €€€

Housed in an historic building with many rooms overlooking the Plaza Mayor, this is a tastefully modern boutique hotel. The stylish en-suite rooms are well equipped, with ADSL connections and flat screen TVs.

➕ 211 D5 ⊠ Calle Concejo 4 ☎ 923 212 100; www.petitpalacelastorres.com

Hostal Sara €

With comfortable en-suite rooms and a good, central location, close to the Plaza Mayor, this friendly hostal is a good budget option. Be sure to ask for one of the internal rooms as the pedestrian road outside can get quite noisy.

➕ 211 D5 ⊠ Calle Meléndez 11 ☎ 923 281 149; www.hostalsara.org

LEÓN

Hotel La Posada Regia €€

The welcome is warm and the level of comfort high in this small, mid-range hotel. It is ideally situated just off the pedestrian-only main street in the old town. The hotel has comfortable brick-clad rooms

Where to...
Eat and Drink

Prices

Expect to pay per person for a meal, including wine and service

€ up to €12   €€ €12–€35   €€€ over €35

BURGOS

Casa Ojeda €€

This long-established, popular place offers classic Burgos fare in a cosy setting of Moorish tiles and low ceilinged rooms full of interesting nooks and crannies. The upper restaurant is in two sections. Typical dishes include Basque-style hake, roast lamb or chicken in garlic. A house speciality is *alubias con chorizo y morcilla* (white beans and spicy sausage).

➕ 205 E3 ⊠ Calle Vitoria 5 ☎ 947 209 052; www.restauranteojeda.com 🕓 Mon–Sat 1:30–4, 9–11:30; Sun 1:30–4

Gaona Jardín €€

Hidden in an alleyway just round the corner from the cathedral and Calle de la Paloma, a street that is lined with tapas bars, is this little Andalucian-style garden. Its bar is laden with tasty *pinchos*, renowned as some of the best in town. There are plenty of these tapas-like snacks to choose from: try the sliced dried tomato with anchovy or the quails egg with wild mushroom sauce. If you want to order warm tapas try the *bacalao* (salt cod) or *foie gras*.

➕ 205 E3 ⊠ Calle de la Sombrerería 29 ☎ 947 206 191; www.gaonajardin.com 🕓 Tue–Sun 1–4, 9–midnight

---

of Logroño. Downstairs there are touches of contemporary design, while the comfortable guest rooms are well decorated in tasteful colours and the swish bathrooms are a treat. The staff are friendly and helpful, and can offer advice on parking. The extensive breakfast buffet is extra.

➕ 206 B4 ⊠ Calle Marqués de Vallejo, Logroño ☎ 941 248 333; www.hotelmarquesdevallejo.com

Hotel Villa de Laguardia €€€

Just over the border in the Rioja Alavesa, this elegant hotel provides the perfect base from which to explore the surrounding villages and wine cellars. Rooms are simply but elegantly furnished, with all the amenities that you would expect of a luxury hotel. Facilities include a top-notch pool, luxurious spa and excellent restaurant – all for very reasonable prices.

➕ 206 B4 ⊠ Paseo de San Raimundo 15, Laguardia ☎ 945 600 560; www.hotelvilladelaguardia.com

---

decorated in warm, bold colours, and its own restaurant specializing in local dishes.

➕ 204 B3 ⊠ Calle Regidores 9–11 ☎ 987 213 173; www.regialeon.com

Parador Hostal San Marcos €€€€

One of Spain's great hotels, this luxurious Parador dates from the 16th century, but the facilities are entirely contemporary. Most of the rooms are in a more modern annexe, but the public rooms of this former pilgrims' hostel have tapestries, carpets and pictures that create a living museum, while the superb cloisters reflect a monastic calm. Service and comfort are of the highest standard.

➕ 204 B3 ⊠ Plaza San Marcos 7 ☎ 987 237 300; www.parador.es

LA RIOJA

Hotel Marqués de Vallejo €€€

This stylish little hotel is in an historic building right in the centre

SEGOVIA

El Descanso de Juan Pacheco €€

The tapas at this typical Segovian bar, just off the Plaza Mayor, are top-notch and the prices good value. It is attached to José María, one of the town's top restaurants, which offers new takes on the traditional classics of the area.

➕ 211 F5 ⊠ Calle Cronista Lecea 11
☎ 921 461 111; www.rtejosemaria.com

Mesón de Candido €€

Eating is a serious matter in this historic 15th-century building beneath the Roman aqueduct. The traditions of the best Castilian country cooking are upheld in this long-established restaurant. The local *judiones de la Granja*, oversize broad white beans, often served with pigs' ears and trotters, are a speciality. As are roast suckling pig and baby lamb. The suckling pig is so tender that the waiters traditionally carve it at your table using the edge of a plate. Try the *tarta de ponche segoviano*, an alcohol-soaked cake, to complete the feast. The restaurant is extremely popular, so make reservations in advance.

➕ 211 F5 ⊠ Plaza Azoguejo 5 ☎ 921 425 911; www.mesondecandido.es ⓦ Daily 1–4, 9–midnight

SALAMANCA

Meson Las Conchas €–€€

Eat very inexpensively at this tapas bar and restaurant surrounded by enticing shops on one of the city's most attractive pedestrian-only streets. Fronted by a spit-and-sawdust bar dishing up wedges of tortilla and cheese, upstairs is the surprise of a restaurant with black bow-tied waiters and elegant furnishings. The menu is vast including salads, vegetarian, seafood and more meat dishes.

➕ 211 D5 ⊠ Rúa Mayor 16,
☎ 923 212 167; www.mesonlasconchas.es
ⓦ Daily 9–9

Restaurante El Mesón €€€

A flight of steps leads down into the pleasant vaulted dining rooms of this temple of Salamancan gastronomy, founded more than 50 years ago. The air-conditioned interior is restrained, with well-spaced tables, and the service attentive. *Cochinillo asado* (roast suckling pig) is one of the restaurant's specialities, but other meat dishes, mainly roasts, reflect the attention paid to the highest quality ingredients. If you have room, round off with one of the tempting desserts.

➕ 211 D5 ⊠ Plaza del Poeta Iglesias 10 ☎ 923 217 222 ⓦ Mon–Sat 1–4, 9–midnight, Sun 2–5

LEÓN

Boccalino €–€€

Perfectly placed for a relaxing meal after a trip to the complex of San Isidoro, this attractive restaurant, airy and spacious inside, also has tables for outside dining in the beautiful square. Choose from the good selection of local cold meats (*embutidos*), salads, or ring the changes with one of the tasty pizzas, pastas or tortillas on the menu. There is a wide choice of better-than-usual desserts and ice-cream if you crave something sweet to finish your meal. Service is professional and friendly.

➕ 204 B3 ⊠ Plaza de San Isidoro 9
☎ 987 223 060; www.hostalboccalino.com
ⓦ Daily 1–4, 9–midnight

Restaurante El Palomo €€

Pass through the pretty bar area to the welcoming, though slightly cramped, dining room, meticulously run by the highly professional owner. There are two well-priced set menus of typical Leónese dishes, with the chance to eat fresh trout and some traditional vegetable specialities. The wine list is of a high calibre, including some outstanding Riojas.

➕ 204 B3 ⊠ Calle Escalerilla 8
☎ 987 254 225 ⓦ Daily 1–4, 9–11:30

Where to...
Shop

There are shops selling local handicrafts – textiles, ceramics and leatherwork – throughout the region but the fine Rioja wines and various regional wines make some of the most memorable gifts to take home.

CAKES AND SWEETS

The *ponche segoviano* (a liqueur-dipped, custard-filled cake topped with marzipan) is sold throughout Segovia. In Avila, look out for *yemas de Santa Teresa*, sticky yellow sweets traditionally made in the town's convents and sold everywhere.

In Salamanca the specialities are *turrón* (hard nougat made from honey and almonds), *paciencias* (almond cakes) or *chochos* (almond and chocolate cakes).

BUYING RIOJA

You are unlikely to find any real bargains in the Rioja region, just good wines, the price of which reflects their quality and the renown of the label. Understanding a few Spanish viniculture terms will help: Gran Reserva wines are aged for at least two years in oak casks and a further three in the bottle. Next in quality come the Reservas, select wines that have spent three years maturing, one of which has been in oak. Crianzas are in their third year, after spending at least one year aging in wood. *Cosecha* or *vino del año* are young wines often with a light, fruity character. Recent "very good" years include 1998 and 2006, while 2001 and 2004 are deemed "excellent years".

Where to...
Be Entertained

Burgos, Segovia, Salamanca and León all have sizeable university populations so there's always a street in town that will get going from midnight onwards.

Salamanca, in particular, is renowned for its raucous nightlife, fuelled in part by the many foreign students that attend the university and language schools in the city. Lively areas include the lanes around the Convento de las Úrsulas, Plaza de San Justo, around Calle Varillas near the market and the arcades of Gran Via. The tables outside Clavel Ocho at Calle Clavel 6 are a good place to start the evening. Remember to opt for an internal room in your hotel if you want the option of sleeping before the small hours.

Beyond the major cities, most visitors are happy to while away the evening enjoying the *paseo* (the early-evening promenade) with the locals and having a drink and a good dinner in the balmy evening air gazing at some stupendous facade – after dark, the main buildings are often floodlit. In some smaller towns and villages, this will probably be all that is on offer.

If you're looking for local culture, ask at the **tourist offices** (www.turismocastillayleon.com) for information on the major fiesta weeks. Apart from Semana Santa (Easter Week), which is big in León, most festivals take place during the summer, when the whole town or village will come alive in a riot of noise, festivity, food and drink.

Atlantic Northern Regions

Getting Your Bearings

The Atlantic and the mountains define Spain's northern
coastal regions; the tides rising and falling, the weather
systems beating in from the west, the very different rhythm of
life from the sun-drenched south, all adding up to utter magic.

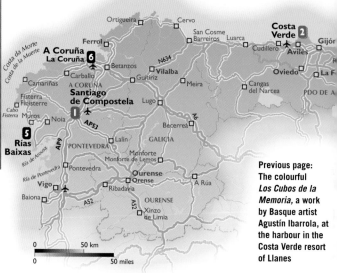

Previous page:
The colourful
*Los Cubos de la
Memoria,* a work
by Basque artist
Agustín Ibarrola, at
the harbour in the
Costa Verde resort
of Llanes

The scenery is stunning, an ever-changing pattern of water and coastline,
green fields and woodland, hills and mountains. This is countryside for
exploring – walking on a near-empty beach, dawdling in some laid-back Costa
Verde village, following the indented shores of the Rías Baixas. It includes
Galicia, with its distinctive character and scenery – hills, white-sand beaches
and deep fjord-like inlets. East lies the enchanting Costa Verde, with its
verdant turf, smooth sandy beaches and aquamarine sea. This lovely coast is
backed by the green hills of Asturias and Cantabria and the superb mountains
of the Picos de Europa.

East again lies the Basque heartland, thriving and individual, with its
friendly people and instantly recognizable sense of identity. The Basque
country spills inland from the coast into neighbouring Navarra (Navarre), well
worth exploring if you've got time. Its diverse landscape is dotted with historic
cities and towns such as Pamplona and tiny Puente la Reina.

Apart from all this, the region has some lovely towns and great cultural
treasures. Santiago de Compostela is one of Spain's most perfect medieval
cities, Santillana del Mar one of its prettiest villages, Bilbao an increasingly
dynamic centre, while the Paleolithic cave paintings at Altamira are of
worldwide importance.

It is a big area, its roads slow, its tourist infrastructure less developed than
elsewhere. Take it slowly and enjoy its charms.

★ **Don't Miss**

Tranquil Playa del Tero, near Llanes

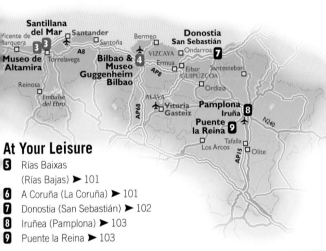

At Your Leisure

Santillana del Mar's Romanesque *colegiata* (collegiate church), which dates from the
12th to 13th centuries

In Five Days

If you are not quite sure where to begin your travels, this itinerary recommends five practical and enjoyable days in the Atlantic Northern Regions, taking in some of the best places to see using the Getting Your Bearings map on the previous page. For more information see the main entries.

Day 1

Morning
Spend the morning visiting **❶**Santiago's **cathedral** (➤ 92), the **Museo y Tesoro de la Catedral** (➤ 92) and the buildings around the **Praza do Obradoiro** (➤ 92–93).

Afternoon
Once the museums open up after lunch, head for the **Museo das Peregrinacións** (➤ 93), perhaps following this up with an hour in the **Museo do Pobo Gallego** (➤ 93–94).

Evening
Don't miss the *paseo* before dining in the old town. After dinner, head for the Praza do Obradoiro to see the **floodlighting** and perhaps to listen to some buskers playing Galician music.

Day 2

Morning
Leave Santiago after breakfast and take the E01 *autopista* towards **❻A Coruña (La Coruña,** ➤ 101), picking up the N-VI on the outskirts of A Coruña towards Lugo, where the N640 heads northeast towards the coast. At Ribadeo, turn east on to the N634.

Afternoon/Evening
Once on the **❷Costa Verde** (➤ 95–96), head for **Luarca** (below, ➤ 95) and spend a couple of hours pottering about enjoying the resort's relaxed atmosphere, then head further along the **Costa Verde** to **Llanes** (➤ 96), where you could spend one or more nights.

Day 3

Head for **Cangas de Onís**, the starting point for a superbly scenic day's drive in the **Picos de Europa** (➤ 180–181). Return to Llanes for a second night or head further east and spend the night at the picturesque village of **Santillana del Mar** (➤ 98).

Day 4

Morning
Leave Llanes early or, if you've spent the night at Santillana, head straight for the **8 Museo de Altamira** (➤ 97–98) to enjoy this superb attraction before the crowds arrive.

Afternoon
Spend the afternoon exploring the villages and beaches along the **Costa Verde**, popping into the museum in Lastres to see its collection of dinosaur remains if you have time (➤ 96), then return to Santillana for the evening.

Day 5

Morning
Head to **4 Bilbao** (above, ➤ 99–100) on the N634. As you come in, look out for the purple signs to the **Museo Guggenheim Bilbao** (➤ 99). Spend the rest of the morning at the Guggenheim, then have a light lunch in the museum's restaurant.

Afternoon
Take in Bilbao's **Casco Viejo** and then hit the shops – Bilbao has some of the best in the region, and there's usually evening entertainment on offer.

Ⓞ Santiago de Compostela

Santiago de Compostela, one of the three great shrines of medieval Christendom, has attracted millions of pilgrims over the centuries. They have walked the Camino de Santiago (► 26–28) to worship at the shrine of St James, the patron saint of Spain. It is one of Spain's most perfect medieval cities, a glorious mix of religious and secular buildings, with an ancient and thriving university, and a unique atmosphere.

Catedral de Santiago

Santiago's star turn is indubitably the cathedral. It dates from the 11th to the 13th century, the simple Romanesque lines of the interior providing a superb contrast to the ornate 1750 facade, the main access. Behind, stands the original 12th-century entrance, the **Pórtico de la Gloria** (Doorway of Glory), one of the sculptural glories of Spain. Carvings on this triple doorway depict prophets and apostles surrounding Christ the Saviour and the Four Evangelists, with St James below. The pillar beneath St James is worn from the millions of pilgrims' hands which have touched it in thanksgiving for their safe arrival. The interior's huge proportions and the ambulatory behind the altar were designed to accommodate as many pilgrims as possible, and give them room to move around. You'll notice a rope-pulley system high above the transept. This operates the *botafumeiro*, a monster incense burner used on major feast days, which needs eight men to swing it through an immense arc above the transept. In marked contrast to the plain granite spaces of the cathedral, the high altar glitters, the lights of the candelabra flashing off the embossed silverwork and gilded figures.

Reached from the cathedral, the **Museo y Tesoro de la Catedral** (Cathedral Museum and Treasury) is housed around the magnificent 16th-century cloisters, and includes the Romanesque old cathedral beneath the Pórtico de la Gloria and the chapel of San Fernando. Stairs lead up to the gallery, completed in 1590, a good vantage point over the square.

Exploring Santiago

The cathedral, superbly set on the sweeping **Praza do Obradoiro**, lies at the heart of the old city. From here, the two main streets,

Rúa do Franco and Rúa do Vilar, lined with shops, bars and restaurants, lead to the Porta Fexeira. All around lies the **Barrio Antiguo** (old quarter), its lovely arcaded streets lined with beautiful granite buildings in the traditional Galician style. Praza do Obradoiro is surrounded on its other sides by three harmonious buildings. The oldest, the **Hostal dos Reis Católicos** (Hostel of the Catholic Monarchs) was founded by Ferdinand and Isabella (► 9) as a lodging house for pilgrims and is now the flagship of the national Parador hotels (► 84). In the centre of its elegantly plain facade is a superb plateresque doorway. Opposite, the **Colegio de San Jéronimo**, with its charming balcony, dates mainly from the 17th century, while the **Ayuntamiento** was built in the 18th century. East of here, the spacious **Praza de Quintana** is surrounded by notable buildings – the lovely arcaded **Casa de la Canónica**, facing a gracious flight of steps leading up to the 17th-century **Casa de la Parra**; opposite is the austere facade of **San Pelayo de Antealtares** monastery. On the other side of the cathedral you'll find the huge complex of the **Monasterio de San Martiño Pinario**, with its church and three cloisters.

Santiago's Museums

The first choice must be the pilgrimage museum, **Museo das Peregrinacións**, a few minutes' walk through the back streets to the north of the cathedral. The museum tells the story of pilgrimage in general, and the Santiago pilgrimage in particular. There's a copy of the fascinating *Codex Calixtinus*, a 12th-century guide to the route, full of tips about travel and information about Santiago; look out too for the collection of souvenirs – 14th-century pilgrims took home much the same keepsakes as people do today. East from here, the fascinating **Museo do Pobo Gallego** (Museum of the Galician People) concentrates on Galician history and culture. Its galleries are housed in the church of Santo Domingo outside the walls of the old city. Interesting rooms encircle the 17th-century cloister, in one corner of which a superb staircase, with three intertwining flights of steps, rises to the different floors of the building.

TAKING A BREAK

A few steps from the cathedral is **Sant-Yago** (Rúa da Raiña 12, tel: 981 582 444), housed in a traditional old stone building where Alfonso Fraga concentrates on ham and cheese dishes of superb quality, as well as a range of Galician specialities.

➕ 202 B4

Tourist Information Office
✉ Rúa do Vilar 63 ☎ 981 555 129; www.santiagoturismo.com
🕐 Jun–Sep daily 9–9; Oct–May 9–2, 4–7

Cathedral
✉ Praza do Obradoiro ☎ 981 583 548
or 981 560 558 🕐 Daily 7:30am–9pm;
hourly rooftop tours Tue–Sat 10–1,
4–7; times may vary 💷 Free

Museo y Tesoro de la Catedral
✉ Praza do Obradoiro ☎ 981 569 327
🕐 Summer Mon–Sat 10–2, 4–8, Sun
10–2; winter Mon–Sat 10–1:30, 4–6:30,
Sun 10–1:30 💷 Moderate

Museo das Peregrinacións
✉ Rúa San Miguel 4 ☎ 981 581
558; www.mdperegrinacions.com
🕐 Tue–Fri 10–8, Sat 10:30–1:30, 5–8,
Sun 10:30–1:30 💷 Inexpensive

Museo do Pobo Gallego
✉ Rúa de San Domingos de Bonaval
☎ 981 583 620;
www.museodopobo.es 🕐 Tue–Sat
10–2, 4–8, Sun 11–2 💷 Free

Santiago's streets are lined with granite buildings

SANTIAGO DE COMPOSTELA: INSIDE INFO

Top tips The best time to visit Santiago is around 25 July, the feast of St James, which coincides with the two-week long Gallego folklore festival. Reserve well in advance as the city is packed at this time.

- To get a true taste of what the Santiago experience means to the pilgrims, look in on the Pilgrim's Mass, celebrated daily at noon in the cathedral.
- Be prepared for heavy rain in Santiago – the city's situated in one of the wettest corners of Galicia, the rainiest region in Spain.
- Try to see the Praza do Obradoiro after dark to witness the dramatic floodlighting and strolling musicians.
- For an overall view of Santiago, stroll along the Paseo da Ferradura in the pleasant public gardens southwest of the old town.

2 Costa Verde

The Costa Verde – the Green Coast – is, as far as foreigners are concerned, one of Spain's best-kept secrets. Stretching right along the Asturian coastline into Cantabria, this chain of fishing villages and low-key resorts, golden beaches and tumbling cliffs offers something for everyone. Pines, eucalyptus, springy turf and the clear green sea give it its name, while its natural beauty is enhanced by the wooded hinterland with mountains rising behind.

West of Gijón

Travelling along the coast from the west, make **Luarca** (Lluarca) your first stop. This lovely little town, set at the mouth of the River Negro, combines the charms of an old-fashioned resort with its true function as a working fishing port. Attractive houses line its streets and squares and encircle the harbour, which is sheltered by a rocky headland crowned with a church and lighthouse.

Cudillero, one of the Costa Verde's charming towns

East of here, **Cudillero** (Cuideiru) is another charmer, with colour-washed arcaded houses curving around its port and a plethora of excellent fish restaurants. Neighbouring **Salinas** is a more developed resort, its chief draw is its pinewoods and beach, one of the longest on the coast. You could take the AS328 out over the moorland to the **Cabo de Peñas**, the northernmost point of the Asturian coast.

East of Gijón

Beyond the lively provincial town of Gijón (Xixon), it's worth pausing at **Lastres** (Llastres), huddled beneath steep cliffs. It is home to the **Museo del Jurásico de Asturias**, which contains the world's most complete collection of dinosaur remains. **La Isla**, a small resort, has a great reputation for cider and seafood. **Ribadesella** (Ribesella), at the mouth of the River Sella, is much larger, a working port and holiday town with an fine beach. East of here, **Llanes** is a delight, and one of the best bases for exploring the Costa Verde. The old town stands at the river mouth, and there's a clifftop *paseo*, all green turf and tamarisk trees, with superb views.

Into Cantabria

Across the border into Cantabria, **San Vicente de la Barquera** is worth visiting for its situation alone. The old town perches above the sea and is approached by a causeway. **Comillas**, where pretty cobbled streets lead to two wonderful beaches, makes a good stop. There's a tiny nature reserve for wildfowl and seabirds, and El Capricho, a grandiose villa designed by Gaudí, which is now an expensive restaurant. From here, it's not far to **Santillana del Mar** (➤ 98) and the charms of **Santander**, a stunningly sited, elegant resort, with some of the best beaches in Spain.

El Capricho in Comillas, architect Antoni Gaudí's flight of fancy

TAKING A BREAK

At **Playa de Comillas** try **La Caracola** (Playa de Comillas, tel: 942 720 741) bar-cum-restaurant.

Tourist Information Office, Llanes
🔲 204 C5 ✉ La Torre, Calle Alfonso IX ☎ 985 400 164; www.infoasturias.com; www.llanes.com 🕓 Summer daily 10–2, 5–9; winter Mon–Sat 10–2, 4–6:30, Sun 10–2

Tourist Information Office, Santander
🔲 205 E5 ✉ Jardines de Pereda s/n ☎ 942 203 000; www.turismodecantabria.com 🕓 Mid-Jun to mid-Sep daily 9–9; mid-Sep to Easter Mon–Fri 8:30–7, Sat 10–2; Easter to mid-Jun Mon–Fri 8:30–7, Sat–Sun 10–7

Museo del Jurásico de Asturias, Lastres
🔲 204 C5 ✉ La Rassa de San Telmo ☎ 902 306 600; www.museojurasico.com 🕓 Jun–Sep daily 10:30–2:30, 4–8; Oct–May Wed–Sun 10–2:30, 4–7 🎟 Moderate

COSTA VERDE: INSIDE INFO

Top tips Very few off-the-beaten-track beaches have any facilities, so take a picnic and be prepared to walk from where you leave the car.
■ The N632 and N634 are relatively fast roads but are set back from the coast; if you use them you'll get little sense of the Costa Verde. Instead take side roads wherever possible.
■ The Costa Verde is best explored outside the peak holiday months of July and August, when it's busy with Spanish and French holidaymakers.

3 Museo de Altamira and Santillana del Mar

The winning combination of the stunning Altamira museum, which tells the story of one of Europe's greatest Paleolithic treasures, with the mellow charms of the tiny, picturesque village of Santillana del Mar, makes this little corner of Cantabria unmissable.

So significant are the Paleolithic cave paintings at Altamira that only replicas are now open to the public

Museo de Altamira

In 1879, the archaeologist Marcelino de Sautuola discovered the extraordinary pictures and engravings at Altamira – the first **Paleolithic cave paintings** to be found. Astoundingly, some date back to 25,000BC, art speaking to us from the dawn of mankind. The chamber depicting bison (15,000–12,000BC) established Altamira's reputation and visitor numbers soared. Throughout the 20th century, concern grew at the effect the presence of the crowds was having on these fragile masterpieces, a concern balanced by the realization that these extraordinary works should be accessible. The result was the admirable **Museo de Altamira**, opened in 2001, which incorporates a replica of the painted caves with a state-of-the-art exhibition space, museum and audiovisual facility.

The tour of the **Neocave**, as the replica is called, tells the entire story of man's habitation of the caves, the highlight being a superbly accurate duplicate of the painted rocks themselves. You'll see how these ancient artists used the rock formations to suggest shape and movement – bison galloping, curled in sleep and crouched together. Look out too for deer, wild boar and a primitive horse. The artists outlined the shapes, as big as 1.5m (5ft), with charcoal and coloured them using natural pigments, mainly ochre, mixed with animal fat.

Santillana del Mar

You have to see the chocolate-box-pretty village of Santillana del Mar, just 3km (2 miles) from Altamira, which, despite its name, is not on the sea. This architecturally homogenous gem grew up around the monastery of Santa Juliana, waxing rich in the 15th century. The majority of the balconied houses date from between the 15th and 18th centuries, while the *colegiata* (collegiate church), with its Romanesque cloister, dates from the 12th and 13th centuries. Santillana is tiny, and a real tourist hot spot – come early or late in the day, when the bus tours have gone and the returning cattle prove that this is still a functioning farming community.

TAKING A BREAK

The best place to stop is the museum's light and airy coffee shop and restaurant. Alternatively, there is the hotel/restaurant Altamira (➤ 105).

➕ 205 D5

Museo de Altamira
✉ Santillana del Mar ☎ 942 818 005; http://museodealtamira.mcu.es
🕐 Summer Tue–Sat 9:30–7:30, Sun 9:30–3; winter 9:30–5, Sun 9:30–3
💶 Inexpensive

Tourist Information Office, Santillana del Mar
✉ Jesús Otero 20 ☎ 942 818 251; www.santillana-del-mar.com 🕐 Daily 9:30–1:30, 4:30–7:30

MUSEO DE ALTAMIRA AND SANTILLANA DEL MAR: INSIDE INFO

Top tips If you have the chance, spend time first in the **exhibition** before visiting the Neocave – it's the best way to get the most out of your visit.

■ Entry to the Neocave is timed; your time will be printed on your ticket as it is issued. Be prepared for a **lengthy wait** at busy times. Advance reservation is strongly recommended. You can buy tickets with a pre-reserved entry time by phone (tel: 902 242 424) or at Banco Santander ATMs (follow the on-screen instructions).

■ It is no longer possible to visit the original caves due to a protracted, ongoing survey of contamination levels. Check online for the latest information on future opening.

In more detail The limestone **caves at Puente Viesgo**, 24km (14.5 miles) from Santander, are also worth visiting, both for their rock formations and the cave paintings, which are believed to be even older than the ones at Altamira. The visitor centre has an excellent interactive exhibition. Tours are in Spanish only.

4 Bilbao and Museo Guggenheim Bilbao

In the early 1990s few people would have earmarked Bilbao (Bilbo), the ex-industrial Basque capital, as a potential major tourist draw. Today, it's precisely that, thanks to the vision of the Basque government and the Museo Guggenheim Bilbao. This astonishing structure is the vanguard of a huge and imaginative urban renewal scheme, which has seen the regeneration of the whole of downtown Bilbao.

Museo Guggenheim Bilbao

Designed by Canadian-born architect Frank Gehry, the Guggenheim opened in 1997 as a European showcase for some of the Guggenheim Foundation's collection of 20th-century art. Standing on the banks of the River Nervión, the sinuous curves, glass and glittering titanium of this astounding building dominate the city's heart. The building centres round an atrium, 55m (180ft) high, with irregular-shaped galleries leading off – one over 130m (142 yards) long. Glass lifts whisk you up to higher levels, where curving walkways hang from the roof and give access to the upper exhibition spaces. Outside, a terrace overlooks a reflecting pool above the river, while on the other side of the building, a flight of shallow steps leads down to the main entrance. Inevitably, it's the building itself that attracts the crowds, but the permanent collection includes works by most major 20th-century artists and the temporary exhibitions staged here are among the most diverse and stimulating on show anywhere in Europe.

Museo Guggenheim Bilbao, architect Frank Gehry's spectacular creation

The City

Don't ignore the rest of Bilbao, a thriving, friendly city stretching along a river valley, from whose streets you can always glimpse green hills. The **Casco Viejo** (old quarter), across the river, is home to the Gothic cathedral, the elegant arcaded Plaza Nueva and the fascinating **Museo Vasco**. This is housed in a lovely old building surrounding a cloister and will fill you in on the history and culture of the Basques. The Casco Viejo is also home to Bilbao's best bars and restaurants. Back across the river, you might also want to take in the **Museo de Bellas Artes**, a few minutes walk from the Guggenheim, set in a tranquil park. Here, you'll find paintings by El Greco, Goya and Murillo, as well as a number of works by Basque artists. Nearby, the huge Palacio Euskalduna, built on the site of an old shipyard, is part of Bilbao's ongoing redevelopment.

TAKING A BREAK

Head for the streamlined **Guggenheim Bilbao Restaurant** (Anandoibarra Etorbidea 2, tel: 944 239 333, www.restauranteguggenheim.com). There is an excellent range of snacks or some of the lightest and most innovative "new Basque" cooking imaginable. You must book, however, and the restaurant is closed on Mondays.

➕ 206 C5

Museo Guggenheim Bilbao
✉ Abandoibarra Etorbidea 2
☎ 944 359 080;
www.guggenheim-bilbao.es 🕐 Daily
10–8 💲 Expensive

Tourist Information Offices, Bilbao
✉ Abandoibarra Etorbidea 2 (near
Museo Guggenheim) ☎ 944 795
760; www.bilbao.net 🕐 Summer
Mon–Sat 10–3, 4–7, Sun 10–3;
winter Tue–Fri 11–2:30, 3:30–6, Sat
11–3, 4–7, Sun 11–2

✉ Plaza Ensanche 11 ☎ 944 795
760; www.bilbao.net 🕐 Mon–Fri
9–2, 4–7:30

Museo Vasco
✉ Plaza Miguel de Unamuno 4
☎ 944 155 423;
www.euskal-museoa.org 🕐 Tue–Sat
11–5, Sun 11–2 💲 Inexpensive

Museo de Bellas Artes
✉ Plaza del Museo 2 ☎ 944 396
060; www.museobilbao.com 🕐 Tue–
Sun 10–8 💲 Moderate

BILBAO AND MUSEO GUGGENHEIM BILBAO: INSIDE INFO

Top tips You'll find a good range of books and gifts in the museum shop.
- Vision Bilbao is a jump-on, jump-off tourist bus which loops round the main areas of the city throughout the day.
- Bilbao has an efficient metro system linking the Casco Viejo with the rest of the city.

In more depth Jeff Koons's *Puppy*, a 24m (79ft) figure of a puppy made of brightly coloured flowering plants, was installed as a temporary exhibition when the museum first opened. He's still there – the Bilbainos loved the figure so much they petitioned for it to stay. *Puppy* is re-planted every May.

Getting in The entry ticket to the Guggenheim is valid for the whole day, so you can come and go more than once.
- Advance reservations in Spain are available through the BBK Teleka system or La Caixa banks cashpoint system – follow the instructions on screen. Alternatively, book online at the museum's website, www.guggenheim-bilbao.es.

At Your Leisure

The fjord-like Rías Baixas

⑤ Rías Baixas (Rías Bajas)

The Rías Baixas, beautiful fjord-like inlets, run inland from the Atlantic on Galicia's western coast. There are four: Vigo, Pontevedra, Arousa and Muros e Noia. Vigo and Pontevedra are the most developed, with an increasingly sophisticated tourist infrastructure. The northern *rías* (inlets) are more low-key, and fishing villages and agriculture still predominate. All four enjoy a mild climate and a stunning coastline, backed by tree-clad hills. The resorts are friendly, the sailing and seafood superb, making this area ideal for a few days' relaxation.

➕ 202 A3 ☎ www.riasbaixas.depo.es

Tourist Information Office, Vigo

➕ 202 B3 ✉ Rúa Teofilo Llorente 5 ☎ 986 224 757; www.turismodevigo.org ⏰ Jul–Aug Mon–Fri 10–2, 4–7, Sat–Sun 10–2, 5–6:30; Sep–Jun Mon–Fri 9:30–2, 4:30–6:30, Sat 10:30–3:30

Tourist Information Office, Pontevedra

✉ General Gutiérrez Mellado ☎ 986 850 814; www.turismeenpontevedra.es ⏰ Mon–Fri 9:30–2, 4:30–6:30, Sat 10–12:30

⑥ A Coruña (La Coruña)

The town of A Coruña sits on a defensive peninsula facing the *ría* on one side and the open sea on the other. The city saw Roman occupation – the lighthouse known as Torre de Hércules dates from the second century AD – and was the departure point for the ill-fated Spanish Armada in 1588. In 1809, during the Peninsular Wars, it was the site of a British retreat – the commander, Sir John Moore, was killed and buried here. Behind the medieval quarter is the lovely colonnaded Praza de María Pita. Cut

OFF THE BEATEN TRACK

If you love places on the edge, a sense of isolation and superb scenery, head for the Costa da Morte (Costa de la Muerte), the stretch of wild, dangerous coast west of A Coruña and Santiago de Compostela. This is a place of legend, barren headlands and remote fishing communities; its name, which means "Death Coast", comes from the hundreds of ships that were wrecked along its shores by powerful Atlantic storms. Beautiful and deserted beaches are strewn along the coast, backed by sweeping sand dunes and granite hills beneath which huddle windswept fishing villages. Fisterra (Finisterre), the Romans' "end of the world", is as far west as you can go in mainland Europe, a bleak cape with a lighthouse perched high above the roaring surf. Softer options are the small towns along this stretch; attractive Camariñas, with its glassed-in balconies, and Noia in its marvellous natural setting, are the pick of the bunch.

Boats moored at the elegant Basque resort of Donostia (San Sebastián)

through west to the Praia del Orzán, where Atlantic waves break on a beach in the heart of the city.

➕ 202 C5

Tourist Information Office
✉ Plaza de María Pita s/n ☎ 981 184 344; www.turismocoruna.es 🕐 May–Oct Mon–Fri 9–8:30, Sat 10–2, 4–8, Sun 10–3; Nov–Apr Mon–Fri 9–2:30, 4–8:30, Sat 10–2, 4–8, Sun 10–3

🏧 Donostia (San Sebastián)

The Basques are rightly proud of San Sebastián, an elegant city whose setting has to be one of the finest enjoyed by any resort. Two green headlands shelter a crescent-shaped beach, complete with off-shore island; while to the east, graceful bridges span the mouth of the River Urumea. The headland on the east of the main Bahía de la Concha is home to the medieval town. Its narrow streets packed with bars and restaurants are centred around the Plaza de la Constitución. Monte Urgull dominates this old quarter; there are wonderful views from its summit, which is topped by a figure of Christ. The city has grown along the river, while at the other end of the bay rises Monte Igueldo. Ride up to the top on a funicular for more panoramas or enjoy the summer crowds and the four great beaches. San Sebastián rose to prominence during the 19th century, when it became a fashionable resort. Its arts festivals draw the crowds in summer, while its cuisine is revered nationwide.

➕ 206 C5

Tourist Information Office
✉ Calle Boulevard 8 ☎ 943 481 166; www.sansebastianturismo.com;

GALICIAN FARMING

Driving through Galicia you'll notice at once the tiny fields, a legacy of ancient inheritance laws which sub-divided the land for generations. Look out, too, for *hórreos* (granite-built granaries), complete with air vents and holy statues, standing on pillars to keep out the damp and rodents. Favourite crops are bizarre cabbages on stalks and allotments full of turnip tops, both of which feature prominently in local cooking. The *rías* are intensively farmed for shellfish of all sorts; the raised platforms of the *mejilloneiras* (mussel rafts) can be seen above the waterline.

www.gipuzkoaturismo.net ⏰ Jun–Sep Mon–Sat 8–8, Sun 10–2; Oct–May Mon–Sat 9–1:30, 3:30–7, Sun 10–2

🎱 Iruñea (Pamplona)

Ernest Hemingway put Pamplona firmly on the map when he described the fiesta of San Fermín in his novel *The Sun Also Rises*. From 7–14 July the entire city gives itself over to 24-hour, non-stop mass celebration in honour of its patron saint with parades, fireworks, bands, funfairs, dancing in the streets and above all the *encierro*, the running of the bulls.

At 8 o'clock each morning during the festival, six bulls are released from their corral to run through the narrow streets to the bullring. Ahead of them run hundreds of people, fleeing in excitement and fear, trying to escape the occasionally maddened animals yet staying as near them as possible, while the watching crowds cheer, yell and push would-be escapers firmly back into the bulls' path. It's dangerous, primitive, skilled and, for the runners, addictive. Every year there are numerous casualties, and sometimes even fatalities. The bulls are killed each evening.

Outside San Fermín, Pamplona is a pleasant, historic city, filled with open green spaces, one of which contains the ruined Ciudadela (citadel). The Gothic cathedral boasts some lovely cloisters and a fine museum containing sacred art from the province of Navarra. Behind it is the Judería, the only vestige of the city's once-large Jewish community, and the Navarrería, the oldest part of Pamplona, which gives access to the city walls high above the River Arga.
🗺 206 C4

Tourist Information Office, Pamplona
✉ Eslava 1 ☎ 848 420 420;
www.sanfermin.com ⏰ Summer daily 9–8;
winter Mon–Sat 10–2, 4–7, Sun 10–2

🎱 Puente la Reina

Few places in Navarra (Navarre) are as evocative of the age-old history of the Camino de Santiago (▶ 26–28) as Puente la Reina, a tiny town sited where the two trans-Pyrenean branches of the pilgrim route meet. A perfect example of how towns grew up along the Camino, it gets its name from the superb 11th-century bridge, built by royal decree to facilitate the pilgrims' passage.

There are two fine churches, the Iglesia del Crucifijo, once a Templar church, and another dedicated to St James himself. Just east of the town, the 12th-century octagonal Romanesque church of Eunate is one of the loveliest on the route. Come here in the late afternoon to see pilgrims arriving in the village, as they've done for over 800 years, with the Pyrenees safely behind them and over 600km (372 miles) still to go.
🗺 206 C4

Tourist Information Office, Puente la Reina
✉ Calle Mayor 105 ☎ 948 341 301; www.pamplona.es, www.turismo.navarra.es
⏰ Jun–Aug Tue–Sat 10–2, 4–7, Sun 11–2

Historic Puente la Reina, on the Camino de Santiago pilgrim route

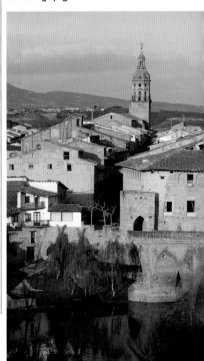

Where to...
Stay

Prices

Expect to pay for a double room per night:

€ up to €100   €€ €101–€180   €€€ €181–€240   €€€€ over €240

SANTIAGO DE COMPOSTELA

Casa Hotel As Artes €€

Hospitable owners run this sparkling inn near the cathedral, a delightful budget option with stone features and wooden shutters. Each of its seven rooms has a name, such as Vivaldi or Picasso, and an appropriately arty theme. All are stylishly decorated, with wooden floors and wrought-iron beds. Embroidered bed-linen adds a touch of luxury. Most rooms have showers. Breakfast, served in the small café, includes fruit salad and a range of tempting breads and cakes.

🚹 202 B4 ✉ Travesia Dúas Portas 2 ☎ 981 572 590; www.asartes.com

Parador Hostal de los Reyes Católicos €€€€

The Catholic Monarchs, Ferdinand and Isabella (▶ 9), founded a hostel next to Santiago's cathedral for pilgrims at their journey's end; today, it is one of Spain's most famous *paradors*, still housed in the original magnificent 16th-century building. Centred around four courtyards, this historic and supremely comfortable hotel, with its terrace, restaurant and splendid public rooms, has to be one of the finest places in Spain to stay.

🚹 202 B4 ✉ Praza do Obradoiro 1 ☎ 981 582 200; www.parador.es

COSTA VERDE

Hotel Luzón €€

This fine hotel stands in its own garden, just set back from the seafront in the attractive town of San Vicente de la Barquera, just across the border in Cantabria. The smart rooms are attractively furnished, with wooden floors. Many have large windows with views out to sea.

🚹 205 D5 ✉ Avda Miramar 1, San Vicente de la Barquera ☎ 942 710 050; www.hotelluzon.net

Hotel Sablón €€

Beside the old city walls, and built on low cliffs overlooking a sandy beach, this hotel's position alone merits a stay here. Add spacious, comfortable rooms – many with sea views – plus an excellent restaurant, and it all adds up to one of the Costa Verde's most attractive places to stay.

🚹 204 C5 ✉ Playa del Sablón 1, Llanes ☎ 985 400 787; www.hotelsablon.com

SANTILLANA DEL MAR

Parador Gil Blas €€€

In one of the quieter squares of Santillana, this pair of lovely old mansions has been transformed into a luxurious *parador*. The traditional beamed ceilings, antique furniture and supremely comfortable rooms make this a top choice.

🚹 205 D5 ✉ Plaza Ramón Pelayo 8 ☎ 942 818 000; www.parador.es

BILBAO

Pensión Mardones €

Simple but stylish, this inexpensive hotel lies in the narrow streets of the atmospheric old town of Bilbao, near the river.

🚹 206 A5 ✉ Calle Jardines 4 ☎ 944 153 105; www.pensionmardones.com

Where to...
Eat and Drink

Prices

Expect to pay per person for a meal, including wine and service

€ under €12   €€ €12–€35   €€€ over €35

SANTIAGO DE COMPOSTELA

O Beiro €€

Wash down the tempting selection of *empanadas* (savoury pasties), cheeses and hams with a local wine in this atmospheric *bodega* a short walk from the cathedral. There's also a fine range of local produce and national wines to take away.

➕ 202 B4 🖂 Rúa da Raíña 3 ☎ 981 581 370 🕐 Mon–Sat 10–10

Don Gaiferos €€

This long-established place beside the church of Santa María Salome (not far from the cathedral) is extremely popular. Its cellar-like dining room has a classy but unpretentious feel, and is renowned for its excellent seafood. Steaks are good too, as are the desserts. Seafood prices are on the high side, but the quality amply justifies the expense.

➕ 202 B4 🖂 Rúa Nova 23 ☎ 981 584 796 🕐 Tue–Sat 1:30–3:45, 8:15–11:30

COSTA VERDE

Casa Eutimio €€

Tucked down by the port, and part of the hotel of the same name, this restaurant serves up fish straight off the boats. Hake cooked with local cider, grilled fish and shellfish, and a splendid dessert menu are the house specialities – wash it down with a recommended wine.

➕ 204 C5 🖂 San Antonio s/n, Lastres ☎ 585 850 012; www.casaeutimio.com 🕐 Tue–Sun 1–4, 9–midnight

El Barómetro €€

The décor may be functional, but this is the real thing, a waterfront restaurant where the fish menu is dictated by the seasons and what comes off the boats. The huge range of fish landed here includes everything from octopus to sardines, hake to lobster – choose what's recommended by the staff.

➕ 203 F5 🖂 Paseo del Muelle 5, Luarca ☎ 985 470 662 🕐 Thu–Tue 1–4:30, 9–midnight, Wed 1–4:30

SANTILLANA DEL MAR

Altamira €€

A lovely 16th-century townhouse, also home to an hotel, is the setting for this classily simple restaurant. Cooking here is mainly Cantabrian, with local specialities such as game and plenty of fish on the menu, as well as Castilian roast piglet and a good *fideuá* (noodles). The summer terrace is an added bonus.

➕ 205 D5 🖂 Calle Cantón 1 ☎ 942 818 025 🕐 Daily 1–4, 8–11

BILBAO

Victor Montes €€–€€€

If you've been exploring the old quarter of Bilbao, head for Plaza Nueva, home to one of Bilbao's great traditional restaurants. Victor specializes in true Basque cooking; here you'll find dishes like *bacalao* (cod) served in different ways, superb hake and shellfish and traditional potato and pepper dishes. Choose between the formal restaurant, the bar or the outside terrace.

➕ 206 A5 🖂 Plaza Nueva 8 ☎ 944 157 067; www.victormontesbilbao.com 🕐 Mon–Sat 1–4, 9–midnight

Where to...
Shop

If you're looking for holiday souvenirs, the best bet in the Northern coastal regions are traditional goods such as pottery and ceramics – local styles differ throughout the region, with a variety of shapes and glazes.

A Coruña and Santiago de Compostela both have shops selling a good selection of **ceramics** from all over the region, and it's worth looking in smaller local potteries wherever you see them.

Galicia is big on **basketware**, woven from chestnut and wicker – look out for *olas*, narrow-necked jugs, lined with plastic, used to serve wine. You can still pick these up sometimes in markets.

Jet has been used for centuries for jewellery-making; the best place

for this is Santiago de Compostela, where you'll also find religious souvenirs, all carrying the scallop shell symbol of St James. Santiago is also a good place for bookshop browsing, particularly if you're interested in books on the Camino (▶ 26–28). Moving east along the coast into the Asturias, you'll start to see traditional *madreñas* (clogs) in the shops, along with **berets**, checked handkerchiefs and knitted jackets decorated with tassels. Head for good foodshops to track down **local specialities** – cheeses, cakes and biscuits and aromatic mountain honey. If you're intent on less ethnic shopping, Bilbao and San Sebastián are the best bets – huge shopping malls on the outskirts, department stores and a full range of fashion boutiques in the downtown areas.

Where to...
Be Entertained

Local tourist offices are the first stop to find out what's happening in the way of entertainment. Summer sees festivals throughout the region, and even the smallest resorts will have lots on and bars serving all night.

GALICIAN CULTURE

In late July Santiago de Compostela celebrates the **feast of St James** with a two-week festival of Galician culture, including concerts, parades, street music and markets.

OPERA, THEATRE AND CONCERTS

In **Bilbao** and **San Sebastián**, things are considerably more sophisticated. Bilbao has a good cultural scene with opera, theatre

and concerts – pick up a copy of the bi-monthly *Bilbao Guide* from the tourist office, or look in the local newspaper, *El Correo*.

July sees **San Sebastián's Jazz Festival** (www.heinekenjazzaldia. com), followed in August by the **Semana Grande** – a week of special events and fireworks – and in September by the **International Film Festival** (www. sansebastianfestival.com). Contact the tourist offices for full details.

BULL-RUNNING

The region's biggest and most famous festival is **Pamplona's San Fermín** (www.sanfermin.com), a riotous week of bull-running and much more besides, which runs from 7–14 July.

Barcelona and Catalunya

Getting Your Bearings

Dazzling, self-confident Barcelona, the capital of Catalonia (Cataluña), has all a big city needs – and more. Prosperous and beautifully situated, it boasts some of Spain's finest museums and architecture. Beyond the city, there is much else to make Catalans proud. From the stunning peaks of the Pyrenees, to the pretty resorts of the Costa Brava and the historic cities of Tarragona and Girona.

In Barcelona, stretching back from the redeveloped waterfront runs the Ramblas, a magnetic thoroughfare choked with crowds, vendors and street performers. Eastwards lies the heart of the ancient city, the Barri Gòtic (Gothic quarter), home to the cathedral. Here, fine medieval churches and mansions line a warren of narrow, historic streets, and several of the city's best museums are sited. To the north stretches the late 19th-century L'Eixample, a grid-pattern of elegant streets, where you'll see stunning examples of Barcelona's Modernista architecture. Art lovers will find the best of the rest museum-wise at Montjuïc to the west of the harbour area; this is also home to the Olympic sports complex.

Around the city stretches the autonomous region of Catalonia, of which Barcelona is the capital. Northeast, the coast extends from the city to lovely cliffs, beaches and villages of the Costa Brava; the main inland centre in

this area is the ancient walled city Girona. Further north, only a few hours away from central Barcelona, are the splendid granite peaks of the Pyrenees. Catalonia's other famous holiday area is the Costa Daurada to the southwest. Here good beaches are centred around Tarragona, an attractive small city rich in Roman remains. Inland, the scenery is mountainous, its drama typified by the spectacular rocky massif on which stands the monastery of Montserrat.

Above:
Narrow streets
characterize the
Barri Gòtic

Previous
page: Gaudí's
spectacular
gatehouse at
the entrance
to Park Güell

The Passion Facade, La Sagrada Família

In Three Days

If you are not quite sure where to begin your travels, this itinerary recommends three practical and enjoyable days in Barcelona and Catalonia, taking in some of the best places to see using the Getting Your Bearings map on the previous page. For more information see the main entries.

Day 1

Morning
Spend the morning soaking up the atmosphere and taking in the sights of the **❶ Barri Gòtic** (➤ 112–115). After you've visited **Plaça de Sant Jaume** (➤ 112) and the 13th-century **Catedral** (La Seu, ➤ 112–114), a visit to the **Museu d'Història de la Ciutat** (➤ 114) will help put what you've seen into perspective. Have lunch at one of the bars in the squares around **Santa Maria del Pí** (➤ 115).

Afternoon
Spend a couple of hours at the **❸ Museu Picasso** (➤ 118–119) before heading for **❷ Las Ramblas** (below, ➤ 116–117), the heart of Barcelona, with its vibrant street life. Pause for a break and a drink in the elegant **Plaça Reial** (➤ 117).

Evening
Have dinner in the **Barri Gòtic** before a late-night stroll and a nightcap overlooking the waterfront in the **Port Vell** (➤ 182–183).

Day 2

Morning
Head for **5 Montjuïc** (➤ 123–124) to visit the **Museu Nacional d'Art de Catalunya** (➤ 123), one of Barcelona's top attractions. For a change of pace, take a stroll through Montjuïc's leafy spaces and pause for a drink at a shady café or pick up the new Telefèric cable car, which departs from opposite the Fundació Joan Miró, up to the old castle for breathtaking views. Alternatively, inspect the impressive Olympic facilties (➤ 134). True art aficionados might prefer to tackle the collection at the **Fundació Joan Miró** (➤ 123).

Afternoon
Take the funicular down Montjuïc and hop on the metro at Parel·lel to head to **4 La Sagrada Família** (➤ 120–122), Gaudí's final masterpiece. For a taste of Gaudí's secular style, then head for the **6 Park Güell** (below, ➤ 125), from where there are fabulous views over the city.

Evening
Spend the evening in **7 L'Eixample** district (➤ 125). There are excellent shops, the best bars, many restaurants and more Modernist architecture.

Day 3

Morning
For a taste of Catalonia outside Barcelona, take a trip to the monastery at **14 Montserrat** (➤ 129) in its spectacular mountain setting. If the day's fine, you could pick up a picnic on your way to enjoy along one of the paths that wind around the mountainside.

Afternoon
Return to Barcelona and spend the rest of the day on one of the **9 beaches** (➤ 126) or wandering along the seafront promenade, finishing up with a fish dinner in **Barceloneta** (➤ 183).

🛈 Barri Gòtic

Redolent of Barcelona's long history and still the spiritual heart of Catalonia, the Barri Gòtic is a maze of narrow streets, sun-dappled squares and ancient monuments to Barcelona's golden age. Here you'll find grand buildings housing wonderful treasures, local markets, antiques shops, bars and restaurants in an area that's as much a draw for the natives as it is for visitors.

Plaça de Sant Jaume

The present Barri Gòtic dates principally from the 14th and 15th centuries, the years that marked the city's commercial zenith as one of the Mediterranean's prime maritime and merchant powers. This tightly packed, labyrinthine quarter was built inside the old Roman walls, and the Barri's main open space, the Plaça de Sant Jaume, lies on the site of the Roman forum and marketplace. On its south side stands the **Ajuntament** (Town Hall), a wonderful 14th-century Catalan-Gothic building, which is home to the city's government. The first floor contains the splendid old council chamber, the Saló de Cent. Across the square is the **Palau de la Generalitat** (Generalitat Palace), the seat of the government of Catalonia. Begun in 1403, it has an elegant Renaissance doorway facing the square, while round the corner you can see its 15th-century facade – look out for the statue showing St George (Sant Jordi), the patron saint of Catalonia, and the Dragon.

Catedral (La Seu)

From the square you can walk up Carrer del Bisbe,

with its overhanging, intricate bridge and down the side of the cathedral, La Seu, to the Plaça de la Seu in front of this great Gothic building. The cathedral is dedicated to St Eulàlia, martyred for her Christian beliefs by the Romans in the fourth century, whose tomb lies in the crypt below the high altar. La Seu was begun in 1298 on the foundations of an earlier church, and more or less finished by 1448 – though the facade took a further 500 years to complete. The interior, with its carved choir and 28 side chapels, is ablaze with dazzling lighting which illuminates the soaring splendours of the columns and flashes off the gold and silver, while myriad twinkling candles punctuate the darker corners. Don't miss the beautiful 14th-century **cloister**, which encircles a lush green space complete with palm trees, magnolias and

The Bridge of Sighs across Carrer del Bisbe, modelled on the famous Venetian bridge

a charming flock of white geese, said to symbolize St Eulàlia's virginal purity.

Plaça del Rei

East of La Seu you'll find the Plaça del Rei, surrounded by a pleasing clutch of historic monuments. The square was originally the courtyard of the palace of the Counts of Barcelona, the **Palau Reial Major**, whose main hall, the spacious 14th-century Saló del Tinell, still survives. It was on the steps of the palace that King Ferdinand and Queen Isabella are said to have received Christopher Columbus on his return from his first voyage to America in 1493. The five-storeyed, arched structure is the Mirador del Rei Martí (King Martin's Tower), built during the Renaissance; you can also see the Capella de Santa Agata (St Agnes' Chapel), with its stained glass and single nave. The Saló del Tinell and the chapel are part of the wonderful **Museu d'Història de la Ciutat** (City History Museum), which tells Barcelona's story through 2,000 years of history. Perhaps the most fascinating parts of the museum are the Roman and Visigothic streets lying beneath the square itself, which were discovered during the 1930s.

Below: The five-storey Mirador del Rei Martí, on medieval Plaça del Rei

Santa Maria del Pí

A few minutes' walk will take you back past La Seu to the charming series of winding streets and linked squares surrounding the 14th-century Gothic church of **Santa Maria del Pí**, named for the pine trees that once grew here. The serene simplicity of the interior is offset by some glowing stained glass. These squares are among the nicest parts of the Barri Gòtic, an ideal place to enjoy the weekend artists' market or have an evening drink while you watch the street entertainers who frequently perform here.

Above: The rose window at Santa Maria del Pí, claimed to be the largest in the world

Left: Plaça del Pí, a popular place to stop for a leisurely drink

TAKING A BREAK

Bar Bilbao-Berria (Plaça Nova 3, tel: 933 170 124). Grab a table outside and choose from a delicious array of *pintxos*.

➕ 201 D2

Catedral (La Seu)
➕ 201 D2 ✉ Plaça de la Seu ☎ 933 428 260; www.catedralbcn.org 🕐 Daily 8–1:30, 5:15–7:30 (access to all sections pm only) 💶 Moderate 🚇 Jaume I/Liceu

Museu d'Història de la Ciutat
➕ 201 E2 ✉ Calle Beguer s/n ☎ 933 153 053; www.museuhistoria.bcn.cat 🕐 Jun–Sep Tue–Sat 10–8, Sun 10–3; Oct–May Tue–Sat 10–2, 4–7, Sun 10–3 💶 Moderate 🚇 Jaume I/Liceu

---

BARRI GÒTIC: INSIDE INFO

Top tips Remember to **cover your arms**, shoulders and the tops of your legs before you visit the cathedral.
- Try to catch one of the concerts that are sometimes held in the Plaça del Rei. Check with the tourist office for details.
- There's often a display of the *sardana*, the Catalan folk dance, in the Plaça de La Seu at noon on Sunday.
- The narrow streets of the Barri Gòtic are best explored on foot. It's easy, though, to get lost in the warren of streets; remember, any street leading downhill will get you out of the area.

Hidden gems Don't miss the remnants of the old Roman walls; you'll find them between the east side of the cathedral and Via Laietana. Built between 270 and 310, they marked the confines of the city until the 11th century.
- Check out the Casa de l'Ardiaca (Archdeacon's House) and the Palau Episcopal (Bishop's Palace) on Carrer del Bisbe next to the cathedral. You can't go into the buildings themselves, but both have lovely courtyards with outer stairways, a typical feature of old palaces in Barcelona. There are Romanesque frescoes in the patio at the top of the Palau's staircase.

② Las Ramblas

Las Ramblas is one of the Mediterranean's great streets – the heart of Barcelona for locals and visitors alike, a place to see and be seen, where you'll return time and again. Choose to spend your time strolling its tree-lined length, sitting in its cafés, watching the crowds and street entertainers, or browsing the news-stands and flower stalls.

The Ramblas kicks off at the **Plaça de Catalunya**, which links medieval Barcelona with the 19th-century grid of L'Eixample (➤ 125) and runs south to the harbour, cutting through the Ciutat Vella (Old Town). The pedestrian-only centre is overlooked by fine buildings and planted with plane trees; traffic is restricted to the outside strip. Each section of the Ramblas – it is divided into five – has a distinctive character, most marked by the subtle changes in what's sold at the kiosks.

The Northern Reaches
Start at the northern end, the **Rambla de Canaletes**. The big iron fountain is the focal point for post-match celebrations when Barça, the city's famous football team, triumphs and a drink here reputedly ensures you'll return to

WHAT'S IN A NAME
Ramla is the Arabic word for the sandy stream bed which once ran parallel with the city walls. Dry in summer, it became the link between the harbour and the town, and was first paved during the 14th century. So dear is it to Barcelonan hearts that it has coined two words: *ramblejar*, to walk down the Rambla, and *ramblista*, someone who loves to *ramblejar*.

Barcelona. After the first crossroads you enter the **Rambla dels Estudis,** known locally as the Rambla dels Ocells, a name it gets from the caged birds sold here. The church on the right is the Església de Betlem, built for the Jesuits in 1681.

Rambla de Sant Josep

Beyond here, lined with flower stalls, you're in the Rambla de Sant Josep. On the right is the wrought-iron entrance arch to the glorious 19th-century **Mercat de la Boqueria** (officially the Mercat de Sant Josep). A profusion of colour, scents and textures, La Boqueria is one of the Mediterranean's finest food markets.

Above: Street entertainers help to create a lively atmosphere

Left: A stroll along Las Ramblas is an essential Barcelona experience

Rambla dels Caputxins and Rambla Santa Monica

Further down on the right, past the round pavement mosaic designed by Joan Miró, is the facade of the **Gran Teatre del Liceu,** Barcelona's opera house, first built in 1847 and re-opened for the second time (fire twice destroyed it) in 1999. Another 100m (110 yards) along on the left, where the street becomes the Rambla dels Caputxins, you'll find the arched entrance to the **Plaça Reial,** an elegant 19th-century arcaded square, complete with palm trees and quirky iron lamps designed by the young Gaudí.

The final stretch is the Rambla de Santa Mònica, which ends at Plaça del Portal de la Pau, with its slender monument to Colombus, erected in 1888.

TAKING A BREAK

The bars in **La Boqueria** serve excellent lunches in an animated, authentic atmosphere. **Bar Pinotxo** (tel: 933 171 731, Mon–Sat 6–5), just to the right of the main entrance, is one of the most popular.

➕ 201 D3 🚇 Catalunya, Drassanes, Liceu

LAS RAMBLAS: INSIDE INFO

Top tips To experience **La Boqueria** market in full swing, visit in the morning. Try to avoid Mondays, when the impressive fish stalls will be closed.

- Gaudí's **Palau Güell** (Carrer Nou de la Rambla 3–5, tel: 933 173 974, Tue–Sun 10–2:30, free) lies just off the Ramblas. It's an astoundingly imaginative building, giving a taste of the architect's originality. Restoration is ongoing until 2011, but parts of the interior are still open to the public.
- Early evening is a good time for a drink in the **Plaça Reial**. Try to avoid it late at night, as it's popular haunt for drug addicts and levels of crime are high.
- Watch your valuables at all times, particularly in crowds and late in the evening; petty theft is common. At the lower end of the Ramblas, near the port, prostitution is rife.

3 Museu Picasso

More people visit the Museu Picasso (Picasso Museum) than any other attraction in Barcelona, drawn here by the mystique of the most towering artistic figure of the 20th century. The museum is housed in a series of converted medieval buildings and, along with the newer Museo Picasso in Málaga (➤ 170), contains one of the most important collections of the artist's work globally.

It is perhaps important to note that the collection isn't fully representative; don't come expecting to see any of Picasso's most famous works, or much in his Cubist style. What you will find here is the most marvellous opportunity to trace how he developed as a painter, from early pictures made when he was a young boy to canvases produced just a few years before his death.

The museum opened in 1963 based on the collection of Jaume Sabartés, friend and secretary to Picasso – you can see him in many of the portraits, including one splendid abstract. There's a wealth of early work, all still influenced by his father's naturalistic style, dating from before Picasso's first visit to Paris in 1900, including drawings, family portraits (don't miss *Tía Pepa*, his aunt), and landscapes and seascapes. Look out for the menu he designed for the Els Quatre Gats café, very much in the style of Toulouse-Lautrec. He then moved into his Blue Period, beautifully typified by *Los Desemparados*, through the Rose Period towards Cubism, which was to dominate much of his mature style. Another of the museum's highlights is *Las Meninas*, a series of some 50 works inspired by Velázquez's famous 17th-century painting in the Prado (➤ 50–53), which Picasso painted in 1969 and donated to the museum.

Opposite: The inner courtyard

Below: The museum's collection includes bold ceramics

PABLO PICASSO

The son of a drawing teacher, Pablo Ruiz Picasso was one of the most important figures of 20th-century art. He was born in Málaga in 1881 (▶ 170) and moved to Barcelona in 1895. Throughout his life he felt himself to be Catalan rather than Andalusian, and the years he spent in Barcelona were some of his most formative. In 1900 he first visited Paris, where the influence of Toulouse-Lautrec was the inspiration for the pictures of his Blue Period (1901–1904). His work developed through different styles until his key work, *Les Demoiselles d'Avignon* (1909), marked a break with representational style. From 1910 he developed Cubism, a style which depicts objects as seen from different angles at the same time. By the early 1930s, he was combining Cubism with Surrealism, while spiritually he was becoming increasingly involved with art as a means of protest, a philosophy which reached its climax in *Guernica* (▶ 54). Prolific and innovative right to the end of his life, his work is full of astonishing power and beauty. He died in 1973.

TAKING A BREAK

Head down Carrer de Montcada to **El Xampanyet** (Carrer de Montcada 22, tel: 933 197 003, Tue–Sun 1–4, 8:30–midnight), a classic, tile-lined, standing-room-only tapas bar. The house *cava* is rather sweet but the beer is well pulled and the anchovies delicious.

🔶 201 E2 ✉ Carrer de Montcada 15–19 ☎ 933 196 310; www.museupicasso.bcn. cat ⏰ Tue–Sun 10–8 💶 Moderate; free Sun afternoons 🚇 Jaume I

MUSEU PICASSO: INSIDE INFO

Top tip The best times to visit are early morning and around lunch time; avoid Sunday afternoons when entrance is free.

In more depth Take time to admire the building itself – five specially converted medieval mansions on the Carrer de Montcada.

Must see In 1982 Jacqueline, Picasso's widow, donated over 40 ceramic vases, dishes and plates, made by Picasso in the 1950s. Leave time to admire these stunningly vibrant works.

4 La Sagrada Família

Antoni Gaudí's great unfinished church of the Sagrada Família (Holy Family) is Barcelona's most famous building, a monument both to this visionary architect and to the Catalan spirit. Soaring, complex, ebullient, it towers above the surrounding buildings in the east of the Eixample. Love it or hate it, the sheer scale and vibrancy of this unique building is unforgettable.

Gaudí's Vision

Conceived by a publisher, Josep Bocabella, in 1882 as an expiatory building to atone for Barcelona's increasingly left-wing ideas, the Sagrada Família was originally designed as a

modest, traditional, neo-Gothic church. In 1884, the project was given to Gaudí, and remained in his hands until his death in 1926. His vision, inspired by his deep nationalist and religious fervour, was revolutionary. Rather than a simple church, he envisaged a vast cathedral, incorporating symbols of all the main tenets of Catholicism. His structure was to have three facades representing the birth, death, and Resurrection of Christ, above which would rise 18 organically inspired towers, glistening with mosaics. These would be reminders of the Twelve Apostles, the Four Evangelists, the Virgin Mary and Christ. The facades would be covered with scenes from the life of Christ, their porches dedicated to the cardinal virtues of Faith, Hope and Charity.

The Passion Facade, the work of modern Catalan sculptor Josep Maria Subirachs

The Nativity Facade

The east facade, the Nativity, has three richly carved and decorated doorways representing the three virtues. Above these, sculpted figures, all rendered with vivid naturalism, portray scenes

ANTONI GAUDÍ

The most famous architect of the Modernista movement was born in 1852, just before Barcelona's expansion in size and economic prosperity. Fuelled by growing Catalan nationalism, the time was ripe for an explosion of home-grown creativity which found its expression in Modernisme, with Gaudí as its most famous exponent. Heavily influenced by Moorish and Gothic architecture, he was also fascinated by the building potential of the new industrial technologies and the beauty of the natural world, fusing these elements in a unique style. Individual examples of his vision are found throughout Barcelona; the Sagrada Família is his mightiest monument. He died in 1926, run over by a tram, and was initially unrecognized. He was buried amid national Catalan grief.

from the Nativity and the Joyful Mysteries of the Rosary, the only real guidelines to Gaudí's ultimate vision.

The Passion Facade

After Gaudí's death, many people argued that the Sagrada Família should be left unfinished, while others maintained that Gaudí had always intended others to continue his project. Work started again in the 1950s and still continues; completion is as much as 30 years away, but eight spires now soar heavenwards and another facade is nearing completion. The new, and controversial, work on the Passion Facade is that of Josep Maria Subirachs, who is also at work on the main entrance. Gaudí left no detailed plans, and many critics feel that Subirachs' sculptures bear no resemblance to what the master envisaged. A Japanese sculptor, Etsuro Sotoo, is thought to be adhering better to Gaudí's original intentions.

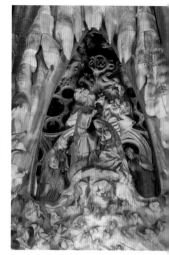

A detail of Gaudí's Nativity Facade, dedicated to the birth and early life of Jesus

TAKING A BREAK

There are splendid views of La Sagrada Família from the outdoor tables at **Ardevol** (Avinguda Gaudí 8) or you can settle inside next door at **La Llesca** (Avinguda Gaudí 12, tel: 934 553 139, Fri–Wed) for tasty home cooking.

✚ 201 F4 ✉ Plaça de la Sagrada Família ☎ 932 080 414; www.sagradafamilia.org 🕐 Apr–Sep daily 9–8; Oct–Mar 9–6 💷 Moderate; expensive with guided tour 🚇 Sagrada Família 🚌 10, 19, 33, 34, 43, 44, 50, 51

LA SAGRADA FAMÍLIA: INSIDE INFO

Top tips Be prepared for crowds and plan your visit early or around lunchtime when the site will be less crowded.

■ The main entrance is on the west of the building, fronting the Plaça de la Sagrada Família. Before you go in, walk to the end of the square and examine the church from a distance – it's the best way to get your first impression before you zoom in for a closer look.

In more depth If you want to examine things at close hand, take the lift up the tower near the rose window. You get great close-ups of the extraordinary stonework and ceramics, and can clamber around the walls and other towers – though it is not recommended for vertigo sufferers.

■ To learn more about the history of the church, its place in Gaudí's architectural development, and its construction, leave time for the on-site Museu de la Sagrada Família, where photos, models and sketches will fill you in.

5 Montjuïc

To the west of the old city and the harbour area, the steep hill of Montjuïc (The Hill of the Jews) is Barcelona's biggest open space, where you could easily spend an entire day. Site of the main area for the 1992 Olympic Games, Montjuïc is also home to two important museums, as well as verdant gardens and a modern cable car with fabulous city views.

The Palau Nacional, home to the Museu Nacional d'Art de Catalunya (MNAC)

MNAC

The main draw for many is the superb Museu Nacional d'Art de Catalunya (MNAC), housed in the Palau Nacional, which was constructed for the 1929 International Exhibition. It has undergone an extensive overhaul and is now one of the largest museums in Europe. Its highlight is the superb collection of **Romanesque art**, vibrant frescoes and sculpture brought from remote churches in the Pyrenees, dating from the sixth to the 13th centuries. The Gothic collection comes from all over Spain, including paintings and sculpture from the 1400s to the 1600s, and there are other treasures from all over Europe.

Fundació Joan Miró

Nearby stands the striking white structure that's home to the Fundació Joan Miró (Joan Miró Foundation), opened in 1975 and expanded in 2001 as one of the world's greatest collections of this famous Catalan artist's work. Miró was born in 1893 and his paintings and drawings, which link Surrealism and abstract art, are instantly recognizable. Most of the works here were donated by the artist before his death in 1983 – more than 225 paintings, 150 sculptures and his whole graphic output. There are works by other artists on display too, many donated by their creators, including Alexander Calder's *Mercury Fountain*, and pieces by Ernst, Balthus and Moore.

Castell de Montjuïc

Further up the hill, on the topmost point of Montjuïc stands the 18th-century Castell de Montjuïc. It was here that Lluís Companys, first president of the Generalitat, was executed on Franco's orders in 1940. Before he was shot, he asked permission to remove his shoes and socks so he could die in contact with the soil of Catalonia. The castle can be reached by Telefèric cable-car, which departs from opposite the Fundació Joan Miró.

Poble Espanyol

For a change of pace, head downhill and take a lively crash course in Spanish regional architecture at the Poble Espanyol. Built for the 1929 International Exhibition, the streets and squares of this enclave are lined with replicas of famous or characteristic buildings from all over Spain – everything from whitewashed Andalusian patios to the arcaded granite streets traditional in Galicia. The buildings contain shops, bars and restaurants and the whole area stays open late, late, late.

A re-creation of an Andalusian street at the Poble Espanyol

TAKING A BREAK

Stop at the Fundació Joan Miró's courtyard restaurant and café or check out the various seasonal *chiringuitos* (café-bars) that are dotted around the park overlooking the city below.

Museu Nacional d'Art de Catalunya (MNAC)
🚩 200 A2 ✉ Palau Nacional ☎ 936 220 376; www.mnac.es 🕐 Tue–Sat 10–7, Sun 10–2:30 📋 Moderate; free first Sun of month 🚇 Espanya 🚌 13, 50, 55

Fundació Joan Miró
🚩 200 B2 ✉ Parc de Montjuïc ☎ 934 439 470; www.fundaciomiro-bcn.org 🕐 Jul–Sep Tue–Sat 10–8 (also Thu 8–9:30pm), Sun 10–2:30; Oct–Jun Tue–Sat 10–7 (also Thu 7–9:30), Sun 10–2:30 📋 Moderate 🚌 50, 55

Poble Espanyol
🚩 200 A3 ✉ Avinguda del Marquès de Comillas ☎ 935 086 300; www.poble-espanyol.com 🕐 Mon 9–8, Tue–Thu 9am–2am, Fri 9am–4am, Sat 9am–5am, Sun 9–midnight 📋 Moderate 🚇 Espanya 🚌 13, 50

MONTJUÏC: INSIDE INFO

Top tips If time is short, the one museum you really should see is the Museu Nacional d'Art de Catalunya, in particular its Romanesque collection.

■ Make for Montjuïc on weekend evenings to enjoy the Font Màgica (Magic Fountain), a free sound-and-light show as the fountains on the steps leading from the Palau Nacional to Plaça de Espanya come to life.

■ For fabulous views, take the Transbordador Aeri cable car from Barceloneta or the Moll de Barcelona up Montjuïc to the Jardins de Miramar.

■ A funicular runs from Paral·lel metro to halfway up Montjuïc and connects with the Telefèric cable car to the castle.

At Your Leisure

6 Park Güell

Intended as a private housing estate, Park Güell was Gaudí's largest secular project, commissioned by wealthy industrialist Eusebi Güell in 1900. Only two houses were eventually built, but the recreational areas, paths and ornamental monuments were all completed by 1914 when work stopped. You can wander the hillside setting, with its wonderful views over the city, and admire this extraordinary ensemble of riotously imaginative pavilions, stairways and mosaic benches – among the most light-hearted of all Gaudí's work. Be prepared for large crowds on weekends and in the summer.

201 off E5 Carrer d'Olat 934 132 400 Daily 10–sunset Park free; Casa Museu Gaudí moderate Vallcarca (followed by a steep, 20-minute walk), Lesseps 24

7 L'Eixample

The Eixample area of Barcelona was designed in 1859 as an extension to the overcrowded medieval city. It's laid out on a grid shape, intersected by long, straight streets, with the wide avenue of the Avinguda Diagonal slicing through the middle. Right from its inception, L'Eixample became the fashionable place to live, with the moneyed classes moving out from the old city into its spacious new buildings and wide avenues. Once here, the rich bourgeoisie commissioned the Modernista architects to build them ever more fantastic edifices, and today this legacy has turned the whole district into a sort of glorious urban museum.

The main thoroughfares are the Passeig de Gràcia and the Rambla de Catalunya, still the heart of Barcelona's main commercial and shopping district. Visit the largely pedestrianized Rambla to enjoy the shops and café life; if you're after architecture, head for the Passeig de Gràcia. The stretch between the Plaça de Catalunya and the Diagonal metro contains some outstanding *Modernista* buildings, among them the **Manzana de la Discordia** (Block of Discord). The buildings that make up the block are wildly diverse in style, ranging from the step-gabled **Casa Amatller** to Gaudí's **Casa Batlló**, with its distinctive undulating rooftop and shimmering ceramic-clad walls. Wander a little further along the street and you'll come to **Casa Milà** (No 92), another Gaudí masterpiece. With its sweeping stone work and cascading metal balconies, it's easy to see how this controversial building got its nickname La Pedrera (meaning "the quarry").

201 D4

Casa Amatller

Passeig de Gràcia 41 934 877 217 Wed noon (reservations necessary) Expensive Catalunya 7, 16, 17, 22, 24, 28

Casa Batlló

Passeig de Gràcia 43 932 160 306; www.casabatllo.es Daily 9–8 Expensive Catalunya 7, 16, 17, 22, 24, 28

Casa Milà

Passeig de Gràcia 92 934 845 995 Daily 10–8 Moderate Diagonal 7, 16, 17, 22, 24, 28, 44

RUTA DEL MODERNISME

Self-guiding walks around the city's Modernist monuments, known as the Ruta del Modernisme, are marked with a characteristic round, red paving stone. The packs, which include a map, guide and discount vouchers for entry to the included 115 Modernist works, are available from the Tourist Office under Plaza de Catalunya (tel: 933 177 652, Mon–Sat 10–7, Sun 10–2). Packs cost €18 and are valid for 30 days.

Barcelona and Catalunya

The superb stained-glass skylight in the auditorium of the Palau de la Música Catalana

8 Palau de la Música Catalana

The exuberant Palau de la Música Catalana is perhaps the most quintessential Modernista building of all. Designed by Lluis Domènech i Montaner as a home for the city's famous choir, the Orfeó, it was built between 1905 and 1908. The facade, splendidly decorated with mosaics and busts, gives a taste of what's to come inside – a riot of stucco work, stained glass, mosaics, sculpture and reliefs, all different, all bursting with colour, light and energy. A guided tour and 20-minute film takes you through the building's history. The Palau also presents over 300 immensely varied concerts each year. The lavish foyer bar is a good place to stop for a drink or a bite to eat.

+ 201 E3 ✉ Sant Francesc de Paula 2 ☎ 932 957 200; www.palaumusica.org **🎧** Guided tours in Spanish and English Jul–Aug daily 10–7; Sep–Jun 10–3:30 **🎫** Moderate **🚇** Urquinaona **🚌** 17, 19, 40, 45, 120

9 Barcelona's Beaches

Thanks to 20 years of regeneration, Barcelona is now bordered by a long strip of blonde sand stretching over 4km (2.5 miles), lined with a promenade and dotted with beach bars, restaurants and marinas. Sant Sebastià and Barceloneta, closest to central Barcelona, are the busiest stretches, backed by traditional paella restaurants and stylish new bars. The beach at Port Olímpic is also very popular, not least because it is the closest to a metro station. Bogatell is one of the hippest parts of the sands and Mar Bella has a small nudist section. Barceloneta and Bogatell are popular with families, as the sands shelve gently to the sea.

+ 201 E1–F1 **🚇** Barceloneta, Ciutadella-Vila Olímpica, Poblenou **🚌** 14, 16, 17, 36, 39, 45, 51 57, 141

10 Museu FC Barcelona

FC Barcelona – affectionately known as Barça by its 107,000 worldwide fans – is one of Spain's most successful soccer clubs. During the Franco years, the club was a symbol of Catalan nationalism, and the lads in red and blue still inspire intense passion. Seating 98,000, Camp Nou stadium was built in 1957, a steeply raked, all-seated venue which is reckoned to be one of the world's great soccer stadia. Fans of the beautiful game should try to catch a match here, but failing that should visit the stadium. Even empty of fans, the huge space is impressive, while the museum is crammed with trophies, cups and memorabilia of every kind.

+ 200 off A5 ✉ FC Barcelona, Avenida Arístides Maillol s/n ☎ 934 963 608; www.fcbarcelona.com **🎧** Mon–Sat 10–6:30, Sun 10–2 **🎫** Expensive **🚇** Collblanc/Maria Cristina **🚌** 15, 43, 59, 70, 72, 75, 113

Further Afield

🔟 Pirineos (Pyrenees)

The Pyrenees, the spectacular mountain range that divides Spain from France, stretches from Catalonia across through Aragón to Navarra. The stunning peaks, lakes and glaciated valleys offer unlimited opportunities for hiking, skiing, rafting, climbing and much more besides. The Parc Nacional d'Aigüestortes i Estany de Sant Maurici stretches 140sq km (54sq miles), its landscapes encompassing glaciated lakes, waterfalls, fir-tree forests and splendid peaks, the highest reaching 3,000m (9,843ft).

Just off the western reaches of the park leads the Valle de Boi, dotted with the finest examples of Romanesque architecture in the country. Dozens of slender-towered churches are recognized as a collective World Heritage Site. The Centre d'Interpretació del Romànic gives interesting historical background plus information on opening times and guided tours.

To make the most of a visit to the area you'll need your own transport.
🔁 208 A5–209 E5

Parc Nacional d'Aigüestortes i Estany Sant Maurici
☎ http://reddeparquesnacionales.mma.es/parques;
www.lleidatur.com

Casa del Parc Nacional de Boí
✉ Carrer de les Graieres 2, Boi
☎ 973 696 189; www.vallboi.com

Casa del Parc Nacional d'Espot
✉ Prat del Guarda 4, Espot ☎ 973 624 036

Centre d'Interpretació del Romànic
✉ Carrer del Batalló 5, Erill-la-Vall ☎ 973 696 715; www.vallboi.com

🔢 Girona (Gerona)

The inland city of Girona, its narrow stepped streets crammed with lovingly preserved old buildings, stands on the banks of the River Onyar. Its province is among Spain's richest, so you'll find plenty of expensive restaurants, shops, bars and galleries, making it one of Catalonia's most tempting towns. Culturally, it's Girona's Arab and Jewish influences that provide the main interest; the maze of narrow

The Pyrenees offer unlimited opportunities for winter- and summer-sports enthusiasts

streets and superb Banys Àrabs (Arab Baths) attesting to its 200-year history as an Arab town, while its Jewish quarter, El Call, occupied for over six centuries, is a warren of tall thin houses and inter-connecting alleys. The impressive Gothic cathedral, with its superb single-vaulted nave and lovely cloister, stands on the site of an earlier mosque. You can learn more in the Museu Arqueològic, from where you can also reach the walls and ramparts surrounding the old city.

➕ 209 E4

Tourist Information Office

✉ Rambla de la Llibertat 1 ☎ 972 226 575; www.girona.cat/turisme ⏰ Mon–Fri 8–8, Sat 8–2, 4–8, Sun 9–2

Banys Àrabs

✉ Portal de Sobreportas ☎ 972 213 262 ⏰ Apr–Sep Mon–Sat 10–7, Sun 10–2; Oct–Mar Tue–Sun 10–2 💶 Inexpensive

Catedral

✉ Plaça Catedral ☎ 972 215 814 ⏰ Cathedral: daily 10–8. Cloister and museum: Tue–Sun 10–8 💶 Moderate

Museu Arqueològic

✉ Sant Pere de Galligants ☎ 972 202 632 ⏰ Jun–Sep Tue–Sat 10:30–1:30, 4–7, Sun 10–2; Oct–May Tue–Sat 10–2, 4–6, Sun 10–2 💶 Inexpensive

🔢 Costa Brava

South from the French border, mountain valleys running headlong to the sea have carved out the Costa Brava, the Rugged Coast, where pine tree-clad headlands shelter sandy coves and deep azure water. Such scenic beauty attracted the developers, and the southern reaches of the area is now a dense strip of mass-tourism hotels and apartment blocks. Blanes, Lloret de Mar and Tossa de Mar are the main resorts, brash and cheerful in character. Tossa de Mar is the pick of the three: enjoy the walled medieval quarter or embark on a cruise, the best way to appreciate the coastline. Northwards, the coast is less developed. Roses is the biggest resort, but nicer by far is L'Escala with its low-key local tourism and rocky coastline, or Cadaqués, a picturesque, if touristy, coastal village famous in the 1920s and 1930s as a literary-artistic colony. Salvador Dalí lived at neighbouring Portlligat, where you can visit his bizarre house. He later moved back to Figueres (Figueras), his birthplace; the Dalí Theatre-Museum is here and contains the broadest range of works spanning the artist's career.

➕ 209 F4 🌐 http://es.costabrava.org

Casa-Museu Salvador Dalí

➕ 209 F5 ✉ Portlligat, Cadaqués ☎ 972 251 015; www.salvador-dali.org ⏰ Mid-Jun to mid-Sep Mon–Sun 9:30–9; mid-Sep to mid-Jun 10:30–6 💶 Expensive

Dalí Theatre-Museum

➕ 209 E5 ✉ Plaça Gala-Salvador Dalí, Figueres (Figueras) ☎ 972 677 500; www.dali-estate.org ⏰ Jul–Sep daily 9–8; Mar–Jun and Oct 9:30–6; Nov–Feb 10:30–6 💶 Expensive

The distinctive, egg-topped exterior of the Dalí Theatre-Museum at Figueres

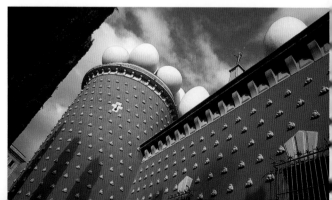

The monastery at Montserrat, long a place of pilgrimage

14 Montserrat

Some 50km (31 miles) northwest of Barcelona, the craggy outcrop of Montserrat rises above the undulating landscape. A short train and cable-car hop from the city, it's both a natural park, criss-crossed with paths and walkways, and the most important pilgrimage centre in Spain after Santiago de Compostela (➤ 92–94). Geologically, Montserrat was formed around 25 million years ago; legend says its Virgin, La Moreneta (The Black Virgin), was brought here by St Peter. In the ninth century a powerful Benedictine monastery grew up around the shrine; with a brief break in the 19th century, the monks have been here ever since. Services are held throughout the day – you can hear the famous boys' choir at 1pm (noon on Sunday, except July) – and you can climb the steps behind the main altar of the basilica to see the gilded 12th-century Madonna at close quarters. Don't miss the audiovisual show, Montserrat Portes Endins, which tells the story of the shrine and the life of the Benedictine community, and leave time to stroll along some of the mountain paths away from the crowds. There is accommodation if you want to stay.
🔢 209 D3

Monestir de Montserrat
✉ Montserrat ☎ 938 777 701; www.montserratvisita.com 🕐 Late Jun–late Dec daily 7–8:30; late Dec–late Jun 7–7:30
🚆 Barcelona, Plaça d'Espanya–Manresa line. Aeri de Montserrat stop for the exhilarating 5-minute cable-car ride up the mountain face; every 15 min (tel: 938 35 00 05, www.aeridemontserrat.com). Next stop, Cremallera de Montserrat (tel: 902 312 020, www.cremallerademontserrat.com) for the rack railway for a 20-minute wind up the mountain side 🎫 Church: free. Museum and audiovisual show: moderate

Montserrat Portes Endins
✉ Montserrat ☎ 938 777 701 🕐 Daily 9–6
🎫 Moderate (joint ticket to the museum)

15 Sitges and the Costa Daurada

South of Barcelona a string of sandy beaches have given this stretch its name, the Costa Daurada (Costa Dorada), the golden coastline. Sitges is the main resort, a vibrant town with excellent beaches and famed for its boisterous gay nightlife. Further south, Salou attracts thousands of holidaymakers looking for good beaches, cheap beer and the entertainment at nearby Port Aventura, (➤ panel, below).

Further south, the long open beaches give way to sheltered coves and the Parc Natural del Delta de l'Ebre (Ebro Delta), one of Spain's largest wetland areas, which shelters thousands of wintering birds. To visit it, head for Deltebre where you'll find boats running into the park.

Inland, the two Gothic Cistercian monasteries of **Poblet** and **Santes Creus**, both founded in the 12th century, provide a complete contrast. Poblet is slighty older and far more evocative, a stunning ensemble cradled by massive walls and set in lovely open countryside. Its late Romanesque cloisters are the high spot, a delicious contrast with the Gothic style of those at Santes Creus.

✚ 209 D3

Tourist Information Office, Sitges

✉ Sínea Morera 1, Sitges ☎ 938 109 340; www.sitges.org ⏰ Mid-Jun to mid-Sep daily 9–9; mid-Sep to mid-Jun Mon–Fri 9–2, 4–6:30

FOR KIDS

■ The **beaches** on these stretches of coast are generally clean, there are lifeguards on duty and fresh-water showers and toilets available in season. Parasols, water-sports equipment and pedalos are available for rental on many of the popular and urban beaches.

■ **Coastal cruises** on the Costa Brava are popular with people of all ages.

■ Older children will enjoy exploring the Roman ruins, the medieval lanes and ancient walls of **Girona** and **Tarragona**.

■ **Port Aventura** on the Costa Daurada is an extensive theme park resort with rides, water sports and hotels aimed at families (tel: 902 202 220, www.portaventura.es, Jun to mid-Sep daily 10–midnight; mid-Sep to Jun 10–7).

🔟 Tarragona

Tarragona, Roman Tarraco, with its splendid Roman monuments, medieval quarter, and pleasant *ramblas*, is beautifully – and strategically – sited high above the sea. It was the capital of Roman Spain, a grand and rich city, and its surviving Roman buildings reflect the city's ancient power and prestige. The pick of these include the necropolis, the circus, two forums and a magnificent amphitheatre backing on to the sea – Tarragona's excellent museums will give you more information. Further out the remarkable Roman aqueduct is among Spain's finest Roman relics. A wander through the narrow streets of the medieval old town, with its serene cathedral, dating from the 12th to the 14th centuries, is a must. Stroll down the Rambla Nova and see the lovely view from the Balcón del Mediterraneo at the seaward end. You could round off your visit with some wonderfully fresh fish – Tarragona is Catalonia's second largest port.

✚ 208 C2

Tourist Information Office

✉ Carrer Mayor 39 ☎ 977 250 795; www.tarragonaturisme.es; www.costadaurada.info ⏰ Jul–Sep Mon–Sat 9–9, Sun 10–3; Oct–Jun Mon–Sat 10–2, 4–7, Sun 10–2

Tarragona's Roman aqueduct

Where to... Stay

Prices

Expect to pay for a double room per night:

€ up to €100   €€ €101–€180   €€€ €181–€240   €€€€ over €240

Note: All listings entries given in this chapter are in Barcelona.

5 Rooms €€–€€€

This Modernista apartment building offers intimate accommodation right in the heart of town. Choose from one of the impeccable rooms or apartments and enjoy the informal, friendly atmosphere.

🕂 201 E3 ⊠ Pau Claris 72, 1° ☎ 933 427 880; www.thefiverooms.com Ⓜ Catalunya, Urquinaona

Chic & Basic Tallers €–€€

This new generation budget *hostal* in El Raval offers more extras than its name suggests. All the white, minimalist rooms are en suite, air-conditioned and equipped with the latest audiovisual equipment, plus there's a kitchen for preparing free drinks and sandwiches.

🕂 201 D3 ⊠ Carrer Tallers 82 ☎ 933 025 183; www.chicandbasic.com Ⓜ Plaça de Catalunya

Hotel Banys Orientals €–€€

The Banys Orientals provides the perfect mix of stylish, attractive accommodation and a great location on a pedestrian street in the Born district. And all at unbeatable prices. Good-value suites are also available in a nearby building. Reserve in advance.

🕂 201 E2 ⊠ Carrer Argenteria 37 ☎ 932 688 460; www.hotelbanysorientals.com Ⓜ Jaume I

Casa Camper €€€

The Mallorcan shoe company Camper extends their ethos of relaxed, stylish comfort to this boutique hotel in the hip streets of El Raval. Thoughtfully conceived, each room has its own small living area. There's also a 24-hour snack bar, plus a sunny rooftop terrace.

🕂 201 D3 ⊠ Carrer d'Elisabets 11 ☎ 933 426 280; www.camper.com Ⓜ Catalunya, Liceu

Gat Xino €

The small en suite rooms at this simple, modern hotel are bright and funky. This branch just about has the edge on the sister *hostal* Gat Raval because of its roof terrace.

🕂 201 D2 ⊠ Carrer de l'Hospital 155 ☎ 933 248 833; www.gatrooms.es Ⓜ Liceu, Sant Antoni

Praktik Rambla €€

This attractive boutique hotel lies on one of l'Eixample's treelined boulevards, just off Plaça de Catalunya. The bright airy rooms blend contemporary lines with original mosaic flooring. Bathrooms are luxurious and there's a quiet, sunny terrace for guests. The café-restaurant is also recommended.

🕂 201 D3 ⊠ Rambla de Catalunya 27 ☎ 933 436 690; www.hotelpraktikrambla.com Ⓜ Plaça de Catalunya, Passeig de Gràcia

W Barcelona €€€€

You won't want for luxury in Barcelona's latest star turn. The enormous building, which rises out of the waves at the very tip of Barceloneta, has changed the face of the city's waterfront and courted much controversy. Facilities include a Bliss spa, hi-tech gym, pool, rooftop bar and top-class restaurant.

🕂 201 D1 ⊠ Plaça de la Rosa dels Vents 1, Passeig de Joan de Borbó ☎ 932 952 800; www.starwoodhotels.com Ⓜ Barceloneta

Where to...
Eat and Drink

Prices

Expect to pay per person for a meal, including wine and service

€ up to €12   €€ €12–€35   €€€ over €35

Bar Pinotxo €

Enjoy some of the best food in the city at this rowdy, authentic place in La Boqueria market (▶ 117). Pull up a stool, order a glass of *cava* and choose from the daily specials cooked in front of your eyes.

🚹 201 D2 ⊠ Mercat de la Boqueria ☎ 933 171 731 🕒 Mon–Sat 8–6 🚇 Liceu

Café de la Academia €€–€€€

With a handful of outside tables overlooking pretty Plaça Sant Just, this intimate Barri Gòtic restaurant offers a balanced mixture of well-executed Catalan dishes, imaginative salads and tasty cod specialities. The lunchtime menu is particularly good value. Reservations are advised.

🚹 201 E2 ⊠ Carrer Lledó 1 ☎ 933 199 253 🚇 Jaume I

Cal Pinxo €€€

Cal Pinxo is one of the best choices on the beachfront at Barceloneta for traditional fish and seafood dishes. The crunchy *chiperones* (baby fried squid) and the *rape* (monkfish), a house speciality, are both mouth-watering. There are tables dining in summer and an upstairs dining room with unbroken ocean views for cooler days.

🚹 201 E1 ⊠ Carrer de Baluard 124, Barceloneta ☎ 932 215 028; www.pinxoplatja.com 🕒 Tue–Sun 12:30–4:30, 7:30–11:30 🚇 Barceloneta

Cerveseria Catalana €€

The bar groans with tempting *montaditos* (canapés) at this popular local bar. It's standing room only unless you manage to bag one of the tables on the pavement terrace.

🚹 201 D1 ⊠ Carrer de Mallorca 236 ☎ 932 160 368 🕒 Daily 8am–1:30am 🚇 Passeig de Gràcia

Cuines Santa Caterina €€

Try different types of cooking under one roof at this open-plan restaurant in Mercat Santa Caterina. The daily specials range from Catalan staples to well-executed Oriental dishes, with a variety of excellent vegetarian options.

🚹 201 E2 ⊠ Mercat Santa Caterina, Avinguda Francesc Cambó 16 ☎ 932 689 918; www.grupotragaluz.com/santacaterina 🕒 Thu–Sat 1–4, 8–12:30, Sun–Wed 1–4, 8–11:30 🚇 Jaume I

Tapas 24 €€

This venture by award-winning chef Carles Abellan aims to address the poor quality of tapas served in so many bars. Enjoy traditional tapas and seafood alongside the likes of his signature ham and cheese toastie (or *bikini*). The cool decor and open kitchen are complemented by friendly, helpful service. Book ahead for one of the few outside tables.

🚹 201 D3 ⊠ Carrer de Diputació 269 ☎ 934 880 977; www.carlesabellan.com 🕒 Mon–Sat 8–midnight 🚇 Passeig de Gràcia

Els Quatre Gats €€

Works by Picasso and other great artists of the day once hung on its walls, and this legendary restaurant and meeting place has preserved its art nouveau look well. As you eat unpretentious Catalan cooking in the large dining room, imagine this as the setting for poetry readings, piano recitals and lively debates.

🚹 201 E3 ⊠ Carrer de Montsió 3 ☎ 933 024 140 🕒 Daily 8am–2am 🚇 Catalunya

Where to...
Shop

Shops in the city range from small, independent businesses and local markets to trendy boutiques and top-rank international chain stores.

FASHION AND ACCESSORIES

The Passeig de Gràcia is lined with all the big names in international fashion. Chain stores like Zara, Mango and H&M are located at the bottom reaches, near Plaça de Catalunya, while designers such as Hermès, Jimmy Choo and Chanel have outlets several blocks north. The further towards Avinguda Diagonal you go, the smarter things get. Some shops are located in stunning Modernista buildings: note particularly **Bagués**, the art nouveau jewellers in Casa Amatller (Passeig de Gràcia 41, tel: 932 160 173, www.bagues.com, metro: Passeig de Gràcia) and the **Loewe** leather accessories showroom in Casa Lleó Morera (Passeig de Gràcia 35, tel: 932 160 400, www.loewe. com, metro: Passeig de Gràcia).

The lanes of El Born and El Raval are the place to head for younger, independent fashion and design. Bold patterns and prints are the signature look at **Custo** (Plaça de les Olles 7, tel: 932 687 893, www.custo-barcelona.com, metro: Jaume 1), while **Desigual** (Carrer Argenteria 65, tel: 933 103 015, www.desigual.com, metro: Jaume 1) offers deliberately clashing colourful garments and **Vialis** (Carrer Vidrieria 15, tel: 933 199 491, www.vialis.es, metro: Jaume 1) specializes in stylish footwear.

There's a branch of Mallorcan shoe store **Camper** next to the company's designer hotel (▶ 131) at Carrer d'Elisabets 11. More traditionally, hand-sewn espadrilles are available in every hue at **La Manuel Alpargatera** (Carrer d'Avinyo 7, tel: 933 010 172, metro: Liceu).

FURNITURE AND DESIGN

Vinçon (Passeig de Gràcia 96, tel: 932 156 050, www.vincon. com, metro: Passeig de Gràcia) is an essential stop for any design-conscious visitor. Inside this splendid Modernista building, you'll find contemporary classics alongside fairly priced designer homeware, furniture and well-chosen seasonal ranges.

FOOD AND WINE

The bustling **La Boqueria** market (▶ 117), the refurbished **Mercat Santa Caterina** (Avinguda Francesc Cambó 16, tel: 933 195 740, www. mercatsantacaterina.net, metro: Jaume 1) and **Barceloneta market** (Plaça Font, tel: 932 216 471) are natural stops for anyone putting together a picnic. **La Ribera** (Plaça Comercial 11, tel: 933 195 206, www.laribera-sa.es, metro: Jaume 1) offers an array of olives and salted cod as well as shelves groaning with tins of anchovies, mussels and the like. Complement your purchases with some wine from **Vila Viniteca** (Carrer Agullers 7, tel: 932 327 777, www.vilaviniteca.es, metro: Jaume 1), one the city's leading wine sellers. And round off at **Bubó** (Caputxes 10, tel: 932 687 224, metro: Jaume 1), which sells the most wonderful confectionery. For those with a sweet tooth, the humbugs at **Papabubble** (Carrer Ample 28, tel: 922 688 626, metro: Drassanes) will appeal, as will the goodies on sale at **Escribà** (La Rambla 83, tel: 933 016 027), one of the finest cake and chocolate makers in town, whose Rambla shop is a Modernist gem.

Where to...
Be Entertained

On Fridays, *La Vanguardia* newspaper has a good cultural supplement in Catalan but the best listings magazine is the Catalan-language *Time Out* which comes out on Thursdays and is also available online at www.timeout.cat.

CLUBS

Many of the better *bares de copas* (▶ 40) and small clubs are found in the lanes of El Raval, El Born and the Barri Gòtic, although Gràcia also has some local favourites. Glitzier places can be found in the Port Olímpic, while Montjuïc offers the popular, long-established La Terrazza (Avinguda del Marqués de Comillas, tel: 934 231 285, www.laterrrazza.com,

metro: Espanya), just behind the Poble Espanyol (▶ 124). To see it at its best don't turn up before 3am.

A few blocks in l'Eixample Esquerra around Carrer de Villarroel and Carrer de la Diputació are the focus of the city's gay life, with gay-friendly bars, restaurants and clubs.

Most clubs open around midnight and recent attempts to control noise mean that many in central Barcelona have to close at 3am. In less residential areas like Montjuïc and the Port Olímpic, they are allowed to stay open later.

OPERA AND MUSIC

The Gran Teatre del Liceu (La Rambla 51–59, tel: 934 859 913, www.liceubarcelona.com, metro:

Liceu) is one of the world's biggest and most celebrated opera houses. The Palau de la Música Catalana (▶ 126) offers spectacular *Modernista* architecture, as well as high-quality music.

THEATRE AND DANCE

Drama in the city is mostly Catalan or Spanish language. However, ballet, dance and mime are all well represented, particularly during the annual Festival del Grec (June, July or August; www.bcn.cat/grec). The Mercat de les Flors (Carrer de Lleida 59, tel: 934 261 875, www.mercatflors.org, metro: Poble Sec) also has a varied programme of dance performances.

SPORT

It's worth taking a look at the Anella Olímpica on the west of Montjuïc (▶ 123–124). The sports complexes and swimming pools were purpose-built for the 1992

Olympic games, though the Estadi Olímpic de Lluís Companys dates from the 1929 Exhibition. Piscines Bernat Picornell leisure complex (Avinguda de l'Estadi; tel: 934 234 041, www.picornell.cat) has a pool and gymnasium. The outside heated pool at the Club Natació Athletic-Barceloneta (Plaça del Mar, tel: 932 210 010, www.cnab.org, metro: Barceloneta) is open year-round, with sunbathing areas and a leisure pool for warmer weather.

For jogging or walking look no further than Barceloneta's beachfront promenade. The paths up on Montjuïc are also popular for their shade and greater variety.

At the Base Nautica de la Mar Bella (tel: 932 210 432) along the Avinguda Litoral, you can rent windsurfing and snorkelling equipment and small craft, and even learn to sail. The nearby beaches offer some of Europe's cleanest city sea-bathing. There is an official nudist beach here and a beach popular with gay couples.

Southern Central Spain

Getting Your Bearings

South of Madrid, the great empty landscapes of Extremadura and Castilla-La Mancha roll on seemingly endlessly. This is classic Spain, the land of the high *meseta* (plateau) of windmills, Don Quixote and castles. It's easy here to visualize the great early battles to expel the Moors, to get a sense of the stark beauty and loneliness of the land, to understand the sheer scale of the country. Nearer the Mediterranean, in València, the contrast is sharp, the coastal mountain ranges sheltering lush valleys and the sea lapping along the shores of one of Europe's major holiday areas.

Similarly, there could hardly be a greater contrast between the region's major cities; Toledo, the epitome of the Spanish fusion of Moorish, Jewish and Christian cultures; Cuenca, an extraordinary cliff-hanging town set in some of Castile's most dramatic scenery; and prosperous, big-city València. The gem-like towns of Cáceres and Trujillo in Extremadura, monuments to the days of the *conquistadores*, contrast with the Roman splendours of Mérida and the religious fervour embodied in the great monastery of Guadalupe, making this remote area well worth exploring. To the east, the resorts of the Costa Blanca are the perfect antidote, offering international-

Toledo is renowned for the quality of its ceramics

★ Don't Miss

Right: Toledo's distinctive Alcázar dominates the city

Previous page: Cuenca, dramatically sited on a gorge

At Your Leisure

standard resorts that attract visitors from all over Europe.

The landscape is on a grand scale, its appeal lying mainly in its subdued tones and harsh beauty. Towards the coast, the mountains shelter lush valleys, while València's *huerta* (fertile, irrigated land) is one of Europe's most productive market garden areas. This fronts on to the coast, where the golden beaches and rocky coastline have helped ensure the Costa Blanca's popularity.

In Five Days

If you are not quite sure where to begin your travels, this itinerary recommends five practical and enjoyable days in Southern Central Spain, taking in some of the best places to see using the Getting Your Bearings map on the previous page. For more information see the main entries.

Day 1

Morning
Start your exploration of ❶ **Toledo** (➤ 140–141) at the **cathedral** (left, ➤ 141), then head west to marvel at El Greco's masterful *Burial of the Count of Orgaz* in **Santo Tomé**, before visiting the 14th-century **Taller del Moro**.

Afternoon
After lunch, you could concentrate on the **Judería**, the old Jewish quarter, visiting the **Casa-Museo del Greco**, the two synagogues and **San Juan de los Reyes**. If you're up to it, late afternoon is the time to admire more great paintings in the **Museo de Santa Cruz**.

Evening
Take an evening stroll before dinner, then a walk or drive along the **Carretera de Circunvalación,** on the south bank of the Tajo, to admire the **floodlit city** from afar.

Day 2

Morning
Leave Toledo and head east on the N400 to ❷ **Cuenca** (➤ 143–144), a drive of 185km (115 miles). Get your bearings and have lunch in or around the **Plaza Mayor**.

Afternoon
The afternoon should give you enough time to enjoy Cuenca, including visiting the historic **cathedral**, the **museums** and the **Museo de Arte Abstracto Español**, housed in one the town's famous Casas Colgadas.

Evening
Soaking up the atmosphere, while enjoying a drink and leisurely meal, should provide the perfect end to your day.

Day 3

Morning
From Cuenca take the N320 south to join the AP36 to **❸València**
(➤ 145–147), a distance of approximately 190km (118 miles).

Afternoon
Spend the afternoon taking in València's main central sights – the area
running from **Plaza Ajuntament** to the **cathedral** and the **Barrio del Carmen**.
It's worth remembering that both the **IVAM** and **Bellas Artes** museums are
open till 8pm – and there'll still be time to shop.

Day 4

Morning
Don't miss València's superb **Mercado Central** before taking in **La Lonja**
(➤ 145), just across the street. Then head out from the centre to the
Ciutat de les Arts i les Ciències (➤ 146).

Afternoon
Take the A7 motorway south towards the **❽Costa Blanca** (➤ 150). Stay
on the coast; either the resort of **Dénia**, **Calp** or **Moraira** (above) would be a
good bet, leaving you poised for the next day.

Day 5

Morning
Spend the morning exploring some of the **Costa Blanca**, or take a drive
inland to the mountains of the Sierra de Aitana, before hitting **Alacant**
(**Alicante**, ➤ 150) in time for a typically Spanish late lunch.

Afternoon
Drive the 18km to **❾Elx (Elche**, ➤ 151) and spend the afternoon
wandering in Europe's biggest palm forest.

❶ Toledo

The town of Toledo has got a great deal going for it – historical richness, superb architecture, a dramatic situation, all of which contribute to making it one of Spain's most visited cities. This golden city perches dramatically on a granite crag above the encircling gorge of the River Tajo (Tagus), its skyline little changed in more than three centuries. Moors and Jews left their mark on the bones of the earlier Roman and Visigothic settlements, contributing to a unique and fascinating cityscape.

Once a Roman town, Toledo became the Visigothic capital, an important trading and cultural centre, which was taken by the Moors in 712. From then on, Mozárabes (Christians subject to Moorish rule), Moors and Jews lived amicably together, a situation which remained unchanged even after the city was re-taken by the Christians in 1085. This fusion of cultures, which made Toledo unique, came to an end in the 16th century with the expulsion of the Moors and Jews and the establishment of Madrid as the Spanish capital.

EL GRECO (THE GREEK) 1541–1614

El Greco – real name Domenicos Theotocopoulos – arrived in Spain from his native Crete via Italy, where he had been influenced by the angular forms, sinuous composition and virulent colours of Mannerism. He arrived in Toledo in 1575, having failed to find work at the Escorial. Here he remained, painting religious works for the city's churches and portraits of the nobility. His fusion of Mannerist forms with an intense spiritualism was perfectly attuned to the contemporary Spanish mood, to the extent that, despite his foreign birth, he is thought of as a quintessentially Spanish painter. His work became increasingly abstract and idiosyncratic, aspects which more than anything else make his pictures fresh and relevant for modern viewers.

he arched
uente de
an Martin,
panning the
iver Tajo

From the Cathedral to San Juan de los Reyes

Mind-blowingly ornate, Toledo's **cathedral** was built between 1227 and 1493, and thus combines Gothic, Renaissance and baroque elements. Four aisles flank the **central nave**, running down to the *coro* (choir), which stands opposite the **Capilla Mayor**. Its huge altarpiece tells the story of the entire New Testament and is backed by the exuberant **Transparente**. Round the walls are over **20 chapels** and the cathedral's treasures include stunning stained glass and pictures by El Greco, Velázquez and Goya.

Santo Tomé contains El Greco's greatest masterpiece, *The Burial of the Count of Orgaz*, a perfect illustration of his ability to combine the spiritual with drama and technical mastery. The church stands on the edge of the **Judería**, the old Jewish quarter, where you'll find the **Casa-Museo del Greco**, home to some superb paintings by El Greco, including his *View and Map of Toledo*. Nearby is the 14th-century **Taller del Moro**, worth seeing for the doorways and decoration. Both the Casa-Museo del Greco and the Taller del Moro are closed for renovation. Toledo's two remaining **synagogues**, the **Tránsito**, a galleried 14th-century building housing the Jewish museum, and **Santa María la Blanca**, should not be missed. The horseshoe arches and tiled floor of 14th-century La Blanca are a good example of cultural fusion, as much reminiscent of a mosque as a synagogue or church. Further on, **San Juan de los Reyes**, built in 1476, is typically Isabelline; the chains on the exterior are those reputedly taken from the Christian prisoners freed from the Moors in Andalucía.

Other Sights

To the east of San Juan, and almost right across town, is Toledo's main square, the **Plaza de Zocódover** – its name, intriguingly, comes from the Arabic word *souk* – which is dominated by the bulk of the **Alcázar**, built and rebuilt over the centuries. In 1936 it was held by Colonel José Moscardó against the Republicans, who threatened to shoot his son, their prisoner, if he did not surrender. Moscardó told his son "If it be true, commend your soul to God, shout *Viva España*, and die like a hero". The threat was carried out. Just two months later the Alcázar was relieved by Nationalist troops. Nearby is the superb **Museo de Santa Cruz**, a collection of some of Toledo's greatest El Grecos and other masterpieces, housed in a former 16th-century hospice with an exquisite plateresque facade. Outstanding here is El Greco's febrile *Assumption*, his *Crucifixion* featuring a backdrop of Toledo, and a vast collection of tapestries and carpets.

TAKING A BREAK

Sip an ice-cold creamy *horchata* and watch the world go by at the **Toledo Café Bar** in the Plaza de Zocódover, right across from one of the best marzipan shops in town.

➕ 212 A3

Tourist Information Office
✉ Puerta de Bisagra ☎ 925 220 843; www.toledo-turismo.com ⏰ Summer Mon–Sat 9–7, Sun 9–3; winter Mon–Sat 9–6, Sun 9–3

Cathedral
✉ Plaza Mayor ☎ 925 222 241 ⏰ Cathedral: daily 10–12, 3:30–6:30. Museum: Mon–Sat 10–6:30, Sun 2–6:30 💶 Moderate; free Wed pm for EU citizens

Santo Tomé
✉ Plaza de Conde ☎ 925 256 098 ⏰ Daily 10–6:45 💶 Inexpensive; free Wed pm for EU citizens

Sinagoga del Transíto
✉ Calle Samuel Leví ☎ 925 223 665 ⏰ Summer Tue–Sat 10–2, 4–9, Sun 10–2; winter 10–2, 4–6, Sun 10–2 💶 Inexpensive; free Sat pm and Sun

Santa María la Blanca
✉ Calle de los Reyes Católicos ☎ 925 227 257 ⏰ Daily 10–6 💶 Inexpensive; free Wed pm for EU citizens

San Juan de los Reyes
✉ Plaza de San Juan de los Reyes ☎ 925 223 802 ⏰ Summer daily 10–7; winter 10–6 💶 Inexpensive

Museo Santa Cruz
✉ Calle Cervantes 3 ☎ 925 221 402 ⏰ Mon–Sat 10–6:30, Sun 10–2 💶 Free

Casa-Museo del Greco
✉ Calle Samuel Leví 3 ☎ 925 224 046 ⏰ Closed for renovation

Museo de Arte Visigótico
✉ Calle San Clemente 4 ☎ 925 227 872 ⏰ Tue–Sat 10–2, 4–6:30, Sun 10–2 💶 Inexpensive; free Sat pm and Sun

Taller del Moro
✉ Calle Taller del Moro ☎ 925 227 115 ⏰ Tue–Sat 10–2, 4–6:30, Sun 10–2 💶 Closed for renovation

Alcázar
✉ Cuesta del Alcázar ☎ 925 221 673 ⏰ Closed for renovation

TOLEDO: INSIDE INFO

Top tips To see Toledo at its best you should spend the night there – with the day trippers gone and the city floodlit, it gets back its soul.
■ Finding somewhere to park in the city can be a nightmare; head straight for the underground car park near the Alcázar.

Must see You'll get the **best views of Toledo** by walking along the south bank of the Tajo on the Carretera de Circunvalación – it's amazing how little the skyline has altered from that shown in so many paintings by El Greco. The classic view depicted in his *Storm over Toledo* was painted from roughly where the Parador stands today.

② Cuenca

Cuenca's setting is extraordinary, perched on a crowded ridge enclosed by the deep gorges of two rivers, the Huécar and the Júcar. Ancient houses teeter on the gorges' edges, steeply stepped streets, lined with tall, narrow houses, meander ever upwards, while around the city spreads a mountainous landscape. Exploring the maze of lanes is a delight, the views are stupendous, and there's the bonus of one of Spain's leading modern art museums.

Cuenca's famous Casas Colgadas (Hanging Houses) cling to the rim of the gorge

Ciudad Antigua

Everything you'll want to see lies in the **Ciudad Antigua** (old city), a densely packed warren, mainly dating from the city's 14th to 16th-century heyday, high above the river gorges. Start in the **Plaza Mayor**, the main square, with its 17th-century arcaded Ayuntamiento (Town Hall) and shady cafés. It's dominated by the **cathedral**, whose unfinished facade hides a 12th to 13th-century building, Anglo-Norman in inspiration. Inside, there's a plethora of Renaissance and baroque monuments, modern stained glass and some extraordinary wrought iron grilles, an artisan speciality of Cuenca, examples of which you can see throughout the city. Nearby are two religious museums, the **Tesoro Catedralicio**, whose chief treasures are some ornate gold and silver plate, and the **Museo Diocesano**. This beautifully restored old building has two El Grecos and a moving 13th-century Byzantine diptych, encrusted with silver and gems, unique in Spain. There are more reminders of the past at the **Museo** de Cuenca, housed opposite in the city's old granary, ranging from local Roman finds to exhibits on geology and prehistory. There are other churches and lovely old mansions scattered throughout the streets and plazas – spend time simply wandering, walk along the gorge and soak up the atmosphere, for Cuenca is much more than the sum of its parts.

Casas Colgadas and Museo de Arte Abstracto Español

In the 14th century the rim of the gorge was lined with **Casas Colgadas** (Hanging Houses), wood and plaster houses whose balconies were cantilevered dizzyingly out into space. Today only three remain, one of which has been beautifully restored and converted to house the **Museo de Arte Abstracto Español** (Museum of Spanish Abstract Art). The gallery was established in the 1960s by Fernando Zóbel, a leading light among Spanish abstract artists, and acquired in 1980 by the Juan March Foundation, an institution devoted to 20th-century art. The museum has a core selection of paintings and sculpture by artists such as José Guerrer, Antonio Saura and Lucio Muñoz, and also stages temporary exhibitions.

TAKING A BREAK

Grab an outside table at the **Taberna El Botijo** in the medieval Plaza Mayor and enjoy a glass of local wine and a plate of crumbly Manchego cheese.

✚ 213 D3

Tourist Information Office
✉ Plaza Mayor ☎ 969 241 050;
www.cuenca.org 🕐 Summer Mon–
Sat 9–9, Sun 9–2:30; winter Mon–Sat
9–2, 5–8, Sun 9–2

Museo de Arte Abstracto Español
✉ Casas Colgadas, Calle
Canónigos s/n ☎ 969 212 983
🕐 Tue–Fri 11–2, 4–6, Sat 11–2,
4–8, Sun 11–2:30 💵 Inexpensive

Cathedral
✉ Plaza Mayor ☎ 969 224 626
🕐 Daily 9–1:30, 4:30–7:30 💵 Free

Tesoro Catedralicio
✉ Plaza Mayor 🕐 Tue–Sat 11–2,
4–6, Sun 11–2 💵 Inexpensive

Museo Diocesano
✉ Palacio Episcopal, Calle
Obispo Valero 1 ☎ 969 224 210
🕐 Summer Tue–Sat 11–1:30,
4:30–6:30, Sun 11–1:30; winter
Tue–Sat 11–1:30, 4–6, Sun 11–1:30
💵 Inexpensive

Museo de Cuenca
✉ Calle Obispo Valero ☎ 969 213
069 🕐 Tue–Sat 10–2, 4–7, Sun 10–2
💵 Inexpensive

CUENCA: INSIDE INFO

Top tips Don't miss the view of the floodlit **Casas Colgadas** from the Puente de San Pablo at night.
■ Even if abstract art leaves you cold, you should visit the Museum of Abstract Art for the beauty of the building alone.
■ Try to visit during the week – Cuenca is a popular weekend excursion from Madrid and can get very busy.

③ València

Rich, stylish València, Spain's third largest city, has to be one of the great party towns, with a year-round series of festivals, culminating in the Fallas, and some of the country's best nightlife. Add to this a balmy climate, fine buildings, excellent museums and elegant shops, and you've got the recipe for a city with plenty going for it.

L'Umbracle garden, designed by architect Santiago Calatrava, in the Ciutat de les Arts i les Ciències

The old part of València is encircled by the dry river-bed of the Turia, which was diverted in 1956 after some catastrophic flooding. Within this area you'll find the atmospheric Barrio del Carmen, the oldest part of the city, and most of the interesting sights.

Plaza Ajuntament

Start exploring at the Plaza Ajuntament, the main square, a large open space complete with a spectacular fountain (visit at night when it is illuminated), palm trees and flower stalls. It's dominated by the solid mass of the Ajuntament (City Hall), which is home to the **Museu Histórico Municipal**. From here head northwest to take in the Modernista **Mercado Central** (Central Market), one of the biggest in Europe, where you can buy seemingly every type of fish, fruit, meat and vegetable that's available. Opposite is one of València's greatest treasures, the beautiful late 15th-century Gothic **Lonja** (Exchange) and its lovely cloister, with soaring vaults and serene space, which was once the city's silk exchange. It still acts as a commercial exchange and comes to life when Sunday stamp and book markets are held here.

The Cathedral Complex

East from here is the cathedral complex, which includes, besides the cathedral, an unfinished tower, the **Miguelete**, the cathedral museum and two plazas. The cathedral has been restored to its simple Gothic splendour, beautifully illuminated by light filtering through the alabaster panels in the lantern above the crossing. The **Plaza de la Virgen** lies behind; here, every Thursday at noon since the Middle Ages, the Tribunal of the Waters meets to regulate grievances about the shared irrigation system in the outlying *huertas*.

City Museums

Museums are scattered all over the city, and if time is short it's hard to decide what to see. Try to take in the **Museo de Cerámica González Martí** (González Marti Ceramics Museum), worth seeing as much for the over-the-top 18th-century baroque facade and ornate interior as for the collection. There are ceramics here from all over Spain, and you'll see some stunning glazes, vibrant *azulejos* (tiles) and a reproduction of a traditional Valencian kitchen. Art lovers should head for the **Museo de Bellas Artes** (Fine Arts Museum), which presents an excellent overall view of Spanish painting, with works, among others, by El Greco, Goya and Velázquez. If modern art's more appealing, the **Instituto Valenciano de Arte Moderno (IVAM)** specializes in temporary exhibitions of 20th-century and contemporary art, while the **Museu Fallero** showcases the prize-winning *ninots* (giant sculptures) from the city's annual Fallas festival (► panel, opposite).

Ciutat de les Arts i les Ciències

The ambitious **Ciutat de les Arts i les Ciències** (Arts and Science City), designed by Valencian architect Santiago Calatrava, lies southeast of the city centre. Funded by the Generalitat to encourage year-round tourism, these dazzling white buildings are set around reflecting pools. **L'Hemisfèric** (Hemisphere) acts as a planetarium, laser screen and IMAX cinema. It's flanked by the **Museu de les Ciències Príncipe Felipe** (Prince Felipe Science Museum), an interactive science museum, and the **Parque Oceanográfico** (Ocean Park), a series of lakes and lagoons constituting one of the world's largest aquariums. The **Palacio de las Artes** (Arts Palace) hosts concerts, opera and theatre.

THE FALLAS

Huge satirical *ninots* (puppets), works of art in themselves, flowers and fireworks, wonderful costumes and music, dancing, bullfights and street parties – this is Fallas week, held in València from 12–19 March in honour of San José. The festival's origins lie in a simple spring rite, when carpenters would burn their spare wood, and it's grown to become an international tourist attraction. Each *barrio* (neighbourhood) commissions its own *ninot*, a giant figure which is judged and is the centre of neighbourhood celebrations throughout the week. There are floral processions to a huge image of the Virgin outside the cathedral, a Fallas queen, and deafening daily firecracker displays in the Plaza Ajuntament. The week's riotous celebration culminates on 19 March, the Nit de Foc, when the giant *fallas* are set on fire, marking the end of festivities for another year.

The Plaza de la Virgen lies at the heart of historic València

TAKING A BREAK

Don't leave town without trying a glass of *horchata*, made from chufa (tiger nuts), and the traditional finger-shaped buns, the snigger-worthy *fartons*. The renowned **Santa Catalina**, just off Plaza de la Reina, is one of the best places to go.

➕ 218 B3

Tourist Information Office
✉ Plaza de la Reina 19
☎ 963 153 931; www.turisvalencia.es 🕐 Mon–Sat 9–7, Sun 10–2

Museu Histórico Municipal
✉ Plaza Ajuntament 1 ☎ 963 525 478 🕐 Mon–Fri 9–2 💷 Inexpensive

Cathedral
✉ Plaza de la Reina ☎ 963 918 127 🕐 Daily 7:30–1, 4:30–8:30
💷 Moderate

Instituto Valenciano de Arte Moderno (IVAM)
✉ Calle Guillem de Castro 118
☎ 963 863 000; www.ivam.es
🕐 Jun–Sep Tue–Sun 10–10; Oct–May 10–8 💷 Inexpensive; free Sun

La Lonja
✉ Plaza del Mercado ☎ 963 525 478 🕐 Tue–Sat 10–2, 4:30–8:30, Sun 10–3 💷 Free

Museo de Bellas Artes
✉ Calle San Pío s/n ☎ 963 870 300
🕐 Tue–Sun 10–8 💷 Free

Museo de Cerámica González Martí
✉ Calle Poeta Querol 2 ☎ 963 516 392 🕐 Tue–Sat 10–2, 4–8, Sun 10–2
💷 Inexpensive; free Sat pm, Sun

Museu Fallero
✉ Plaza Monteolivete 4 ☎ 963 525 478; www.fallas.com 🕐 Tue–Sat 10–3, 4:30–8:30, Sun 10–3
💷 Inexpensive

L'Hemisfèric
✉ Avenida Autopista del Saler
☎ 902 100 031; www.cac.es
🕐 Shows daily hourly from 11–6
💷 Moderate

Museu de les Ciències Príncipe Felipe
✉ Avenida Autopista del Saler 5 ☎ 902 100 031; www.cac.es
🕐 Summer Sun–Fri 10–10, Sat 10–8; winter Sun–Fri 10–6, Sat 10–8
💷 Moderate

Parque Oceanográfico
✉ Avenida Autopista del Saler 5 ☎ 902 100 031; www.cac.es
🕐 Mon–Sun 10–6, closes later on Sat and Jul–Sep 💷 Expensive

VALÈNCIA: INSIDE INFO

Top tips The **Bus Turistic** is a hassle-free way to visit main sights. It leaves half hourly from outside the cathedral and makes 17 stops on its circular route.
■ València is surprisingly big, so be prepared to do a lot of walking.
■ There's a high level of street crime and begging in the city.

In more depth As host to the America's Cup in 1997, the city instigated a facelift to its waterfront, leaving as its legacy kilometres of **beaches** clean and safe enough to merit EU Blue Flag status, a sparkling **marina**, and a host of lively bars and good restaurants all just a quick hop from the old town.
■ If you're looking for a green place in which to relax, head for one of the city's many marvellous **parks** along the Tura riverbed or alternatively the Jardín Botánico or the Jardines del Real-Viveros.

At Your Leisure

The ruins of the Roman amphitheatre at Mérida, built to seat 15,000 spectators

4 Mérida

If you're interested in Spain's Roman past, head for Mérida, which has more Roman remains than any other Spanish city. Mérida was the capital of the Roman province of Lusitania, a rich centre, liberally endowed with superb public buildings. A 60-arched bridge, the Puente Romano, crosses the islet-scattered River Guadiana into the city, and is the best place to start your explorations. Just across the river to the left lie the Morerías archaeological excavations, where you can watch the digging. Ahead lies the heart of Mérida, with its great Arco Trajano (Trajan's Arch), while 10 minutes' walk northeast will bring you to the Teatro Romano (Roman Theatre), Anfiteatro (Amphitheatre), Casa Romana del Anfiteatro (Amphitheatre Roman House) and the Museo Nacional de Arte Romano (National Museum of Roman Art). The Teatro Romano was built around 15BC as a gift to the city from Agrippa, the right-hand man of Augustus, the first Roman emperor. With its two-tier colonnaded stage, it's one of the best preserved anywhere in the Roman empire, and is used during the summer as the venue for a classical theatre festival. Take a look at the Anfiteatro, built to seat 15,000 before admiring the wonderful mosaics in the Casa Romano. The fine collections in the nearby Museo Nacional de Arte Romano, housed in an airy structure designed by the renowned Spanish architect Rafael Moneo, will help you make sense of all you've seen.

✚ 210 C1 ☎ www.merida.es; www.festivaldemerida.es

Tourist Information Office

✉ Paseo José Álvarez Sáenz de Buruaga s/n ☎ 924 009 730; www.turismoextremadura.com ⏰ May–Oct Mon–Fri 9–2, 5–7, Sat–Sun 9:30–2; Nov–Apr Mon–Fri 9–2, 4–6, Sat–Sun 9–2

Museo Nacional de Arte Romano

✉ Calle José Ramón Mélida 2 ☎ 924 311 690; www.mcu.es ⏰ Jul–Sep Tue–Sat 9:30–3:30, 5:30–8:30, Sun 10–2; Oct–Jun Tue–Sat 10–2, 4–9, Sun 10–2 💶 Inexpensive; free Sat pm, Sun

5 Cáceres

Tucked away in the west of Extremadura, the provincial capital of Cáceres is an almost perfectly preserved walled town, a monument to the returning New

World *conquistadores*, whose money funded its construction. Nearly everything you'll want to see lies within the mainly Moorish walls, best approached from the Plaza Mayor through the 18th-century Arco de la Estrella. Once inside, you can wander through streets lined with some of Spain's finest Gothic and Renaissance mansions. These are austere buildings, their appeal lying in their severe lines and beautiful ochre-coloured stonework. Star sights include the buildings around the Plaza de Santa Maria and the lovely Plaza de San Mateo. Keep an eye out for the family crests adorning the different mansions and the storks' nests perched on every available tower. Cáceres' provincial museum is worth a visit for the building alone; it's housed in the Casa de las Veletas, which, with its patio, well-proportioned rooms and horseshoe arches, is a perfect example of the local style.

➕ 210 B2

Tourist Information Office
✉ Plaza Mayor s/n ☎ 927 010 835;
www.turismoextremadura.com 🕐 Summer Mon–Fri 9–2, 5–7, Sat 9:45–2; winter Mon–Fri 9–2, 4–6, Sat 9:45–2

Museo Provincial
✉ Plaza de las Veletas 1 ☎ 927 010 877
🕐 Mid-Apr to Sep Tue–Sat 9–2:30, 5–8:15, Sun 10:15–2:30; Oct to mid-Apr Tue–Sat 9–2:30, 4–7:15, Sun 10:15–2:30 🎫 Inexpensive; free for EU citizens

6 Trujillo

Trujillo is among Extremadura's most enticing towns, a tiny set-piece of narrow streets, tranquil squares, mansions, castle walls and towers complete with storks' nests. Like Cáceres (► above) it's a *conquistador* town, built with New World booty money. Francisco Pizarro, the conqueror of Peru, was born here, and his family built many of Trujillo's finest houses. Spend time exploring its streets, admiring its serene architecture, and sitting in the grandiose Plaza Mayor. If you climb up to the Moorish castle, there

are wide views across the town and surrounding countryside.
➕ 210 C2 ☎ www.trujillo.es

Tourist Information Office
✉ Plaza Mayor s/n ☎ 927 322 677;
www.trujillo.es 🕐 Daily 10–2, 4:30–7

7 Guadalupe

Picturesque Guadalupe, all russet-tiled roofs and flower-hung balconies, is dominated by the great mass of the Real Monasterio de Guadalupe, once one of Spain's most important pilgrimage centres. Established in 1340, the monastery stands on the site of the discovery by a cowherd of a miraculous Virgin, said to have been carved by St Luke. The vast complex, a fascinating mix of architectural styles, was richly endowed with artworks and treasures by returning *conquistadores*, who had taken their devotion to the Guadalupe Virgin with them to the New World – the Caribbean island of Guadalupe is named after the monastery. The richly gloomy church interior, dimly glittering in the candlelight, is a mere foretaste of what's to come. There are two cloisters; the 14th to 15th-

Cobbled streets in picturesque Guadalupe

century Mudejar cloister has a double storey of horseshoe arches and a bizarre central pavilion; the second cloister is pure 16th-century Gothic. Around these lie museums rich in paintings and sculptures, textiles and embroidery, jewels and relics. The finest room is the Sacristía, unaltered since its 17th-century construction and still hung with a magnificent series of paintings of scenes of the life of St Jerome by Zurburán. Right in the heart of the monastery, you reach the Camarín, a tiny, richly decorated room which contains the bejewelled figure of the Virgin herself.

➕ 210 D2

Tourist Information Office
✉ Plaza Mayor s/n ☎ 927 154 128;
www.turismoextremadura.com 🕐 Summer Tue–Fri 10–2, 5–7, Sat–Sun 10–2; winter Tue–Fri 10–2, 4–6, Sat–Sun 10–2

Real Monasterio de Guadalupe
✉ Guadalupe ☎ 927 367 000;
www.monasterioguadalupe.com 🕐 Daily 9:30–1, 3:30–6:30 💶 Moderate

🎱 Costa Blanca

València's southern province is Alacant (Alicante), a wonderfully varied area with historic towns, fertile land and some impressive mountain scenery. It's best known though for its coastline, the Costa Blanca (White Coast), a positive mecca for people from all over Europe seeking sun, sand, sea and good-value holidays. Developed in the 1960s, no resort is better equipped for mass-market tourism than **Benidorm**, a high-rise, brash and noisy resort with great beaches and non-stop entertainment. The coast's other resorts are lower key and have managed to retain some of their Spanish character, and you could do worse if you're looking for a few days by the sea. The stretch of coast from Dénia to Altea still has some unspoiled rocky shoreline, clean beaches and pretty towns – try **Dénia** itself, up-market, residential **Moraira**, or **Calpe** (**Calp**), dominated by the looming mass of the rocky outcrop known

as the Peñon d'Ifach. Old **Altea** is a picturesque, if much-visited village, while inland the mountains of the **Sierra de Aitana** rise above lush valleys dotted with fortress settlements like **Guadalest**.

South of Benidorm, **Alacant** (Alicante) has kept its Spanish soul and character – a dignified, pleasant city with palm-lined promenades, fine beaches and a magnificently sited castle. South again, the coastline is flatter, with rolling dunes, pine woods and resorts catering as much to Spaniards as foreigners.

➕ 218 B1

Tourist Information Office, Alicante
➕ 218 B2 ✉ Avenida Rambla Méndez Nuñez 23 ☎ 965 200 000; www.alicante-turismo.com 🕐 Mon–Fri 9–8, Sat 10–2, 3–8, Sun 10–2

Tourist Information Office, Benidorm
➕ 218 B2 ✉ Avenida Martínez Alejos 16 ☎ 965 851 311; www.benidorm.org 🕐 Mon–Fri 9–8, Sat 10–1:30, 4:30–7:30, Sun 10–1:30

Tourist Information Office, Dénia
➕ 218 C2 ✉ Plaza Oculista Buigues 9 ☎ 966 422 367; www.denia.net 🕐 Summer Mon–Sat 9:30–2, 5–8; winter 9:30–1:30, 4–7

Esplanada de España, Alacant (Alicante)

The 12th-century Moorish Torre Fortaleza de la Calaforra in Elx (Elche)

9 Elx (Elche)

The ancient city of Elche, Roman Illici, stands on the Vinalopó river, surrounded and infiltrated by more than 300,000 palm trees, a veritable forest, unique in Europe. The groves probably date from Phoenician times and are protected by law. Many of the female trees bear dates, often on sale from street vendors, and the fronds of the male trees are sent all over Europe for use in Palm Sunday church processions. The best way to get an idea of the scale of this exotic planting is to visit the Huerto del Cura, or hire a bicycle and explore the plantations around the city's edge.

Elche's main sights are clustered around the vast 16th to 17th-century baroque basilica of Santa Maria, whose blue-tiled dome dominates the centre. In August, this is the scene of the Misteri d'Elx, a medieval mystery play, celebrating in words and music the death and assumption of the Virgin. It has been performed by the townspeople since the 1260s, soon after the Reconquista – there's a museum devoted to it.

Moorish civilization is represented by a splendid watchtower, the Calaforra, and Arab baths. An archaeological museum is devoted to the ancient Iberian settlement of Illici, a few kilometres south, as well as classical and Islamic artefacts.

+ 218 A1

Tourist Information Office
✉ Parque Municipal ☎ 966 658 196; www.turismedelx.com ⏰ Mon–Fri 9–7, Sat 10–7, Sun 10–2

Museu Municipal de la Festa
✉ Calle Major de la Vila 27 ☎ 965 453 464 ⏰ Tue–Sat 10–1:30, 4:30–8 💰 Moderate

THE BIG BLACK BULL
Throughout Spain the silhouette of a huge black bull looms proudly beside main roads. This is the Osborne bull, designed in 1956 by Manolo Prieto to advertise sherry and brandy made by the firm of Osborne. The bull faced a tricky moment in the mid-90s when Spain passed an act banning all roadside advertising. Public outcry won the day and the ubiquitous sign was exempt from the decree. It's said that Prieto died a disappointed man – he would have preferred to be remembered for what he saw as his "real" art, not an advertising hoarding.

Where to...
Stay

Prices

Expect to pay for a double room per night:

€ up to €100   €€ €101–€180

€€€ €181–€240   €€€€ over €240

TOLEDO

Hostal del Cardenal €€

This *hostal* is quintessentially Spanish. Built in the 18th century for the local archbishop, it is wonderfully peaceful with rambling gardens, ponds and ancient walls covered with cascading vines. The interior is furnished with antiques, oil paintings and Mudejar tiles. Feast your eyes, and then your stomach by dining in the excellent hotel restaurant.

🔠 212 A3 ⌂ Paseo de Recaredo 24 ☎ 925 224 900; www.hostaldelcardenal.com

Hotel Santa Isabel €

All the rooms in this small hotel in the old part of Toledo have small balconies – try for one that overlooks the convent opposite. The interior is fresh and modern and although the bathrooms are small they have all the essentials. The basement garage and large breakfast room are definite assets.

🔠 212 A3 ⌂ Calle Santa Isabel 24 ☎ 925 253 120; www.santa-isabel.com

CUENCA

Cueva del Fraile €€

For the facilities that it offers, which run to tennis courts and a swimming pool, this comfortable hotel some distance out of Cuenca is good value. Built around a patio, it occupies a 16th-century building in huge gardens and is furnished in traditional style.

🔠 213 D3 ⌂ Carretera Cuenca–Buenache km7 ☎ 969 211 571; www.hotelcuevadelfraile.com

Posada de San José €€

A former 17th-century convent, this *posada* sits on the rim of Cuenca's remarkable gorge and the view from the rooms is truly unforgettable. Ancient beams, uneven floors, low ceilings and an intriguing warren of rooms on different levels make this an evocative and romantic retreat. Every room is different, but all are furnished with decorative flair and most have a small terrace. The tapas bar is popular with locals and the restaurant welcoming and reliably good.

🔠 213 D3 ⌂ Calle Julián Romero 4 ☎ 969 211 300; www.posadasanjose.com

VALÈNCIA

Ad Hoc €€€

This hotel is right in València's old quarter, surrounded by some of the best bar life in Spain. The owner is an antiquarian and art enthusiast and this is reflected in the interior. Light brick work, vaulted ceilings and sensitive lighting against earthy toned paintwork create a welcoming environment. Meals are available in a cosy dining room.

🔠 218 B3 ⌂ Boix 4 ☎ 963 919 140; www.adhochoteles.com

Venecia €€

This bright, professionally run hotel couldn't be more central with some of the attractive en suite rooms looking out over the Plaza Ayuntamiento. There is a variety of rooms adapted for non-smokers, families and visitors with mobility problems.

🔠 218 B3 ⌂ Plaza Ayuntamiento 3 ☎ 963 524 267; www.hotelvenecia.com

Where to...
Eat and Drink

Prices

Expect to pay per person for a meal, including wine and service

€ up to €12   €€ €12–€35   €€€ over €35

TOLEDO

Casón de los López de Toledo €€€

Prior to its conversion, this former private home was recognised as being one of the most beautiful buildings in Toledo. A vaulted foyer leads to a ground floor café which serves coffee and snacks, while upstairs there is a choice of dining rooms. There are magnificent antiques, paintings and artwork throughout and the market-based menu features fine Castilian and Continental cuisine, such as ravioli and garlic soup and baked cod with Manchego cheese and onions. Diners can enjoy a post-dinner tot at the wood-panelled basement bar where more than 90 varieties of whisky are sold.

➕ 212 A3 🗺 Sillería 3 ☎ 925 254 774; www.casontoledo.com 🕐 Mon–Sat 1:30–4, 8:30–11:30, Sun 1:30–4. Closed Mon Jul–Aug

La Ermita €€€

La Ermita is a place to come for a special treat. Reserve a table by the huge windows and enjoy the wonderful views over Toledo and the surrounding countryside. Dishes are accomplished versions of Spanish and international cuisine, with a tempting selection for vegetarians. There is also a good tasting menu at €48.

➕ 212 A3 ➕ Carretera de Circunvalación s/n ☎ 925 253 193; www.laermitarestaurante.com 🕐 Tue–Sat 2–4, 9–11, Sun 2–4

CUENCA

Mesón Casas Colgadas €€€

In one of the city's famous Casas Colgadas (Hanging Houses), this restaurant enjoys splendid views over the Huécar from its formal but unstuffy dining room. The menu features modern interpretations of traditional fare, like *gazpacho pastor*, *ajoarriero* (cod cooked with eggs and garlic), followed by such Moorish-inspired desserts as *alajú*, made with honey, orange and almonds. Reservations are recommended.

➕ 213 D3 ➕ Calle Canónigos s/n ☎ 969 223 509; www.mesoncasascolgadas.com 🕐 Wed–Sun 1:30–4, 9–11, Mon 1:30–4

VALÈNCIA

Casa Montaña €

This popular café-restaurant was founded in 1836. The seafood dishes are excellent as are the starters, especially the *jamón ibérico* (Spanish ham) and *tostada de queso la Serena* (cheese on toast). The restaurant claims to have one of the longest wine lists in Valencia.

➕ 218 B3 🗺 Calle José Benlliure 69 ☎ 963 672 314 🕐 Tue–Sun 1:30–4, 8:30–11:30, Sun 1:30–4

La Riuà €€

Decorated with ceramic tiles in the local style, this popular place just off Plaza de la Reina is well placed for exploring the old town. Classic local dishes ring the changes on fish in many guises, and there's plenty of home-made paella. Adventurous diners might be tempted to try the eels or baby octopus.

➕ 218 B3 🗺 Calle del Mar 27 ☎ 963 914 571 🕐 Tue–Sat 2–4, 9–11, Mon 2–4. Closed Easter and Aug

Where to...
Shop

Toledo is renowned for its pottery and Valencia for the much sought-after Lladró porcelain and its glassware.

TOLEDO

Jewellery and ornaments made from matte black steel inlaid with gold thread, a Moorish technique known as *damasquinado*, make popular souvenirs. You can see it being made at **Damasquinados Manuel Melendez** at Travesia del Conde 4, a long-established family business.

Marzipan is another local speciality. **Santo Tomé** at Calle Santo Tomé 5 claims to follow the original 13th-century recipe.

The town's main shopping street is **Calle Comercio** where you'll find chains stores such as Zara, Mango, Benetton, Lacoste, Pull & Bear and Camper.

Roadside stores offer the best variety and prices for pottery, although serious bulk buyers may consider a trip to **Talavera de la Reina**, 76km (47 miles) west of Toledo where much of the pottery is produced.

VALÈNCIA

Lladró porcelain originates in Valencia, and the city is also known for its glassware.

Valencia is famous for its *paella*, and one of the best buys here is a **paella pan**. They come in all sizes and can be found at several *ferreterías* (ironmongers) near the **Mercado Central** (▶ 145) on Plaza del Mercado, near the city centre.

Where to...
Be Entertained

Valencia, Spain's third largest city, is famed for its lively nightlife. Evenings in Toledo and Cuenca are more low key.

NIGHTLIFE

Toledo is a great city for taking an evening *paso* stopping en route for a drink and some tapas. In summer, head to little Plaza de la Magdalena, just south of Plaza de Zocódover.

Nightlife in **Cuenca** centres around Calle de San Miguel and Plaza de San Nicolás. There are also more bars and clubs around Calle Fray Luis de León off the Plaza de España in the new part of town.

Valencia offers some of Spain's best nightlife. The city has a significant gay community – the third largest in Spain. Much of the action is centered around the Barrio del Carmen and the hip streets around the Mercado de Abastos. In the summer, the Malvarosa neighbourhood and the regenerated port area are also fun. For something a little more hedonistic, head for the opera and the chandeliers at **Café de las Horas** (Calle Conde de Almodóvar 1, tel: 963 917 336).

THEATRE AND CLASSICAL MUSIC

Toledo's **Teatro Rojas** (Plaza Mayor, tel: 925 223 970) often stages world-class theatre and dance.

In Valencia, check what's on at the **Teatro Principal** (Calle Barcas 15, tel: 963 539 200) or the **Palau de la Música** (Paseo Alameda 30, tel: 963 375 020), which has seasonal classical music recitals.

Andalucía

Getting Your Bearings

Andalucía is hot sun and deep shade, flamenco and fiestas, sweeping landscapes and great Moorish monuments – the epitome of the Spanish dream. No other region so perfectly encapsulates most people's vision of the country, whether you're looking for a hedonistic play area, unspoiled countryside or vibrant, beautiful cities. From its historic centres to its mountains, coast and holiday resorts, Andalucía has something for everyone.

The three major cities of Seville, Córdoba and Granada preserve a clutch of extraordinarily brilliant Moorish monuments, reminders of medieval Europe's most sophisticated civilization. The region's smaller centres are equally fascinating: the little-known Renaissance gems of Baeza and Úbeda, Ronda with its spectacular gorge, and elegant Jerez, famed for its sherry, horses and orange trees. Off the beaten track you'll find whitewashed hill towns, windswept fishing villages and quiet inland communities where strangers are rare.

Andalucía's towns are set in superb landscape, which ranges from the high peaks of the Sierra Nevada and the fertile upland valleys of Las Alpujarras, to the rolling olive-planted hills of the northeast and the cork forests and fertile plains of the west. The coastline stretches from arid Almería through the Costa del Sol, Europe's most developed resort area, to the untouched beaches of the Costa de la Luz. West again is the wetland region of the Coto de Doñana. The surge in tourist development in the late 20th century resulted in some dire mistakes, but did have the benefit of creating good roads, hotels of an international standard and some of the best golf courses and sports facilities in Europe.

Aracena

Cabezas Rubias

HUELVA

Valverde del Camino

A49 E01

Huelva

Mazagón

Sanlúcar de Barrameda

Chipiona

Costa de la Luz

Cádiz

Puerto Real

Conil de la Frontera

Vejer la Fro

E803 A66

SE

Sevil Sevill

A49 E05

AP4 E05

Jerez de Frontera

8

Ta

★ Don't Miss

At Your Leisure

Previous page: Córdoba's Alcázar

Right: A farmhouse on the terraced slopes of Las Alpujarras

Left: Golfers at Torremolinos

In Five Days

If you are not quite sure where to begin your travels, this itinerary recommends five practical and enjoyable days in Andalucía, taking in some of the best places to see using the Getting Your Bearings map on the previous page. For more information see the main entries.

Day 1

Morning
Start your day in ❶ Seville (➤ 160–163) by heading for the cathedral (below) and its treasures, then be sure to climb up the Giralda (➤ 161) for a great view. Next visit the Real Alcázar (➤ 162), where the tranquil gardens are the perfect climax to a hard morning's sightseeing.

Afternoon
Art enthusiasts could visit the Museo de Bellas Artes (➤ 162–163), one of the most important museums in Spain, before wandering through the south and west areas of the city.

Evening
Head for the Barrio de Santa Cruz (➤ 162–163) for a drink and some tapas before dinner and a chance to experience some flamenco.

Day 2

Morning
Leave Seville on the fast NIV for the 143km (88-mile) drive to ❷ Córdoba (➤ 164–165), arriving around 11am. Head straight for the Mezquita.

Afternoon
Wander around the Judería (➤ 165), down to the Alcázar de los Reyes Cristianos (➤ 165), and along the river bank before leaving on the N432 to ❸ Granada (➤ 166–168) – the drive should take two and a half hours.

Evening
Head for the Plaza de San Nicolás in the old Moorish quarter, the Albaicín (➤ 168) for your first view – perhaps at sunset – of the magnificent Alhambra palace.

Day 3

Morning
Be among the first at the Alhambra (➤ 168) and spend the whole morning exploring one of Spain's greatest glories.

Afternoon/Evening
After a late lunch pass the afternoon visiting the cathedral and the Capilla Real (➤ 168), before joining the evening crowds downtown.

Day 4

Morning/Afternoon
Leave Granada and head south on the fast E902 to the coast. Drive along the ⑥ **Costa del Sol** (➤ 170) on the N340/E15 as far as San Pedro de Alcántara. At San Pedro turn inland to Ronda on the A376.

Evening
Stroll through ⑦ **Ronda** (above, ➤ 170) to admire the gorge and spectacular Puente Nuevo, in the evening light before dinner.

Day 5

Morning
Spend the first part of the morning in Ronda before heading southwest on the coast road or the 369 through the mountains of the Serranía de Ronda to reach the coast just east of Algeciras.

Afternoon
Drive along the ⑨ **Costa de la Luz** (➤ 171), a beautiful, undeveloped stretch of coastline, on the coast road or the N340 then pick up the A4 at San Fernando and continue on to ⑧ **Jerez de la Frontera** (➤ 171).

0 Seville

Think "Andalucía" and you'll probably visualize whitewashed streets, Moorish architecture, flamenco dresses, orange trees and proud horsemen. Seville, the region's capital, has all this and much more besides. Packed with diverse treasures, the city is also renowned for its fiestas, relaxed and hedonistic lifestyle and the exuberance of its inhabitants. A truly seductive city, it encapsulates the spirit of the south and the essence of Andalucían allure.

Prosaically, Seville is Spain's fourth-largest city, the seat of a university, an important industrial centre and the heart of a rich agricultural region. In 1992 the World Expo was held in Seville, leaving the legacy of a radically modernized infrastructure and huge civic pride.

> From the Giralda there are bird's-eye views over the cathedral and city

First inhabited by Greeks, Phoenicians and Romans, Seville was among the most important of the Moorish city-states and, later, a favourite residence of the Christian monarchs. With

the discovery of the New World in 1492, the city boomed, becoming one of the richest and most cosmopolitan in Europe. In the 17th century, despite economic and political decline, artists such as Velázquez, Murillo and Zurbarán worked here and by the 1800s the city was firmly on the European tourist map.

The Catedral, Giralda and Real Alcázar

Seville's magnificent cathedral, built on the site of the Moorish mosque, is the third largest in Europe, only outsized by St Peter's in Rome and St Paul's in London. Vast, rich and, despite its size, harmoniously balanced, it was built between 1401 and 1519, a superb blend of Gothic austerity and Spanish flamboyance. Almost as wide as it is long, the interior is dominated by the **Capilla Mayor,** the chapel, its splendid, richly carved Flemish altarpiece glistening with gold leaf behind its immense grilles. Opposite lies the choir, with superb choir stalls and an ornate 17th-century marble and bronze screen. Stand between the two and look up at the transept roof, 56m (184ft) above your head; this riot of stone filigree is supported by massive arches and columns, whose huge size is dwarfed by the scale of the cathedral. Other highlights include Christopher Columbus' grand tomb in the south transept, the treasury and sacristy, packed with paintings and precious altar-vessels, and the domed **Capilla Real** (Royal Chapel), the burial place of Alfonso X of Castile.

When the Christians destroyed the mosque to build the cathedral, they kept the minaret and transformed it into a belltower. Nicknamed the **Giralda** – after the weathervane (*giradillo*) that crowns the structure – the 98m (321ft) high tower was built in the 12th century during the caliphate of the Almohad dynasty. Inside, rather than steps, there is a ramp, wide enough for two horsemen to pass, which leads to the top, where you'll get wide views of the city. Directly below lies the lovely courtyard known as the **Patio de los Naranjos** (Courtyard of the Orange Trees), which once formed part of the mosque and now leads into the cathedral.

FESTIVALS

Seville has two great annual festivals; Semana Santa (Holy Week), held the week before Easter, and the Feria (Spring Festival), usually held about two weeks after Easter. The Semana Santa, a deeply religious event when emotion and passion runs high, is celebrated by *pasos* (processions), held by confraternities from Seville's different districts. The processions consist of huge floats supporting religious statues, sumptuously decorated and carried by up to 60 men; they are accompanied by veiled and shrouded penitents, and extolled by improvised laments from the crowds. By contrast, the Feria is a completely secular affair, a week-long celebration of Andalucía's love-affair with horses, music and beautiful women. Carriages filled with laughing girls in colourful flounced dresses, accompanied by horseback riders in traditional dress, parade the streets, gallons of sherry are drunk, and *sevillanas* are danced all night.

Seville's other great monument lies opposite the cathedral – the unforgettable **Real Alcázar** (Royal Palace). Slightly less swamped with tourists than its cousin in Granada, this palace epitomizes the elegance and charm of Mudejar secular architecture. Little remains of the original Moorish Alcázar, and most of what you see was built by Pedro the Cruel in 1362. His builders were Christianized Moors, the inventors of Mudejar style, and this Arabian Nights complex is one of the purest examples of their art still surviving. It's a labyrinth of courtyards, delicately stuccoed and tiled rooms, terraces and coffered chambers, fountains and arched patios. Later Christian monarchs added their own touches. Charles V added some lavish, tapestry-hung rooms in the 16th century, but his great contribution was the Renaissance elements he incorporated into the existing **gardens**. Pergolas, terraces, pools and arcades, planted with magnolias and oranges, plumbago and jasmine, make this one of Spain's finest gardens.

Santa Cruz and the Museo de Bellas Artes

East of the cathedral lies the **Barrio de Santa Cruz** (Santa Cruz quarter), a maze of narrow white streets and sun-splashed squares shaded by orange trees. Originally the Jewish quarter, the area became popular with the 16th- and 17th-century nobility who added fine mansions along its alleyways. These are inward-looking houses, the windows of the plain walls facing the street barred with superb *rejas* (grilles), the interiors centring on green and shady patios. The finest of all, a little further north, is the **Casa de Pilatos**, built in 1519 and a splendidly unified mixture of Mudejar, Gothic and Renaissance elements. It's built around a succession of superb and lushly planted patios, has brilliant *azulejos* (tilework) and one of the city's most elegant interiors.

West from here, you'll find the **Museo de Bellas Artes** (Fine Arts Museum), housed in a 17th-century convent built around three graceful courtyards, which concentrates on the

Architecture at Casa de Pilatos combines Mudejar, Gothic and Renaissance elements

Golden Age of Spanish painting. The gallery in the former church is devoted to Murillo, and pride of place is given to his *Immaculate Conception*, a perfect example of his deeply religious, idealistic style. Zurbarán, another great master, is also well represented, his masterpiece being a stark, sculptural *Christ on the Cross*; look out too for his *Carthusian Monks at Supper* and Ribero's startling handling of light and dark in his pictures in the upstairs galleries.

South and west of the cathedral lie more delights, notably the buildings, gardens and museums surrounding the Plaza de España, the riverside area, and Triana – traditionally the gypsy quarter, across the Guadalquivir river. Explore them as part of a walk (➤ 184–185), or simply spend time wandering the streets and soaking up the atmosphere.

TAKING A BREAK

Right in the hub of town, **Bar Rincón San Eloy** (San Eloy 24, tel: 954 218 079) is a place to enjoy a breather from shopping – along with a glass of *fino* (sherry). There are *azulejo* (tile) steps for sitting on and a vast tapas menu.

➕ 214 C3
☎ www.turismosevilla.org

Tourist Information Office
✉ Avenida de la Constitución 21
☎ 954 221 404;
www.andalucia.org ⏰ Mon–Fri 9–7,
Sat 10–2, 3–7, Sun 10–2

Catedral and Giralda
✉ Plaza Virgen de los Reyes
☎ 954 214 971;
www.catedraldesevilla.es ⏰ Jul–
Aug Mon–Sat 11–6, Sun 2:30–6;
Sep–Jun Mon–Sat 11–6, Sun 2:30–7;
open for services 🎟 Moderate;
free on Sun

Real Alcázar
✉ Plaza del Triunfo ☎ 954 502 323
⏰ Tue–Sat 9:30–5, Sun 9:30–1:30
🎟 Moderate

Casa de Pilatos
✉ Plaza de Pilatos ☎ 954 225 298
⏰ Mar–Sep daily 9–7; Oct–Feb 9–6
🎟 Moderate; free Tue pm

Museo de Bellas Artes
✉ Plaza del Museo 9 ☎ 954 220
790 ⏰ Wed–Sat 9–8:30, Sun 9–2:30,
Tue 2:30–8:30 🎟 Inexpensive; free
to EU citizens

SEVILLE: INSIDE INFO

Top tips Avoid visiting the cathedral on Sunday afternoons – the free entrance draws huge crowds.
- The Alcázar is very badly sign-posted; pick up an English audioguide to help you find your way around.
- Early afternoon is a good time to visit the cathedral and the Real Alcázar during high season; it may be hot, but it won't be quite as crowded.
- Watch your valuables in Seville; the city has a bad reputation for mugging and petty theft.

Must see If you don't have a lot of time, head for the Barrio de Santa Cruz and the Alcázar for a quintessential taste of the city.

2 Córdoba

Córdoba had a great past, first as the largest Roman city in Spain and later as the capital of the Islamic empire in western Europe. From this era dates its most famous building, the Mezquita (Mosque), one of the world's most spiritual and powerful structures. Around this core, other lovely buildings and picturesque *barrios* are scattered, while the Guadalquivir waterfront is an added bonus.

The Mezquita

Córdoba's original eighth-century mosque was enlarged several times, attaining its present size early in the 11th century. For Spanish Muslims, Córdoba was an important place of pilgrimage, outshone only by Mecca and Jerusalem.

You enter through the **Patio de los Naranjos**, a symmetrical ablutions courtyard. Inside, you find yourself in a forest of pillars and arches. These form 19 aisles, made up of double arches supported by round and square columns. The arches alternate brick and stonework, creating a red-and-white striped pattern which acts as a unifying element to the whole. Through this shadowy maze, against the eastern wall, you can make out the *mihrab* (prayer niche). Right in the centre of this serene, rational building looms a flamboyant cathedral choir, built in 1523 as part of Charles V's scheme for "Christianizing" Moorish places. When he realized what had been done in his name Charles was aghast, declaring "To build something ordinary, you have destroyed something unique in the world".

Around the Mezquita

West from the Mezquita, past the **Palacio Episcopal** (Bishops' Palace), stands the rebuilt **Alcázar de los Reyes Cristianos**

CÓRDOBA: INSIDE INFO

Top tips Arrive as **early as possible** at the Mezquita to beat the tour groups. Buy your **entrance ticket** to the Mezquita at the office underneath the Torre de Alminar in the Patio de los Naranjos.

■ **Stick to the south side** of the Mezquita as you enter and approach the *mihrab* – you'll get a better feel of the building as a mosque.

■ **Opening times are changeable;** check at the tourist office for an update.

In more depth The *mihrab* in the Mezquita was erected in the 10th century by al-Hakam II to indicate the direction of Mecca and to amplify the words of the *imam* (priest). It was used as a model for numerous other mosques in Spain and North Africa. The design combines energy with stillness, a perfect illustration of the basic tenets of Moorish architecture.

Tranquil gardens at Córdoba's Alcázar

and some of Córdoba's most seductive **patios**, all white walls and brilliant flowers. Behind here lies the **Judería**, the old Jewish quarter, a tangle of narrow lanes and tiny squares, with the old **sinagoga** (synagogue) at its heart. This tiny 14th-century building is one of only three in Spain that survived the 1492 expulsion of the Jews.

Across the River

Across the river is the **Torre de la Calahorra,** a Moorish fortress, now containing a museum, built in the 14th century to defend the **Roman bridge**, while along the river you'll see the ruins of the **mills** and **Moorish waterwheels**.

TAKING A BREAK

Begin your evening with a sherry in the bar or cool leafy patio of **El Caballo Rojo** (Calle Cardenal Herrero 28), reputed to be Córdoba's oldest restaurant.

215 E4 www.turismocordoba.org

Tourist Information Office
Palacio de Congresos y Exposiciones, Torrijos 10
957 201 774;
www.turismodecordoba.org Apr–Oct Mon–Fri 9:30–7, Sat 10–2, 5–7, Sun 10–2; Nov–Mar Mon–Sat 9:30–6, Sun 10–2

Mezquita-Catedral
Torrijos 957 470 512
Summer Mon–Sat 8:30–7:30, Sun 2–7; winter Mon–Sat 8:30–7:30, Sun 2–6. Sun am for services
Moderate; free weekdays till 10am

Alcázar de los Reyes Cristianos
Campo Santo de los Mártires
957 420 151 Tue–Sat 10–2, 4:30–6:30, Sun 9:30–2:30
Inexpensive; free Wed

Torre de la Calahorra
Calle Acera Arrecife 957 293 929 Daily 10–6 Moderate

Sinagoga
Calle Judias 20 957 202 928
Tue–Sat 9:30–2, 3:30–5:30, Sun 9:30–1:30 Inexpensive; EU citizens free

❸ Granada

Granada is home to the Alhambra, the most evocative, exciting and sensual of all Spain's monuments, beautifully preserved, lovingly tended, and set in superb natural surroundings. Nothing more perfectly reveals the sophistication and spirit of Moorish Spain, while the city's Christian monuments poignantly illustrate the transience of this, and every, great civilization.

The Alhambra and Generalife

The **Alhambra** was the palace-fortress of the Nasrid Sultans, built around an existing Moorish 11th-century fortress between the 13th and 14th centuries. The complex, encircled by walls and towers, consists of the **Alcazaba**, the old fort; the **Palacios Nazaríes**, the actual palace; and, beyond the walls, the **Generalife**, the summer palace and gardens of the sultans. Hard against the Nazaríes looms the Renaissance bulk of Charles V's palace, built in the mid-16th century.

The **Alcazaba** is dominated by the Torre de la Vela, an imposing tower overlooking the city from where the Cross was first displayed when the city, the last Moorish stronghold, fell to the Christians in 1492. The solidity of this military stronghold is a foil for the grace and delicacy of the **Palacios Nazaríes**, the heart of the Alhambra. Council chambers, reception rooms, throne rooms and the harem are set about a series of patios and gardens. Originally crudely built, the chambers are principally a vehicle for ornamental stucco decoration, where Arabic inscriptions are used to form patterns and *trompe l'oeil* ceiling ornamentation gives an illusion of staggering height. The **Sala de los Abencerrajes**, with its 16-sided honeycomb vault, is the finest of these, closely followed by the **Sala de los Reyes** and the **Sala de las Dos Hermanas**. Marble arcades frame the fish pool in the **Patio de los Arrayanes**, the lions still stand guard around the central fountain in the **Patio de los Leones**, and the whole is encircled with flowering, shady gardens.

Nearby, a series of enclosed gardens, green and well-watered, surround the sultans' summer palace, the **Generalife**. The palace is little more than an elegant pavilion, it's the gardens that take star billing. A series of garden rooms, each opening out to another vista of verdant beauty, succeed one another. Each is beautifully planted to delight the senses – deep cool shade, bright clear colours, fragrance everywhere, and the constant trickle and tinkle of running water. Nowhere better illustrates the Moors' obsession with water – its sound, its movement – than the fountains, pools and cascades in this lovely spot, an earthly vision of the Koran's Paradise.

The Moorish palace of the Alhambra, perched high above the modern city

ENTRY TO THE ALHAMBRA

For conservation purposes, only about 8,000 visitors are allowed daily into the Alhambra. To avoid queuing and probable disappointment, **advance reservation** to the Alhambra is highly recommended and imperative in the summer months. You can do this up to a year ahead:

- **Internet** www.alhambra-tickets.es
- **By telephone** In Spain tel: 902 888 001, daily 8am–midnight. From abroad tel: 34 934 923 750, daily 8am–midnight.
- **At any BBVA bank** in Spain Mon–Fri 9–2; a small commission is charged.
- From many **hotels** within the province of Granada.

In all cases you will be issued with a **reference number** exchangeable for **tickets** at the "Advance Booking" window at the main entrance.

- Tickets are valid for either the **morning** or the **afternoon**. On your ticket a **half-hour period** will be specified during which you **must** enter the Palacios Nazaríes; if you fail to do so you cannot see this part of the complex, though, once inside, you can stay as long as you like.
- You can use the **different sections** of your ticket **in any order** as long as you visit the Palacios Nazaríes during your specified time slot. You will not be allowed into the Alhambra (even with a pre-booked ticket) less than one hour before closing time.

The Catedral and Capilla Real

Granada's **Catedral** was begun in the 1520s and finished in the 1700s; it's big and impressive but easily outshone by the neighbouring **Capilla Real**, the burial place of the Catholic Monarchs, Ferdinand and Isabel. Flamboyantly late Gothic in style, the interior contains a sumptuous marble monument, commissioned by Charles V in 1517. Ferdinand and Isabella lie in the crypt beneath their serene effigies and a candle burns continually at Isabella's dying request.

The Albaicín

The **Albaicín** spreads across the slopes of a hill opposite the Alhambra. It's the largest Moorish city quarter still in existence in Spain, a wonderfully atmospheric place to wander, whose narrow streets give a true sense of Granada as a Moorish city.

TAKING A BREAK

Stop for tapas or the excellent *menus del día* at the palm-shaded terrace at **Café au Lait** (Callejón de los Franceses 31), close to the cathedral.

The vaulted interior of Granada's cathedral

➕ 216 B2

Tourist Information Offices
✉ Calle Santa Ana 2 ☎ 958 225 990; www.andalucia.org; www.granadatur.com 🕐 Mon–Fri 9–7, Sat 9–2, 4–7, Sun 10–2

✉ Plaza Mariana Pineda 10 ☎ 958 247 128; www.turismodegranada.org 🕐 Mon–Fri 9–8, Sat 10–7, Sun 10–3

Alhambra and Generalife
✉ Calle Real de la Alhambra ☎ 902 441 221; www.alhambra-patronato.es 🕐 Mar–Oct daily 8:30–8, 10–11:30; Nov–Feb 8:30–6 (also Fri–Sat 8–9:30pm) 💷 Expensive

Catedral
✉ Calle Gran Via de Colón 5 ☎ 958 222 959 🕐 Mar–Aug Mon–Sat 10:45–1:30, 4–8, Sun 4–7; Sep–Feb 10:45–1:30, 4–7, Sun 4–6 💷 Inexpensive

Capilla Real
✉ Calle Oficios ☎ 958 227 848 🕐 Apr–Sep Mon–Sat 10:30–1, 4–7, Sun 11–1, 4–7; Oct–Mar Mon–Sat 10:30–1, 3:30–6:30, Sun 11–6:30 💷 Inexpensive

---

GRANADA: INSIDE INFO

Top tips Try to **arrive as early as possible** at the Alhambra, before the crowds.
- An **audio-guide** will help you get the most out of your visit.
- The easiest way to reach the Alhambra is to take the minibus service that runs from the Plaza Nueva. If you do come **by car**, follow the **purple signs** from the ring road or city centre.
- The **best view** of the Alhambra is across the valley from the Plaza de San Nicolás in the Albaicín.
- **Watch your valuables** in the Albaicín; there's an escalating number of thefts.

At Your Leisure

A Renaissance gem, Baeza is listed as a UNESCO World Heritage Site

4 Baeza and Úbeda

These elegant Renaissance towns, just 9km (6 miles) apart, overlook a rolling landscape of olive trees in the upper valley of the Guadalquivir. They are crammed with stone churches and palaces set around attractive plazas.

Baeza is the smaller of the two – here you'll find a cluster of Isabelline palaces (► 15), a Romanesque church, a fine cathedral, and some superb views.

Úbeda's principal attraction is the Plaza de Vázquez de Molina, a stunning Renaissance square surrounded by dazzling buildings. Beside the Parador, at the end of the plaza is the Capilla del Salvador, a lovely chapel with an exuberant plateresque facade, and an over-the-top retablo inside.

⊞ 216 B4

Tourist Information Offices

✉ Plaza del Pópulo, Baeza ☎ 953 740 444; www.andalucia.org ◷ Apr–Sep Mon–Fri 9:30–7, Sat–Sun 10–1, 5–7; Oct–Mar Mon–Fri 9:30–2:30, 4–6, Sat 10–2, Sun 10–1

✉ Palacio Marqués de Contadero, Calle Baja del Marqués 4, Úbeda ☎ 953 750 897; www.andalucia.org ◷ Mon–Fri 9–8, Sat–Sun 10–2

Capilla del Salvador

✉ Plaza de Vázquez de Molina, Úbeda ☎ 953 750 897 ◷ Mon–Sat 10–2, 4:30–6:30, Sun 11–2, 4–7 ◉ Moderate

5 Las Alpujarras

The high valleys across the southern slopes of the Sierra Nevada are known as Las Alpujarras. They were first settled by the North African Berbers and later were the final stronghold of the Moors. The area is mountainous, well-watered and fertile, its ancient terraces still used for agriculture. The cube-like houses with flat roofs and secret courtyards are North African in style, and rug-making, introduced by the Berbers, is still an important local industry. The spa town of Lanjarón, whose bottled water is drunk all over Spain, is the gateway, and the market settlement Órgiva the "capital". Most people head for the High Alpujarras and the

picturesque villages of Pampaneira, Bubión and Capileira. All three cling to the steep slopes above the Poqueira gorge, with the snow-capped tops of the southern Sierra rising behind. This is superb walking country, with great views and sparklingly clear air.
⊞ 216 B2

Tourist Information Office
✉ Avenida de la Alpujarra s/n, Lanjarón
☎ 958 770 452; www.andalucia.org
🕙 Summer Thu–Tue 10–2, 4:30–8:30

❻ Costa del Sol

The Costa del Sol (Sunshine Coast) stretches along the Mediterranean coast from Gibraltar to the province of Almería. Its capital is Málaga, an attractive city with an historic quarter, sophisticated shops and the excellent Museo Picasso. To the east are the mass-market resorts of Torremolinos, Benalmádena, Fuengirola and Marbella. This was the first area in Spain to be developed for mass tourism, and attracts northern Europeans looking for good-value vacations and villas in the sun. Marbella, home to the super-rich, is the pick of the bunch on the western stretch; to the east of Málaga, the coast is steeper and prettier and the development less intense.
⊞ 215 E2

Tourist Information Office
Málaga
⊞ 215 F2 ✉ Pasaje de Chinitas 4 ☎ 952 213 445; www.malagaturismo.com 🕙 Mon–Fri 9–8, Sat–Sun 10–2

Marbella
⊞ 215 E2 ✉ Plaza de los Naranjos
☎ 952 868 977; www.marbella.es 🕙 Mon–Fri 9–9, Sat 10–2

❼ Ronda

Ronda's setting is its principal attraction, for the ridge on which it's built is split by a gorge more than 100m (328ft) deep called El Tajo, and spanned by a superb 18th-century arched bridge, the Puente Nuevo. The old town still retains some Moorish buildings – superb baths,

a bridge and a ruined Alcázar. The best way to explore here is simply to wander, but be sure to take in the Casa de Mondragón, a beautiful Moorish palace now housing the local museum. Across the gorge lies the Mercadillo quarter, developed after the Christian reconquest. Here you'll find the theatrical Plaza de Toros, built in 1785, one of Spain's most important bullrings and the birthplace of the modern *corrida*. Behind it runs the Paseo de Blas Infante, a lovely walkway which skirts the edge of the gorge. Aim to spend the night here, to enjoy evening falling and the peace that descends once the crowds of daily coach tours have departed.
⊞ 215 D2 ☎ www.turismoderonda.es

Tourist Information Office
✉ Plaza de España 1 ☎ 952 871 272; www.andalucia.org 🕙 Mon–Fri 10–6, Sat 10–2, 3–5, Sun 10–2:30

Casa de Mondragón
✉ Plaza de Mondragón ☎ 952 870 818
🕙 Apr–Sep Mon–Fri 10–7, Sat– Sun 10–3; Oct–Mar Mon–Fri 10–6 ⓘ Inexpensive

Plaza de Toros
✉ Calle Virgen de la Paz ☎ 952 874 132; www.rmcr.org 🕙 Apr–Sep daily 10–8; Oct–Mar 10–6 ⓘ Moderate

The dramatic Puente Nuevo, Ronda

The elegant dome of Jerez's Gothic-Renaissance cathedral

⑧ Jerez de la Frontera

South of Seville you're in sherry country, and sedate and appealing Jerez is its capital. It's a prosperous and elegant city with streets and plazas shaded by orange trees and lined with the *bodegas* (warehouses) of the great wine-producing dynasties. You can take a tour – González Byass and Pedro Domecq are the best known – and listen to an explanation of the *solera* system of wine production before sampling the finished product. Flamenco enthusiasts might like to pop into the Centro Andaluz de Flamenco in the atmospheric Barrio de Santiago; Jerez is an important centre of the art. Near the central Plaza del Arenal lies the lovely Gothic-Renaissance cathedral and an archaeological museum, while further out of town you can experience Jerez's equine love affair at a musical performance at the Real Escuela Andaluz del Arte Ecuestre (Royal Andalucían School of Equestrian Art).

🔁 214 C2

Tourist Information Office
✉ Alameda Cristina s/n (Claustros de Santo Domingo) ☎ 956 338 874; www.turismojerez. com ⏰ Jun–Sep Mon–Fri 9–3, 5–7, Sat–Sun 8–4; Oct–May Mon–Fri 9:30–3, 4:30–6:30, Sat–Sun 9:30–2:30

González Byass
✉ Calle Manuel María González 12 ☎ 956 357 016; www.gonzalezbyass.es ⏰ English guided visits: Mon–Sat 12, 1, 2, 5 and 6, Sun 12, 1 and 2 💶 Expensive (admission includes tastings and tapas). Advance reservations required

Pedro Domecq
✉ Calle San Ildefonso 3 ☎ 956 151 500; www.domecq.es ⏰ Mon–Sat 10–2. Advance reservations required 💶 Moderate

Centro Andaluz de Flamenco
✉ Plaza San Juan 1 ☎ 856 814 132; www.centroandaluzdeflamenco.es ⏰ Mon–Fri 9–2 💶 Free

Real Escuela Andaluz del Arte Ecuestre
✉ Avenida Duque de Abrantes ☎ 956 318 008; www.realescuela.org ⏰ Performances: Mar–Oct Tue and Thu 12; Nov–Feb Tue 12. Stable visits: Mon, Wed and Fri 10–2 (varies seasonally) 💶 Expensive

⑨ Costa de la Luz

Andalucía's beautiful Atlantic coastline, suffused with radiant light, stretches from Tarifa past vast sandy beaches, pinewoods and cliffs. Wind- and kitesurfers flock to Tarifa, a base for whale and dolphin spotting and visiting the Roman ruins at Baelo Claudia. From here are fantastic views to Gibraltar and across the straits to Morocco. Further west and a little inland lies Vejer de la Frontera, one of the loveliest of the "white towns", with a fabulous hilltop setting and a maze of narrow streets. From here, more laid-back fishing and low-key holiday villages run along the coast west of Cabo Trafalgar, scene of Nelson's great sea victory in 1805. Neighbouring Conil de la Frontera has great beaches, while west again, beyond Cádiz, the little towns of Chipiona and Sanlúcar de Barrameda are a world away from the Mediterranean resorts.

🔁 214 B2

Tourist Information Office, Tarifa
🔁 215 D1 ✉ Paseo de la Alameda ☎ 956 68 993; www.aytotarifa.com, www.tarifainfo.com ⏰ Summer Mon–Fri 10–2, 6–8, Sat–Sun 10–3; winter Mon–Fri 10–2, 5–7, Sat–Sun 10–3

Where to...
Stay

Prices
Expect to pay for a double room per night:
€ up to €100   €€ €101–€180   €€€ €181–€240   €€€€ over €240

SEVILLE

Hostería del Laurel €€
This characterful hotel is on a small square lined with orange trees in the heart of the Barrio de Santa Cruz. The Hostería's *bodega* is mentioned in Zorilla's famed *Don Juan Tenorio*; these days the restaurant and tapas bar are equally famed among locals in the know. The spacious, en suite rooms are spread over two floors. They are bright, basic and spotlessly clean; several have views of the plaza.
➕ 214 C3 ⊠ Plaza de las Venerables 5,
☎ 954 220 295; www.hosteriadellaurel.com

Las Casas de la Judería €€€
This is one of the prettiest hotels in Seville, tucked down an alleyway on the edge of the Barrio de Santa Cruz, but close to the shops and commercial heart of the city. The rooms are set around three classic courtyards, which were once incorporated into three palaces. The predominant colours are warm ochre and white and the rooms, which are individually decorated in subdued pastel colours, are appropriately palatial with high ceilings and plush furniture.
➕ 214 C3 ⊠ Callejón de Dos Hermanas
☎ 954 415 150; www.casaspalacios.com

CÓRDOBA

Casa de los Azulejos €€
This very pretty colonial house stands on a quiet side road a few steps outside the Judería, Córdoba's old Jewish quarter. The original marble flooring and plant-filled patio make this a cool, atmospheric retreat. Crisp white linen complements the colourful walls, old wooden doors and wrought ironwork. A decent breakfast is included in the price.
➕ 215 E4 ⊠ Calle Fernando Colón 5
☎ 957 470 000;
www.casadelosazulejos.com

Los Omeyas €
This hotel is in a superb setting, amid the tangle of back streets in the Judería, the former Jewish quarter. It has been refurbished to reflect the city's Moorish heritage with Mezquita-style arches, white marble and latticework. A central patio provides access to comfortable, though uninspired, rooms with air conditioning. Try for one of the rooms on the top floor for a panoramic view of the Mezquita (▶ 164). Breakfast is a reasonably priced extra.
➕ 215 E4 ⊠ Calle Encarnación 17,
☎ 957 492 267;
www.hotel-losomeyas.com

GRANADA

Casa del Aljarife €€
This hotel is a gem, set in a sensitively refurbished 17th-century house on a tiny square in the heart of the Albaicín (the city's old Moorish quarter), with soul-stirring views of the surrounding rooftops, ninth-century city walls and the Alhambra. Typical of the area, there is a delightful shady central courtyard, as well as a rooftop terrace. The rooms are small but have plenty of character and the space is utilized cleverly.
➕ 216 B2 ⊠ Placeta de la Cruz Verde 2,
Albaicín ☎ 958 222 425;
www.casadelaljarife.com

Where to...
Eat and Drink

Prices
Expect to pay per person for a meal, including wine and service
€ up to €12   €€ €12–€35   €€€ over €35

SEVILLE

Habanita €–€€
Tucked down a side street in the buzzing Alfalfa *barrio*, this is one of the few restaurants in Seville serving vegetarian fare. The menu is vast, and includes some meat-based Cuban and Mediterranean dishes. There are some real one-offs like yucca with garlic, as well as black beans, tamales and strict vegan fare. They're not too pious to serve alcohol and calorific, sugar-laden desserts though!
🚹 214 C3 🖾 Calle Golfo 3, Seville ☎ 954 219 516 🕙 Mon–Sat 12:30–4:30, 8–1:30

La Albahaca €€€
Set on one of the city's prettiest squares, this wonderful old building was once a family manor house. It has been subtly converted into one of the best-known restaurants in the city, with an attractive outdoor patio, as well as four intimate dining rooms, decorated with dazzling *azulejos* (tiles), antique oil paintings, chandeliers and plenty of plants. The well-rounded menu includes several truly decadent puddings.
🚹 214 C3 🖾 Plaza de Santa Cruz 2 ☎ 954 220 714 🕙 Mon–Sat 12–4, 8–midnight

---

Where to...
Stay

Prices
Expect to pay per person for a meal, including wine and service
€ up to €12   €€ €12–€35   €€€ over €35

Hostal Britz €
This welcoming, inexpensive *hostal* close to the Alhambra gives excellent value for money. Rooms, although basic, are comfortable, and some have terraces and en suite bathrooms. On bustling Plaza Nueva, it can be noisy on Saturday nights but central Granada is only a step away
🚹 216 B2 🖾 Cuesta de Gomérez 1 ☎ 958 223 652; www.lisboaweb.com

COSTA DEL SOL

La Fonda €
In the centre of the village of Benalmádena, this hotel doubles as a cookery school which gives it the added attraction of cut-price, top culinary fare. There are cool patios shaded by palms, a swimming pool and fountains. Rooms are light and airy with terraces and sea views.
🚹 215 E2 🖾 Calle Santo Domingo 7, Benalmádena ☎ 952 568 563; www.fondahotel.com

RONDA

Alavera de Los Baños €
This charming little hotel next to the 13th-century Moorish baths is a wonderful bolthole. It has super views of the Serranía de Ronda and city walls. Facilities include a lovely garden and small pool, and there is also a library, reading room and dining room.
🚹 215 D2 🖾 Hoyo de San Miguel ☎ 952 879 143; www.alaveradelosbanos.com

Molino del Puente €€
Only five minutes' drive out of Ronda, this converted mill is set in beautiful countryside with lovely riverside gardens and a large pool. The old olive and flour mill has been refurbished into 10 comfortable, attractive en suite rooms. There is also a very good-value restaurant.
🚹 215 D2 🖾 Fuente de la Higuera, Ronda ☎ 952 874 164, www.hotelmolinodelpuente.com

CÓRDOBA

Mesón de Juan Peña €€

This unassuming restaurant just west of the Mezquita is a diner's delight. Córdoban dishes are given an innovative twist, servings are generous and the quality memorable. The *salmorejo* (thick gazpacho) and home-made *croquetas* are not to be missed. No reservations are taken: arrive early or be prepared for a wait.

➕ 215 E4 ⊠ Dr Flemming 1 ☎ 957 200 702
🕐 Mon–Sat 1–5, 8–1

Taberna Plateros €

Dating from the 17th century, the large patio restaurant leads to more tiled rooms and a traditional marbled bar where blue-collar workers and businessmen meet. Expect home-style cooking with local specialities such as deep-fried aubergines (eggplant) served with a spicy tomato sauce. No credit cards.

➕ 215 E4 ⊠ San Francisco 6 ☎ 957 470 042 🕐 Tue–Sat 8–4, 7.30–midnight

GRANADA

Bodegas Castañeda €€

Granada is famous for its lively tapas bars and this one, reputedly the oldest in town, more so than others. Elbow yourself a little space at the bar and enjoy the atmosphere. Your drink will come with some tasty tapas for you to enjoy or you decide whether to graze on other traditional dishes or a selection of cheeses or cold meats.

➕ 216 B2 ⊠ Calle de Elvira 5 ☎ 958 223 222 🕐 Daily noon–late

Mirador de Morayma €€

Buried in the Albaicín, this restaurant may be hard to find and you have to ring the doorbell to get in. Once inside, you have unbeatable views from the wisteria-covered terrace across the gorge to the Alhambra with the peaks of the Sierra Nevada forming a magnificent backdrop. The menu is mainly traditional with a few surprises, such as *ensalada de remojón granadino* (salad of cod, orange and olives). After your meal wander up to the Mirador San Nicolas for more views.

➕ 216 B2 ⊠ Pianista García Carillo 2 ☎ 958 228 290 🕐 Daily noon–late

COSTA DEL SOL

Bar Logueño €

Shoehorned into a deceptively small space, this is one of Málaga's best-loved tapas bars. There is a tantalizing array of tapas from which to choose, including many Logueño originals, like sautéed oyster mushrooms with garlic, parsley and goats' cheese. There is also an excellent range of Rioja wines. The service is fast and good, despite the lack of elbow-room.

➕ 215 F2 ⊠ Calle Marín García 9, Málaga ☎ 952 223 048 🕐 Mon–Sat 1–4, 7–late

RONDA

Casa Santa Pola €€

The comfortably elegant dining rooms of Casa Santa Pola stretch over three floors, offering breathtaking views across El Tajo ravine. Roast meats cooked in a wood-fired oven are the speciality here; the *cochinillo* (suckling pig) melts in your mouth and the *conejo a la Rondeña* (stewed rabbit with wild herbs and mushrooms) is wonderfully tasty.

➕ 215 D2 ⊠ Calle Santa Domingo 3 ☎ 952 879 208 🕐 Mon–Sat 1–5, 8–1

Tragabuches €€€

This Rondan institution is the place to head if you're looking for a change from traditional Andalusian fare. The refreshingly contemporary surroundings and inventive layering of flavours create a truly unforgettable experience. Dishes like gazpacho ice cream with apple jelly or oxtail ravioli with chestnut purée might tempt you to trust in the taster menu.

➕ 215 D2 ⊠ Calle de José Aparicio 1 ☎ 952 190 291; www.tragabuches.com 🕐 Tue–Sat 1–5, 8–1, Sun 1–5

Where to...
Shop

FASHION

For clothes and shoe shops in **Málaga** head for Calle Marqués de Larios. In **Marbella** try Calle Ramón y Cajal, where you'll find big-name designers such as Versace, Armani, Donna Karan and Gucci within a few doors of each other.

Granada city's Calle Reyes Católicos has plenty of high street chains and boutiques. If you can't find what you want here, try El Corte Inglés off Acero del Darro (a continuation of the same street).

Seville's swanky Calle Sierpes has a number of splendid, if pricey boutiques. For fashion in **Córdoba**, head for the area surrounding the pedestrianized Avenida del Gran Capitán, where you'll find chic dress shops to match any in Seville.

SOUVENIRS AND CRAFTS

You can buy souvenirs that range from tacky T-shirts to traditional pottery in most places. Most shops are wholly dedicated to mass-produced souvenirs are concentrated around major attractions and big resorts. If you head inland, however, you can often find more unusual crafts.

In **Málaga** province the Artesania Grazalema (Plaza de España, Grazalema, tel: 956 132 008) sells an intriguing range of woven goods.

Las Alpujarras in **Granada** province is well known for the brightly coloured woven *jarapas* (rugs and bedcovers). Worth seeking out is Bodega La Moralea (Calle Verónica, Pampaneira, tel: 958 763 225), which carries a

vast stock of souvenirs, as well as tempting local food products.

In **Seville**, head across the river to Triana if you're seeking the colourful tiles and ceramic ware so distinctive of the city. Azulejos Santa Isabel (Alfarería 12, tel: 954 344 608) is just one of several well-stocked outlets.

Córdoba is celebrated for its leather crafts. In the centre, Meryan (Calleja de las Flores, tel: 957 475 902) sells a good range of leather goods, and other artefacts.

ANTIQUES AND ART

If you are looking for interesting pieces with a genuine Spanish pedigree, search the antiques and fine arts shops scattered throughout the centres of **Granada** and **Seville**.

FOOD AND DRINK

The hill regions of the Alpujarras in Granada province and the Sierra Morena in Seville province are famous for their *jamón serrano* (dried ham); villages such as Trevélez in the Alpujarras (▲ 169) have shops devoted to *jamón* and other cured meats.

You can find own-label brands of sherry in the big-name *bodegas* of **Jerez de la Frontera** (▲ 171), while in specialist shops in the main towns and the wine-producing areas, you will find every kind of sherry, wine and liqueur on sale – and you can often sample before deciding what to buy.

MARKETS

The best market for fresh fish is at Sanlúcar de Barrameda (▲ 171), on the Costa de la Luz, although the markets in other coastal towns are also worth visiting.

For mixed fish, meat, fruit and vegetables, try the markets at Cádiz and Málaga (▲ 171), and for clothing and general goods, Fuengirola (▲ 170) and Córdoba (▲ 164–165).

Where to...
Be Entertained

NIGHTLIFE

On the **Costa del Sol**, the mass-market resort of Torremolinos attracts a partying and clubbing crowd in the summer, while the road between Marbella and Puerto Banús offers a glitzy strip of big-name clubs. Málaga's buzzing bars throng around Calle Granada and Calle Beatas, although in summer the beachside neighbourhood of Pedregalejo is the place to head for all-night action. In Marbella, Plaza de los Olivos is good for lively bars and in Puerto Banús the lanes around the marina offer a myriad of partying options.

Granada's nightlife largely caters to the city's sizeable student population, who hang out at bars around Plaza del Príncipe. The caves in the Sacromonte district of the city also offer a range of options from pricey tourist bars to authentic flamenco performances. **El Camborio** (Camino del Sacromonte) is a lively option with several dance floors and views of the Alhambra from the terrace.

Seville's music bars cluster around the Plaza de la Alfalfa and along El Torneo, parallel to the river. The Bulebar and the Barqueta bars are particularly lively in the summer. For more information on nightlife in Seville visit www. exploreseville.com.

Although much less cosmopolitan than Seville, Granada and Málaga, **Córdoba** has some lively dance and music bars on Calle Cruz Conde, just north of Plaza de las Tendillas.

FLAMENCO

In **Málaga**, there are regular flamenco shows at Vista Andalucía (Avenida de los Guindos, tel: 952 231 157) and frequent top calibre performers appear at Teatro Miguel de Cervantes (Calle Ramos Marín, tel: 952 224 100, www. teatrocervantes.com). **Jerez de la Frontera** has a strong flamenco tradition, particularly in the Barrio de Santiago. There are excellent shows at El Laga (Plaza del Mercado, tel: 956 338 384). One of the most popular flamenco venues in **Granada** is Peña Flamenca La Platería (Placeta de Toqueros 7, tel: 958 210 650, www.laplateria. org.es), while **Seville's** La Carbonería (Calle Levíes 18, tel: 954 214 460) is an atmospheric bar with flamenco on Monday and Thursday nights. In **Córdoba**, head to Tablao Cardenal (Calle Torrijos 10, tel: 957 483 320), one of the best venues for "classical" flamenco.

OUTDOOR ACTIVITIES

The windier Atlantic coast, especially at Tarifa between Gibraltar and Cádiz, is one of the world's best wind- and kitesurfing venues, while the opportunities for scuba diving, water-skiing and paragliding are increasing.

Andalucía's mountains provide endless opportunities for adventure holidaying whether it's walking in the fertile landscapes of Las Alpujarras (▶ 169) and the Sierra de Grazalema (▶ 186–187), or horse riding and bicycling on organized trips.

The spectacular Sierra Nevada mountain range is a popular skiing destination during the winter.

You can also go for the wilder extremes of adventure sport and try rock climbing, abseiling, canoeing, paragliding and hang-gliding.

For detailed information on what is on offer enquire at one of the tourist offices.

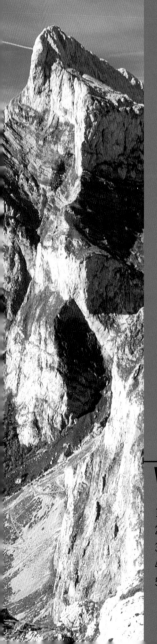

Walks and Tours

1 EL RASTRO, MADRID

Walk

This walk takes you from the elegance of the Plaza Mayor through the exuberant working class districts of El Rastro and Lavapiés, which are now becoming increasingly fashionable. The vibrant weekend street life, with the famous Rastro Sunday market, makes a good contrast with the fine 18th-century architecture and the expanses of green you'll also encounter on this walk.

DISTANCE 3.2km (2 miles) **TIME** 3 hours, allowing time for El Rastro and the Real Jardín Botánico
START POINT Plaza Puerta del Sol 🅜 Sol ➕ 198 C3
END POINT Real Jardín Botánico 🅜 Atocha ➕ 199 D1

1–2

Stand in the **Plaza Puerta del Sol** (➤ 46) with your back to the **Casa de Correos**, built in 1768 and the city's post office until 1847. You're standing at the epicentre of Spain, since all distances are measured from the stone slab below the clock tower, known as Kilometro Cero (Kilometer Zero). Turn left down **Calle Mayor**, and take the fourth turning on the left into the **Plaza Mayor** (➤ 46–47).

2–3

Leave the Plaza Mayor in the southwest corner and head down the **Calle de Toledo**, a typically

Madrileño street with wonderfully idiosyncratic shops. As you reach the Plaza de Segovia Nueva, the huge building on the opposite left-hand corner is the **Iglesia de San Isidro** (Mon–Sat 7:30–12:30, 6–8, Sun 8:30–2:30, 5:30–8:30). The church was built as the Jesuits' Spanish powerhouse in 1622–33 and was part of the Colegio Imperial. Charles V fell out with the Jesuits in 1767, annexing their property, and the church was rededicated to San Isidro, Madrid's patron saint. It served as the city's cathedral from 1886–1993.

3–4

Follow the signposted **El Rastro** route south from San Isidro down Calle de los Estudios to the Plaza de Cascorro and across this into **Calle Ribera de Curtidores**, the heart of the Rastro district and site of the famous flea market. Curtidores is quietish on a weekday, but becomes a sprawling, vibrant market on Sundays, particularly after 10am, when the market really gets going. You'll find everything

Bargain hunters at the Rastro Sunday flea market

imaginable on sale, a great atmosphere, and some of the city's liveliest bars. Watch your bag, and leave valuables back at the hotel.

4–5

Turn left down Calle de San Cayetano and continue until you reach the parallel street, **Calle de Embajadores**, with the 1761 church of **San Cayetano**, one of the area's patrons, ahead of you across the road.

5–6

Head down Embajadores and take the sixth turning left, **Calle de Tribulete**, to walk past **La Corrala**. This traditional 19th-century tenement block, with its balconies opening on to a central courtyard, provides some of the area's most characteristic housing. In summer the patio is used for *zarzuela*, Spain's own version of Gilbert and Sullivan, which incorporates elements of opera with bawdy music-hall songs and jokes.

6–7

From La Corrala, continue along Tribulete until you reach **Plaza Lavapiés**, a square which was the medieval centre of the Jewish quarter. Turn diagonally right into Calle de Argumosa, and

follow it round until the end, where on the left is the new extension to the **Museo Nacional Centro de Arte Reina Sofía** (▶ 54).

7–8

From the Reina Sofía, use the Atocha station underpass system to reach Calle del Dr Velasco on the north side of the Paseo de la Infanta Isabel. Head north to the **Real Jardín Botánico** (daily 10–dusk, inexpensive). The gardens were founded in the 18th century and restored in the 1980s to house over 30,000 plant species from around the world. It is a peaceful spot to while away an hour or so, with shady paths, benches and hothouses crammed with tropical plants and vines.

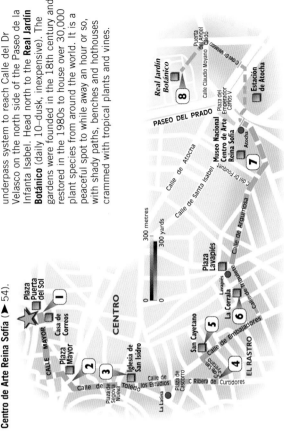

2 PICOS DE EUROPA
Drive

This spectacular drive will give you the best idea possible, without actually trekking into the mountains, of the grandeur and magnificence of the Picos de Europa. The route is immensely varied, covering narrow gorges with precipitous rock walls, upland mountain meadows and woodland, and high plateaux. Along the route there are frequent stretches of narrow road with overhanging rocks and steep drops; nervous drivers who are unused to mountain roads should be prepared for testing driving in places.

DISTANCE 170km (105.5 miles) **TIME** Driving 4 hours, but allow all day to give yourself plenty of time to enjoy the mountains
START POINT Cangas de Onís ✚ 204 C5 **END POINT** Panes ✚ 205 D5

1–2

Start in the town of Cangas de Onís (easily reached from Oviedo) and bear right after the bridge onto the N625 (signposted Riaño 63) and follow the course of the **River Sella**, teeming with trout, past smallholdings and grazing cattle. The valley narrows to the impressive gorge of the **Desfiladero de los Beyos**, said to be the narrowest motorable gorge in Europe. As this eventually widens, the road climbs steeply to the mountain village

of **Oseja de Sajambre**, with great views to the sharp peak of Niaja (1,732m/5,684ft).

2–3

After Oseja, the road continues upwards through a lovely stretch of high woodland and open alpine meadows to the pass at **Puerto del Pontón**, a height of 1,290m (4,231ft).

3–4

Continue along the N625 to Riaño. This is high-plateau country and ahead of you opens out the immense stretch of **the Riaño reservoir (Embalse de Riaño)**, built to irrigate the plains around León and Palencia. The village of Riaño was built to replace the villages lost when the dam was completed in the 1980s.

4–5

Take the N621 from Riaño towards **Portilla de la Reina**. At first little villages punctuate this gentler landscape, which soon becomes increasingly rocky and narrows until the

road reaches the pass, with its bronze statue of a deer, at **Puerto de San Glorio** (1,609m/5,281ft). From the pass there are superb views into Cantabria.

Rugged mountain terrain in the heart of the Picos

5–6

From here the twisting road descends very steeply through rapidly changing vegetation; at **La Vega** follow the N621 to the left towards **Potes.**

6–7

At the town of Potes, you could make a 20km (12.5-mile) detour into the heart of the mountains to the cable car at **Fuente Dé**. This swoops up 900m (2,954ft) to a viewpoint perched to the east of the massif of Torre Cerredo (Tesorero; 2,648m/8,691ft), the Picos' highest peak. It's a popular excursion so be prepared to wait to ride both up and down. Otherwise, follow the road through the dramatic **Desfiladero de la Hermida** gorge, whose sides are so steep that no sunlight touches the tiny village of La Hermida for six months of the year. The road follows the course of the **River Deva**, another salmon and trout river, to arrive at **Panes**. From here the 114 skirts the northern edge of the Picos back to Cangas de Onís.

The medieval bridge at Cangas de Onís

TAKING A BREAK

The 1,000m (3,280ft) high village of Riaño is the best place to stop – try the Hotel Presa (Avenida de Valcayo 12, tel: 987 740 637), where you can fill up on tapas or enjoy mountain home-cooking in the wood-panelled restaurant.

3 BARCELONA'S WATERFRONT

Walk

This walk combines some lovely waterside stretches around Port Vell, one of Barcelona's prime recreational areas, with a glimpse of some interesting older neighbourhoods and the city's loveliest park. There are some fascinating, Catalan-slanted museums en route and the chance to admire one of the city's oldest and most atmospheric churches.

DISTANCE 2.5km (1.5 miles) TIME 1.5 hours without stops
START POINT Monument a Colom 🚇 Drassanes ➕ 201 D1
END POINT Palau de Mar 🚇 Barceloneta ➕ 201 E1

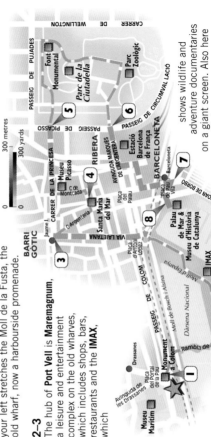

1–2

Start with the **Monument a Colom** (▶ 117) behind you. Before you begin the walk, you could detour to the **Drassanes**, once the hub of Barcelona's ship industry. These 13th-century shipyards functioned through to the 18th century but now house the **Museu Marítim** (Maritime Museum), a fascinating collection of all things nautical, including a lavish replica of the 16th-century Royal Galley. Due to refurbishment, the museum is only partially open.

Cross the busy road and take the Rambla de Mar walkway across the water towards the Maremagnum centre. Along the waterfront to your left stretches the Moll de la Fusta, the old wharf, now a harbourside promenade.

2–3

The hub of **Port Vell** is **Maremagnum**, a leisure and entertainment complex on the old wharves, which includes shops, bars, restaurants and the **IMAX**, which shows wildlife and adventure documentaries on a giant screen. Also here is the **Aquàrium de Barcelona**, a state-of-the-art exhibition focusing on Mediterranean sea life. Leave this area and cross the road at the east end of the Moll de la Fusta to head up the wide Via Laietana. Here you're on the fringes of the Barri Gòtic (▶ 112–115). Continue to Plaça de Jaume I.

3–4

Branch diagonally right down Carrer Argentera to the superb Catalan-Gothic church of **Santa Maria del Mar**. Built between 1324 and 1329 on the orders of Jaume II, it originally stood on the seashore, hence the name, Our Lady of the Sea. A tribute to medieval Catalan maritime power, the soaring columns rise above a wide nave, drawing the eye up to the beautiful vaulting.

4–5

Leave the church and walk north up Carrer de Montcada, a 14th-century street lined with mansions built around central courtyards, which is home to the **Museu Picasso** (▶ 118–119). This area is called **La Ribera** (the waterfront), once medieval Barcelona's trading and maritime district and now buzzing with bars, cafés and galleries. At the top, turn right along Carrer de la Princesa, then cross the Passeig de Picasso to enter the **Parc de la Ciutadella**.

5–6

The Ciutadella park gets its name from the Bourbon fortress, built in 1715 and mostly demolished in 1869. The surviving portion is home to the Catalan parliament. Amid the tranquil formal greenery, you'll find an ebullient baroque fountain, and, in the southeast corner, **Parc Zoològic**, the city's zoo.

6–7

Leave the park, cross the road and walk down Avinguda Marquès de l'Argentera before turning left by the station and crossing the road into **La Barceloneta**. It's an attractive corner, with its long narrow streets and small squares, but the main draw is the plethora of excellent **fish and seafood restaurants**. Turn right towards the sea to emerge on the Passeig de Joan de Borbó.

7–8

Turn right and walk along the landscaped waterfront towards the old warehouse called the **Palau de Mar**. Beautifully renovated, this now houses bars, restaurants and the **Museu d'Història de Catalunya** (Catalan History Museum) which tells the story of the region and the city from neolithic to modern times.

PLACES TO VISIT

Museu Marítim
➕ 201 D2 ✉ Avinguda de les Drassanes 1
☎ 933 429 920; www.mmb.cat ⏰ Daily 10–8
💰 Moderate

Aquàrium de Barcelona
➕ 201 D1 ✉ Moll d'Espanya, Port Vell
☎ 932 217 474; www.aquariumbcn.com
⏰ Jul–Aug daily 9:30am–11pm; Sep–Jun 9:30–9
💰 Expensive

Santa Maria del Mar
➕ 201 E2 ✉ Plaça de Santa Maria 1 ☎ 933
102 390 ⏰ Daily 9–1:30, 4:30–8 💰 Free

Parc Zoològic
➕ 201 F2 ✉ Parc de la Ciutadella ☎ 902 457
545; www.zoobarcelona.com ⏰ Mar–May daily
10–6; Jun–Sep 10–7; Oct–Feb 10–5 💰 Expensive

Museu d'Història de Catalunya
➕ 201 E1 ✉ Plaça de Pau Vila 3 ☎ 932 254
700; www.mhcat.net ⏰ Tue and Thu–Sat 10–7,
Wed 10–8, Sun 10–2:30 💰 Inexpensive

4 HEART OF SEVILLE

Walk

This varied walk takes you along some of Seville's most spacious boulevards, through the shady Parque de María Luisa and along the Guadalquivir river then back to the commercial heart of the city. There's plenty to see en route, so allow time for museum visiting, relaxing in the shade and a spot of retail therapy to finish off.

DISTANCE 3km (2 miles) **TIME** Allow around 3 hours to give time for sight-seeing en route
START POINT Puerta de Jerez
END POINT Calle de Sierpes

1–2

Start your walk in Calle San Fernando with the ritzy Hotel Alfonso XIII on your right. Walk up Calle San Fernando and past the grandiose Fábrica de Tabacos. This massive building, constructed in the 19th century and served as a cigarette factory in the 19th century and was the setting for Bizet's *Carmen*. Today, it houses part of the University. At the junction, turn right down Avenida del Cid to the next busy intersection.

2–3

Cross the road here and bear right along Avenida Isabel la Católica. You're now in the spacious area of the city that was developed for the 1929 Ibero-American Expo. One block down, on the left, is the **Plaza de España**, popular with both locals and tourists. This wide semicircular complex, complete with fountains, waterways, monumental staircases and dazzling tilework, was the centrepiece of the Americas Fair and where Spanish industry and crafts were exhibited.

3–4

Cross the road and walk down Avenida Rodríguez Caso which runs into the **Parque de María Luisa**. The park – shady, green and cool – was laid out in the 19th century, and it's scattered with sumptuous pavilions and mansions that were intended to house more exhibits at the Fair. Take any of the footpaths on the left and head through the park, past the lake, and on to the **Plaza de América**. This is surrounded by opulent 1929 structures, two of which house museums, the **Museo Arqueológico** (Archaeological Museum) and the **Museo de Artes y Costumbres Populares**, devoted to traditional everyday life in Andalucía.

The Torre del Oro on the banks of the Guadalquivir

Calle Sierpes

7

0   300 metres

4–5

From the plaza, walk west (straight ahead) towards the Canal Alfonso XIII then turn right down

Paseo las Delicias. Continue to the second bridge (Puente de San Telmo), where the road becomes Paseo Cristobal Colón.

Across the river lies the vibrant **Triana** district, the traditional home of Seville's gypsy flamenco dynasties. Continue down Paseo Cristobal Colón. On your left is the **Torre del Oro** (Tower of Gold), once aptly covered in gold, which was built in 1220 by the Almohad dynasty as part of a defence system running from

the Alcázar across the river. It now houses Seville's maritime museum. Further down, across the road, lies the **Plaza de Toros**, one of the oldest and most prestigious bullrings in Spain. Once built of wood, the present 14,000-seat ring was constructed around the imposing Prince's Balcony, and is actually oval, rather than round.

5–6

To the south of the bullring, cut down Calle de Antonia Díaz then turn right on to Calle Adriano, and continue straight on until you hit the Avenida de la Constitución with the cathedral across the road in front of you.

6–7

Turn left, cross the road, and walk down to the Plaza San Francisco, where you can turn left to walk down **Calle Sierpes**, a wide pedestrian-only street lined with expensive designer boutiques which lies at the heart of Seville's shopping district.

PLACES TO VISIT

Museo Arqueológico

⊠ Plaza de América ☎ 954 786 474 ⊙ Wed–Sat 9–8, Tue 2:30–8, Sun 9–2 ⊕ Inexpensive, free for EU citizens

Museo de Artes y Costumbres Populares

⊠ Plaza de América ☎ 954 232 576 ⊙ Wed–Sat 9–8, Tue 2:30–8, Sun 9–2 ⊕ Inexpensive, free for EU citizens

Torre del Oro

⊠ Paseo de Cristobal Colón s/n ☎ 954 222 419 ⊙ Sep–Jul Tue–Fri 10–2, Sat–Sun 11–2 ⊕ Inexpensive, free for EU citizens

Plaza de Toros

⊠ Paseo de Cristobal Colón 12 ☎ 902 223 500; www.realmaestranza.com ⊙ Daily 9:30–7; bullfight days 9:30–3; guided tours every half-hour in Spanish ⊕ Moderate

5 THE PUEBLOS BLANCOS AND THE SIERRAS

Drive

This beautiful drive takes you from within a stone's throw of the Atlantic through fertile countryside to the high inland sierras behind the coast. En route you can explore some of Andalucía's prettiest settlements – the *pueblos blancos*, the white towns, and enjoy some of the finest mountain scenery in southern Spain.

DISTANCE 201km (125 miles) **TIME** 4.5 hours driving, but allow all day. You could spread this drive over two days, with an overnight stop at Grazalema or Ronda
START POINT Vejer de la Frontera ✚ 215 D2 **END POINT** Jimena de la Frontera ✚ 215 D2

Vejer de la Frontera, a *pueblo blanco* of white houses

1–2

At the bottom of the hill below **Vejer de la Frontera** (▶ 171), turn left inland off the N340 on to the 396 across rolling, fertile, agricultural land to **Medina-Sidonia**. *Medina* is an Arabic word meaning "city", and Medina-Sidonia is one of the least-known and loveliest of the *pueblos blancos*. It's best to park outside the town and explore the narrow streets on foot, making sure you see the spacious tree-lined main square, the Moorish castle ruins and the parish church, built on the site of a mosque.

Natural Sierra de Grazalema

and the pass at **Puerto del Boyar** (1,103m/3,618ft). This pass is an important funnel for bird migration and you can see griffon vultures wheeling overhead at any time of year. Through the pass, picturesque **Grazalema** lies ahead. Its setting against a rocky backdrop, the ochre tiled roofs, sparkling white houses and its lovely main plaza all combine to make this one of the prettiest of the *pueblos blancos*.

2–3

Take the 389 (signposted **Paterna de Rivera**), then **Arcos de la Frontera**) all the way to **Arcos de la Frontera**, turning left on to the 382 as you approach the town. Dramatically situated Arcos sprawls down a ridge, a warren of dazzling white streets, fine churches and splendid mansions. Walk up through the town, following the signs to the *conjunto histórico* (historic quarter), and you'll arrive in the Plaza del Cabildo, where there's a stunning *mirador* (viewpoint) overlooking the surrounding countryside.

3–4

Leave **Arcos** on the 372 and head east towards **El Bosque**. You'll pass tiny Benamahoma before climbing steadily into the mountains of the **Parque**

4–5

Leave **Grazalema** on the 372. Continue through the cork forest on the 372, turning right on

TAKING A BREAK

Pause in Grazalema, one of the prettiest *pueblos blancos*, and perhaps have lunch at **Restaurante Cádiz el Chico** (Plaza de España 8; tel: 956 132 027. Closed first two weeks in Jun), where you can sample their delicious roast lamb.

to the 374 at the junction just after you leave the Parque (signposted Ronda 17). After 2km (1 mile) turn right towards Montejaque, Benaoján and Cueva de la Pileta. If you want to visit **Ronda** (▶ 170) as part of the drive, continue straight on here and backtrack later. At **Montejaque**, turn left following signs to **Benaoján** and **Ronda** and **Cueva de la Pileta**. Stop for a while to explore this labyrinthine system of caves, where you can see a series of spectacular prehistoric paintings (guided tours hourly).

5–6
Continue on same road for 5.5km (3.5 miles) then turn left (signposted **Jimena de la Frontera**). After 7km (4.5 miles) turn right on to 369, a spectacular ridge route, to **Gaucin**. With its crag-top setting and superb defensive position, it's easy to see why this village was once renowned as a bandit's stronghold – from its castle you can see Gibraltar on a clear day.

6–7
Take the 405 and continue to **Jimena de la Frontera**, topped by a Moorish castle, branching on to the C3331 to reach the town, or continuing on the 405 to the coast

The old Moorish castle rising above the little town of Guacin

Practicalities

BEFORE YOU GO

WHAT YOU NEED

	Some countries require a passport to remain valid for a minimum period (usually at least six months) beyond the date of entry – check beforehand.	UK	Germany	USA	Canada	Australia	Ireland	Netherlands	Spain
● Required ○ Suggested ▲ Not required △ Not applicable									
Passport/National Identity Card		●	●	●	●	●	●	●	●
Visa (regulations can change – check before you travel)		▲	▲	▲	▲	▲	▲	▲	▲
Onward or Return Ticket		▲	▲	▲	▲	●	▲	▲	▲
Health Inoculations		▲	▲	▲	▲	▲	▲	▲	▲
Health Documentation (▶ 194, Health)		○	○	△	△	△	○	○	○
Travel Insurance		○	○	○	○	○	○	○	○
Driving Licence (international/national) for car hire		●	●	●	●	●	●	●	●
Car Insurance Certificate (if using own car)		●	●	△	△	△	●	●	△
Car Registration Document (if using own car)		●	●	△	△	△	●	●	△

WHEN TO GO

Madrid

High season   Low season

JAN	FEB	MAR	APR	MAY	JUN	JUL	AUG	SEP	OCT	NOV	DEC
43°F	50°F	57°F	63°F	68°F	79°F	90°F	86°F	75°F	64°F	53°F	50°F
6°C	10°C	14°C	17°C	20°C	26°C	32°C	30°C	24°C	18°C	12°C	10°C

☀ Sun   ⛅ Sunshine and showers   🌧 Wet   ☁ Cloudy

Because of its size and geography, Spain has a very varied climate. The Mediterranean coast and the south generally have mild, wet winters and long hot summers, with most of the rainfall occurring in the autumn. The winter months, after the rain, are ideal here, where spring comes early. It can rain throughout the year in the northern regions, with Cantabria and Galicia having the highest rainfall in the country. This makes high summer in the north less searingly hot than in central Spain or further south, where the heat is punctuated throughout the summer months by dramatic thunderstorms. July and August in the south bring a hot, dry wind from Africa. Winter in inland Spain can be bitter, with heavy snow and biting winds across the central plateau. Central and southern Spain are at their best in spring, while the optimum time to visit the northern coast and the mountainous regions is the summer.

GETTING ADVANCE INFORMATION

Websites
■ www.tourspain.es
■ www.spain.info is the Spanish National Tourist Office

■ Go Spain (links to a large number of Spanish sites): www.gospain.org

In the UK
Spanish National Tourist Office, PO Box 4009, London W1A 6NB
☎ (020) 7486 8077; brochure line 08459 400 180. Visits by appointment

GETTING THERE

By Air Spain's international airports include Madrid, Barcelona, Alicante, Bilbao, Oviedo, Santiago, Málaga, Seville, València, Jerez and Murcia.

From the UK these are served by Spain's international carrier, Iberia (tel: 807 123 456, www.iberia.com), British Airways (tel: 0845 77 333 77, www.britishairways.com), EasyJet (tel: 0870 600 0000, www.easyjet.com), and numerous no-frills airlines including Ryanair (tel: 807 22 00 222, www.ryanair.com), Air 2000 (tel: 0871 200 7799, www.firstchoice. co.uk) and Jet2.com (tel: 0906 302 0660, www.jet2.com). Flying time is 2–3 hours.

From the US Iberia (tel: toll free 800/772-4642) flies non-stop from New York, Miami and Chicago to Madrid, with connecting flights on to other Spanish airports. Other US airlines fly direct from the east coast to Madrid, while Delta Airlines also operates a non-stop service to Barcelona. Flying time from New York is around 7 hours.

Ticket prices are lower from November to March, excluding Christmas and Easter. All airport taxes are normally included in the ticket price.

By Sea Ferries run from the UK direct to Santander and Bilbao. Brittany Ferries (tel: 0871 244 0744, www.brittany-ferries.co.uk) operates from Plymouth to Santander with a sailing time of 24 hours, while P & O ferries (tel: 0871 664 5645, www.poferries.com) runs from Portsmouth to Bilbao and takes 36 hours. An alternative is to cross the Channel by ferry or through the Eurotunnel and travel through France to Spain.

By Rail UK travellers can get to Spain by train, either making the Channel crossing by ferry or taking the Eurostar as far as Paris. Journey times are around 17 hours to Barcelona by ferry and train, and 19 hours to Madrid. The Eurostar option takes roughly 20–22 hours. If you plan to use trains in Spain, try an InterRail Global FlexiPass, which allows for 5- or 10-days travel within either a 10-day or 22-day period.

TIME

Spain is one hour ahead of Greenwich Mean Time (GMT).

CURRENCY AND FOREIGN EXCHANGE

Currency The Spanish unit of currency is the euro (€). There are seven euro bank **notes**: €5, €10, €20, € 50, €100, €200 and €500. **Coins** come in denominations of 1, 2, 5, 10, 20 and 50 cents and €1 and €2. **Traveller's cheques** are a convenient way to carry money. **Credit cards** are widely accepted and can also be used for cash advances at banks as well as for withdrawing money from ATMs. Photo proof of identity is usually required to use a card in a shop.

Exchange You can exchange foreign currency and traveller's cheques at *bancos* (banks), *cajas de ahorros* (savings banks) and *casas de cambio* (bureaux de change). Banks generally offer better rates and lower commission charges. The department store El Corte Inglés also offers excellent exchange facilities. You will need your passport.

In the USA
Spanish National Tourist Office, 35th Floor, 666 5th Avenue
New York NY 10103
☎ 212/265-8822

Spanish National Tourist Office, 8383 Wilshire Blvd Suite 960
Beverley Hills CA 90211
☎ 323/658-7188

In Canada
Spanish National Tourist Office, 2 Bloor West, Suite 3402, Toronto, Ontario
M4W 3E2
☎ 416/961-3131

WHEN YOU ARE THERE

NATIONAL HOLIDAYS

1 Jan	New Year's Day
6 Jan	Epiphany
Mar/Apr	Good Friday, Easter Monday
1 May	Labour Day
15 Aug	Assumption of the Virgin
12 October	Americas Day
1 Nov	All Saints' Day
6 December	Constitution Day
8 Dec	Feast of the Immaculate Conception
25 Dec	Christmas Day

The autonomous regions have their own additional public holidays, and every town in Spain celebrates its patron saint's feast day.

ELECTRICITY

The power supply in Spain is 220/230 volts AC. Sockets accept two-pin round plugs so British appliances will need a two-pin adaptor. North Americans will need this plus a transformer; these are hard to find in Spain, so it's best to bring one with you.

OPENING HOURS

○ Shops ● Post Offices
● Offices ● Museums/Monuments
● Banks ● Pharmacies

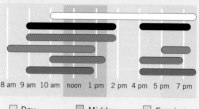

8 am 9 am 10 am noon 1 pm 2 pm 4 pm 5 pm 7 pm

☐ Day ☐ Midday ☐ Evening

Shops Smaller shops often close for lunch and on Saturday afternoon. Tourist-oriented shops and hypermarkets open longer.
Banks Banks close Saturdays April to October. *Casas de cambio* open late daily and some also open on Sunday.
Pharmacies Pharmacies close on Saturday afternoon, but at least one chemist in town remains open at the weekend.

TIPS/GRATUITIES

Tipping is expected for all services. As a general guide, the following applies:

Restaurants (if service not included)	5–10%
Bar Service	Change
Tour Guides	Optional
Chambermaids	€6
Porters	€6

ADDRESSES

In Spain, the abbreviation "s/n" signifies a house or building that does not have a street number (*sin número*). The abbreviation "Urb", short for *urbanización*, is used as part of the address for newer developments.

TIME DIFFERENCES

GMT	Spain	USA New York	Germany	France	Australia
12 noon	1pm	7am	1pm	1pm	Sydney 10pm

STAYING IN TOUCH

Post Post offices (*correos*) are normally central; post boxes are yellow. Buy stamps (*sellos*) at any *tabacos*. *Poste restante* letters can be sent to any Spanish post office; put the surname in capitals and underlined and send them to *Lista de Correos* followed by the name of the town and province.

Public telephones The blue and green public telephones take coins and phonecards (*tarjetas telefónicas*), which are available from post offices, newspaper kiosks and *estancos* (tobacconists). A few also accept credit cards. Some of the cheapest places to make calls from are *locutorios* (phone centres), often found near rail stations. The cheap rate for international calls is 10pm–8am and all day Sunday.

International Dialling Codes
Dial 00 followed by:

UK	44
USA/Canada	1
Ireland	353
Australia	61
New Zealand	64

Mobile providers and services Except for the most remote areas, Spain has good mobile-phone coverage. Network suppliers include Spain's own Movistar, as well as Vodaphone and Orange. 3G networks for mobile broadband are increasingly common. If you intend to use your phone a lot, buy a local SIM card. This will avoid expensive roaming charges. Spain uses GSM 900/1800, like the rest of Europe and Australia; US and Japanese phone systems are not compatible.

WiFi and internet Many hotels and hostels offer broadband internet access including WiFi, as do some rental apartments. Increasingly, cafés, restaurants – and even some parks – have WiFi areas. There are also cheap internet cafés around bus and train stations and immigrant areas of the larger towns and cities. It costs between €1–€3 to go online for 30 minutes.

PERSONAL SAFETY

- Avoid carrying valuables, documents and large amounts of cash and keep a firm hold of bags in bars, restaurants and around major tourist attractions.
- Pickpocketing and bag snatching are rife around major monuments, as well as at train stations, and on crowded buses and metros. Beware of the distraction techniques employed by pickpockets.
- In a busy environment drawing attention to troublemakers may deter them but in quieter streets, it is best not to struggle.
- If you do have something stolen, your insurance company will require a signed copy of a police statement (*denuncia*), which you can get from a local police station or online at www.policia.es. For the latter option you arrange a time to collect the stamped paper from a local police station.

Police assistance: 091 or 112

EMERGENCY	112
POLICE	112
FIRE	112
AMBULANCE	112

HEALTH

 Insurance Citizens of EU countries receive free or reduced-cost medical treatment with relevant documentation (European Health Insurance Card), but private medical insurance is still advised and essential for all other visitors; without this, EU citizens are charged at private rates. Private medical insurance is strongly recommended, particularly for visitors from the US, Australia and New Zealand.

 Dental Services Dental treatment in Spain is expensive, so check your medical insurance before you go to ensure that it includes dental treatment.

 Weather High temperatures and humidity are common throughout the summer months. Protect against sunburn and dehydration by dressing suitably, applying sunscreen with a high SPF and drinking plenty of water – about 1.5–2 litres daily in hot weather.

 Drugs Prescription and non-prescription drugs and homeopathic remedies, as well as medical advice, are available from pharmacies. Many drugs that are on prescription in other countries are also available over the counter in Spain. Chemists operate a rota so there is always one open 24 hours a day; notices in pharmacy windows give details. If you need to renew a prescription, ask your doctor for the chemical name of the drug, as it may be marketed in Spain under another name.

 Safe Water Tap water is generally safe to drink although not always palatable. Mineral water (*agua mineral*) is widely available.

CONCESSIONS

Students An International Student Identity Card (ISIC) will help obtain free or reduced entry to many museums and sites as well as other discounts.

Senior citizens Senior citizens can get reductions on some museum entry charges on production of an identity document.

TRAVELLING WITH A DISABILITY

Major cities and resorts have hotels adapted for people with disabilities and all new buildings are now, by law, disabled-friendly. Transport remains a problem, as as metros are difficult to access and only the more modern trains have wheelchair facilities. Accommodation out of the main tourist centres is also a problem. Tourist Information offices can provide useful addresses.

CHILDREN

Children are welcome everywhere in Spain. The under 4s travel free on RENFE trains and at a 40 per cent discount between 4–12 years. Local tourist boards have lists of child-friendly attractions. Nappies and baby food are widely available.

TOILETS

Public toilets (*Los Servicios*) are highly variable and sometimes lack paper. Those in museums and galleries are generally clean and free.

TOURIST CARDS

Tourist cards are available in many large cities. These give discounted admission to key sights, as well as free travel and vouchers for shops and restaurants. Contact tourist offices for more information.

EMBASSIES AND HIGH COMMISSIONS

UK	USA	Canada	Australia	Germany
☎ 917 146 400	☎ 915 872 200	☎ 914 223 250	☎ 913 536 600	☎ 915 579 000

USEFUL WORDS AND PHRASES

Spanish (*español*), also known as Castilian (*castellano*) to distinguish it from other tongues spoken in Spain, is related to the French and Italian languages. Apart from certain local and regional variations, every letter is pronounced, with the emphasis usually on the last syllable.

GREETINGS AND COMMON WORDS

Do you speak English? **¿Habla inglés?**
I don't understand **No entiendo**
I don't speak Spanish **No hablo español**
Yes/No **Sí/no**
OK **Vale/de acuerdo**
Please **Por favor**
Thank you (very much) **(Muchas) gracias**
You're welcome **De nada**
Hello/Goodbye **Hola/adiós**
Good morning **Buenos días**
Good afternoon/evening **Buenas tardes**
Good night **Buenas noches**
How are you? **¿Qué tal?**
Excuse me **Perdón**
How much is this? **¿Cuánto vale?**
I'd like... **Quisiera/me gustaría**

EMERGENCY!

Help! **¡Socorro!/¡Ayuda!**
Could you help me please? **¿Podría ayudarme por favor?**
Could you call a doctor? **¿Podría llamar a un médico por favor?**

DIRECTIONS AND TRAVELLING

Aeroplane **Avión**
Airport **Aeropuerto**
Car **Coche**
Boat **Barco**
Bus **Autobús**
Bus stop **Parada de autobús**
Station **Estación**
Ticket (single/return) **Billete (de ida/de ida y vuelta)**
I'm lost **Me he perdido**
Where is...? **¿Dónde está...?**
How do I get to...? **¿Cómo llego a...?**
the beach **la playa**
the telephone **el teléfono**
the toilets **los servicios**
Left/right **Izquierda/derecha**
Straight on **Todo recto**

ACCOMMODATION

Do you have a single/double room available? **¿Tiene una habitación individual/doble?**
with/without bath/toilet/shower **con/sin baño/lavabo/ducha**
Does that include breakfast? **¿Incluye el desayuno?**
Could I see the room? **¿Puedo ver la habitación?**
I'll take this room **Cojo esta habitación**
One night **Una noche**
Key **Llave**
Lift **Ascensor**
Sea views **Vistas al mar**

DAYS

Today	**Hoy**
Tomorrow	**Mañana**
Yesterday	**Ayer**
Later	**Más tarde**
This week	**Esta semana**
Monday	**Lunes**
Tuesday	**Martes**
Wednesday	**Miércoles**
Thursday	**Jueves**
Friday	**iernes**
Saturday	**Sábado**
Sunday	**Domingo**

NUMBERS

0	**cero**	20	**veinte**
1	**uno/una**	21	**veintiuno**
2	**dos**	30	**treinta**
3	**tres**	40	**cuarenta**
4	**cuatro**	50	**cincuenta**
5	**cinco**	60	**sesenta**
6	**seis**	70	**setenta**
7	**siete**	80	**ochenta**
8	**ocho**	90	**noventa**
9	**nueve**	100	**cien**
10	**diez**	101	**ciento uno**
11	**once**	110	**ciento diez**
12	**doce**	120	**ciento veinte**
13	**trece**	200	**doscientos/ cienta**
14	**catorce**		
15	**quince**	500	**quinientos/ quinientas**
16	**dieciséis**		
17	**diecisiete**	1000	**mil**
18	**dieciocho**	5000	**cinco mil**
19	**diecinueve**		

RESTAURANT

I'd like to book a table **Quisiera reservar una mesa**

A table for two please **Una mesa para dos, por favor**

Could we see the menu, please? **¿Nos trae la carta, por favor?**

What's this? **¿Qué es esto?**

A bottle/glass of… **Una botella/copa de…**

Could I have the bill please? **¿La cuenta, por favor?**

Service charge included **Servicio incluido**

Waiter/waitress **Camarero/a**

Breakfast **Desayuno**

Lunch **Almuerzo**

Dinner **Cena**

Menu **La carta**

MENU READER

a la plancha grilled
aceite oil
aceituna olive
agua water
ajo garlic
almendra almond
anchoas anchovies
arroz rice
atún tuna
bacalao cod
berenjena aubergines
bistec steak
bocadillo sandwich
café coffee
calamares squid
cangrejo crab
carne meat
cebolla onion
cerdo pork
cerezas cherries
cerveza beer
champiñones mushrooms
chocolate chocolate
chorizo spicy sausage
chuleta chop
conejo rabbit
cordero lamb
crema cream
crudo raw
cubierto(s) cover (cutlery)
cuchara spoon
cuchillo knife
embutidos sausages
ensalada salad
entrante starter
espárragos asparagus
filete fillet
flan crème caramel
frambuesa raspberry
fresa strawberry
frito fried
fruta fruit
galleta biscuit
gambas prawns

gazpacho gazpacho (cold soup)
guisantes peas
habas broad beans
helado ice cream
hígado liver
huevos fritos/ revueltos fried/ scrambled eggs
jamón serrano ham (cured)
jamón York ham (cooked)
judías beans
judías verdes French beans
jugo fruit juice
langosta lobster
leche milk
lechuga lettuce
legumbres pulses
lengua tongue
lenguado sole
limón lemon
lomo de cerdo pork tenderloin
mantequilla butter
manzana apple
mariscos seafood
mejillones mussels
melocotón peach
melón melon
merluza hake
mero sea bass
miel honey
naranja orange
ostra oyster
pan bread
patata potato
patatas fritas chips
pato duck
pepinillo gherkin
pepino cucumber
pera pear
perejil parsley
pescado fish

pez espada swordfish
picante hot/spicy
pimientos red/ green peppers
piña pineapple
plátano banana
pollo chicken
postre dessert
primer plato first course
pulpo octopus
queso cheese
rape monkfish
relleno filled/ stuffed
riñones kidneys
salchicha sausage
salchichón salami
salmón salmon
salmonete red mullet
salsa sauce
seco dry
segundo plato main course
solomillo de ternera fillet of beef
sopa soup
té tea
tenedor fork
ternera beef
tocino bacon
tortilla española Spanish omelette
tortilla francesa plain omelette
uva grape
verduras green vegetables
vino blanco/ rosado/ tinto white/rosé/red wine
zanahorias carrots

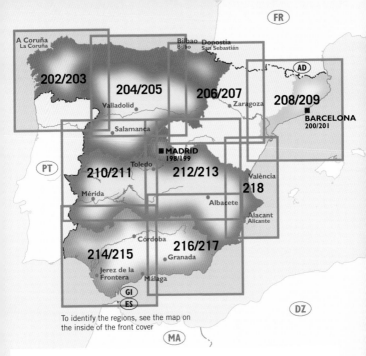

Streetplans

- ══════ Main/other road
- ────── Railway
- ⊙─────⊙ Funicular railway
- ● Metro station
- ─ ─ ─ City wall
- ▮ Important building
- ▮ Park/garden

- ✝ Church
- ☾ Mosque
- *i* Tourist information
- ● Monument/statue
- ✉ Post office
- ▢ Featured place of interest
- ▫ Place of interest

Regional Maps

- ══════ Major route
- ══════ Motorway
- ══════ National dual/single road
- ────── Regional/local road
- ────── Railway
- ▮ National park/ nature reserve

- ✈ Airport
- ▫ Town/village
- ▢ Featured place of interest
- ▫ Place of interest

Atlas

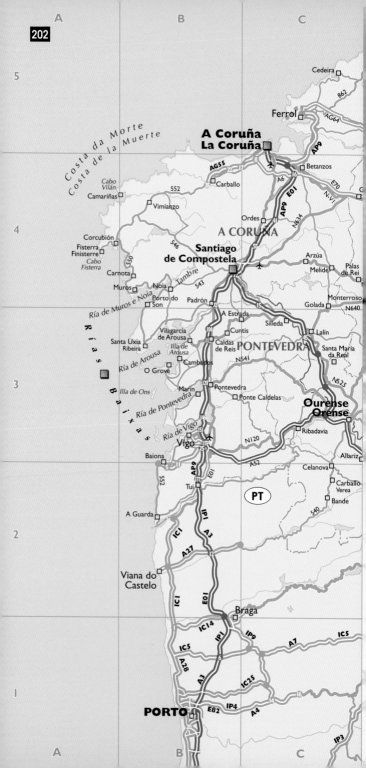

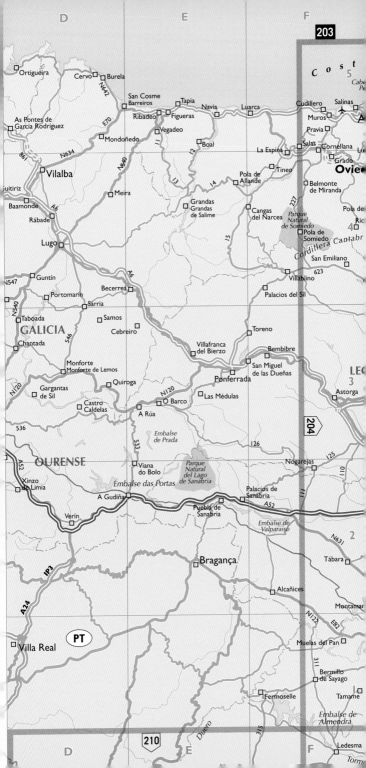

Ortigueira
Cervo
Burela
As Pontes de García Rodríguez
San Cosme Barreiros
Ribadeo
Figueras
Tapia
Navia
Luarca
Cudillero
Salinas
Muros
C o s t
Cabe Pe
Pravia
Vegadeo
Boal
La Espina
Salas
Cornellana
Grado
Ovied
Mondoñedo
Vilalba
Tineo
Pola de Allande
Belmonte de Miranda
Pola de
Ric
4
Baamonde
Rábade
Meira
Grandas
Grandas de Salime
Cangas del Narcea
Parque Natural de Somiedo
Pola de Somiedo
Cordillera Cantabr
uitiriz
Lugo
San Emiliano
Villablino
623
Guntín
Becerreá
Villablino
Palacios del Sil
Portomarín
Sarria
Samos
Cebreiro
Toreno
Taboada
GALICIA
Chantada
Villafranca del Bierzo
Bembibre
San Miguel de las Dueñas
LE
Monforte
Monforte de Lemos
Quiroga
Ponferrada
Astorga
Gargantas de Sil
Castro Caldelas
O Barco
Las Médulas
A Rúa
204
OURENSE
Embalse de Prada
126
125
Viana do Bolo
Parque Natural del Lago de Sanabria
Nogarejas
Xinzo de Limia
Embalse das Portas
Palacios de Sanabria
A Gudiña
Puebla de Sanabria
Verín
Embalse de Valparaíso
N631
2
Bragança
Tábara
Alcañices
Montamar
IP3
A24
Muelas del Pan
PT
Villa Real
Bermillo de Sayago
Tamame
Fermoselle
Embalse de Almendra
210
Duero
Tormo
Ledesma

N642
N634
861
E70
N640
A6
N547
N540
N120
536
A52
533
546
227
11
12
13
14
15
N120
N122
E82
311
315

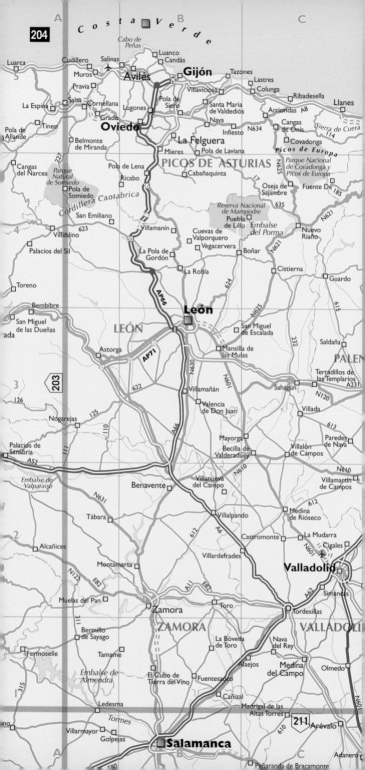

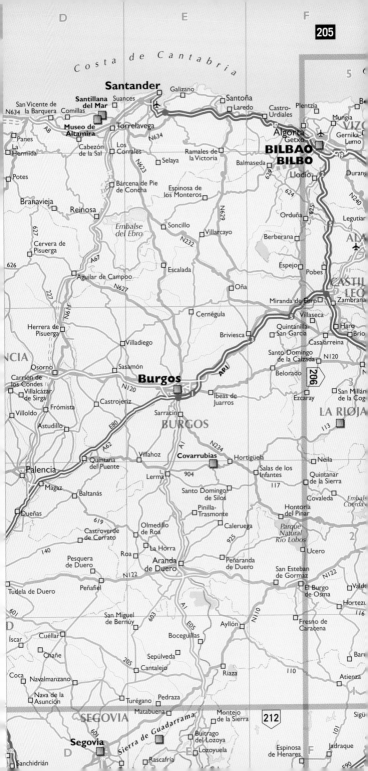

Costa de Cantabria

Santander

Galizano

Santoña

Santillana del Mar

Suances

Laredo

Castro-Urdiales

Plentzia

San Vicente de la Barquera

N634

Comillas

Museo de Altamira

Torrelavega

N634

Algorta Getxo

Mungia

VIZ

Gernika-Lumo

Panes

Cabezón de la Sal

Los Corrales

BILBAO BILBO

La Hermida

Ramales de la Victoria

Selaya

Balmaseda

Potes

Bárcena de Pie de Concha

Espinosa de los Monteros

Llodio

624

Durang

Brañavieja

Reinosa

Soncillo

Villarcayo

N629

Orduña

N240

Legutiar

627

Embalse del Ebro

Berberana

Espejo

ALA

626

Cervera de Pisuerga

N232

Escalada

Pobes

CASTIL LEÓ

227

Aguilar de Campoo

N627

Oña

Miranda de Ebro

Zambrana

Herrera de Pisuerga

Cernégula

Villaseca

N-VI

Villadiego

Briviesca

Quintanilla-San García

Haro

Brio

NCIA

Osorno

Sasamón

Burgos

Santo Domingo de la Calzada

Casalarreina

N120

Carrión de los Condes

N120

AP1

Belorado

206

Villalcázar de Sirga

Castrojeriz

Ibeas de Juarros

Ezcaray

San Millán de la Cog

Villoldo

Frómista

Sarracín

LA RIOJA

Astudillo

E80

BURGOS

113

Palencia

A62

Quintana del Puente

Villahoz

Covarrubias

Hortigüela

Neila

Magaz

Lerma

904

Salas de los Infantes

Quintanar de la Sierra

Baltanás

Santo Domingo de Silos

117

Dueñas

Pinilla-Trasmonte

Caleruega

Hontoria del Pinar

Covaleda

Embals Cuerda

619

Castroverde de Cerrato

Olmedillo de Roa

Parque Natural Río Lobos

Pesquera de Duero

La Horra

925

Ucero

140

Roa

Peñaranda de Duero

Tudela de Duero

N122

Aranda de Duero

San Esteban de Gormaz

N122

Peñafiel

N110

El Burgo de Osma

Valde

Íscar

Cuéllar

San Miguel de Bernúy

603

Ayllón

Hortezu

116

601

505

A1

Fresno de Caracena

Chañe

Boceguillas

Atienza

Coca

Navalmanzano

205

Sepúlveda

110

Bare

Nava de la Asunción

Cantalejo

Riaza

Turégano

Pedraza

SEGOVIA

Matabuena

Montejo de la Sierra

212

Sigü

Segovia

Sierra de Guadarrama

Buitrago del Lozoya

Espinosa de Henares

Jadraque

Sanchidrián

Rascafría

Lozoyuela

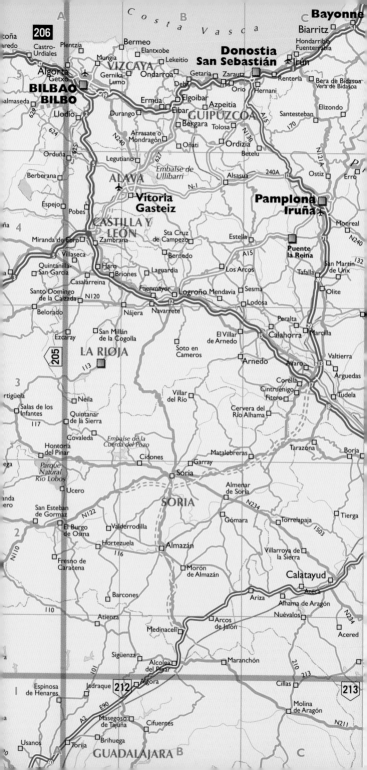

210
203
210

Fermoselle
Tamame

Embalse de
Almendra

315

Duero

Ledesma

Tormes

Vitigudino

517

Villarmayor
Golpejas

Lumbrales

Martín
de Yeltes

Vecinos

SALAMANCA

A62 E80

IP5

E80 A25

Morasverdes

Tamames

205 Las
Veguillas

Fuentes
de Oñoro

Ciudad-Rodrigo

El
Cabaco

Linares
de Riofrío

IP2 E802
E806

El Bodón

Sierra de la Peña Francia

Sequeros
La Alberca

A23

Parque Natural
Las Batuecas

Las Batuecas

Villasrubias 526

Caminomorisco
Las
Hurdes

Lagunilla

Baños

Valverde del Fresno

Embalse de
Gabriel y Galán

Cabezuela
del Valle

Hoyos

Villanueva de
la Sierra

PT

Embalse de
Borbollón

Montehermoso

N110

108 109

Coria 108

Plasencia

Alagón

Parque Natural
Monfragüe

Alcántara

Garrovillas

Embalse de
Alcántara

Torrejón
el Rubio

117

Brozas

CÁCERES

Jaraicejo

Arroyo
de la Luz

Herreruela
N521

Cáceres

Trujillo

Valencia de
Alcántara

Malpartida
de Cáceres

Torrequemada

A5

110

100

Aldea
del Cano

Alburquerque

Montánchez

Puebla de
Obando

Miajadas

106

La Roca de
la Sierra

N430

Villanueva
de la Serena

Aljucén

Embalse de
Los Canchales

Medellín

Don
Benito

E90

Montijo

Mérida

Badajoz

A5 E90

Guareña

A66 N630

Alange

Embalse
de Alange

La Albuera

Almendralejo

Palomas

Olivenza

N432

Villafranca
de los Barros

BADAJOZ

Almendral

Santa
Marta

214

Feria

Villanueva
del Fresno

Zafra

Campillo
de Llerena

Jerez de los

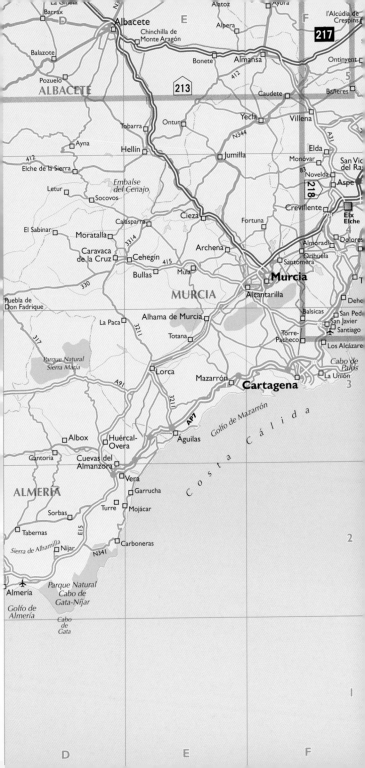

The Automobile Association would like to thank the following photographers, companies and picture libraries for their assistance in the preparation of this book.

Abbreviations for the picture credits are as follows: (t) top; (b) bottom; (l) left; (r) right; (c) centre; (AA) AA World Travel Library.

2i AA/C Sawyer; 2ii AA/M Jourdan; 2iii AA/R Strange; 2iv AA/P Enticknap; 2v AA/S Watkins; 3i AA/M Bonnet; 3ii AA/M Chaplow; 3iii AA/M Chaplow; 3iv AA/M Jourdan; 5l AA/C Sawyer; 5c AA/M Chaplow; 5r AA/M Jourdan; 7 Photolibrary Group; 8 AA; 9 Photolibrary Group; 11 AA/M Bonnet; 14/15 AA/M Bonnet; 14 AA/M Bonnet; 16 The Art Archive/Tavera Hospital Toledo; 17 The Persistence of Memory, 1931 (oil on canvas), Dali, Salvador (1904–89/Museum of Modern Art, New York, USA/© DACS/The Bridgeman Art Library; 18/19 AA/M Jourdan; 20/21 Photolibrary Group; 22/23 AA/J A Tims; 23 AA/P Enticknap; 24t AA/M Jourdan; 24c AA/M Jourdan; 24b AA/M Jourdan; 25 Sipa Press/Rex Features; 26/27 Photolibrary Group; 28 AA/S Watkins; 29l AA/M Jourdan; 29c AA/M Jourdan; 29r AA/T Carter; 41l AA/R Strange; 41c AA/M Chaplow; 41r AA/M Jourdan; 42 AA/M Chaplow; 43 Photolibrary Group; 44 AA/M Jourdan; 45 AA/M Chaplow; 47 AA/M Jourdan; 48 AA/M Jourdan; 49 AA/M Jourdan; 50 AA/M Jourdan; 51 ©The Gallery Collection/Corbis; 52 Execution of the Defenders of Madrid, 3rd May, 1808, 1814 (oil on canvas), Goya y Lucientes, Francisco Jose de (1746–1828)/ Prado, Madrid, Spain/The Bridgeman Art Library; 54 AA/M Chaplow; 55 ©Melba Photo Agency/Alamy; 56 AA/M Jourdan; 57 AA/R Strange; 65l AA/P Enticknap; 65c AA/S Watkins; 65r AA/S Watkins; 67t AA/M Chaplow; 67b AA/M Chaplow; 68 AA/S Watkins; 70 AA/M Jourdan; 71 AA/M Jourdan; 73 AA/M Jourdan; 74/75 AA/M Chaplow; 75 AA/M Chaplow; 76 AA/M Chaplow; 78/79 AA/S Watkins; 80 AA/M Jourdan; 81 AA/M Jourdan; 82 AA/P Enticknap; 87l AA/S Watkins; 87c AA/M Chaplow; 87r AA/M Jourdan; 89t AA/M Jourdan; 89b AA/M Jourdan; 90 AA/M Jourdan; 91 AA/M Jourdan; 92/93 AA/M Jourdan; 93 Photolibrary Group; 94 AA/P Enticknap; 95 AA/M Jourdan; 96 AA/M Jourdan; 97 Photolibrary Group; 99 AA/M Jourdan; 101 AA/P Enticknap; 102 AA/S Watkins; 103 Photolibrary Group; 107l AA/M Bonnet; 107c AA/M Bonnet; 107r AA/M Bonnet; 108 AA/M Chaplow; 109 AA/M Bonnet; 110 AA/M Bonnet; 112/113 AA/M Bonnet; 114t AA/M Chaplow; 114b AA/M Bonnet; 115 AA/S Day; 116 AA/M Bonnet; 117 AA/M Bonnet; 118 AA/M Bonnet; 119 AA/M Bonnet; 120/121 AA/M Bonnet; 122 AA/M Bonnet; 123 AA/M Bonnet; 124 AA/M Bonnet; 126 AA/M Bonnet; 127 AA/M Bonnet; 128 AA/S Watkins; 129 AA/M Bonnet; 130 AA/P Enticknap; 135l AA/M Bonnet; 135c AA/J Edmanson; 135r AA/M Chaplow; 137t AA/M Chaplow; 137b AA/J Edmanson; 138 AA/M Chaplow; 139 AA/M Chaplow; 140/141 AA/J Edmanson; 143 AA/M Chaplow; 145 Photolibrary Group; 146/147 AA/J Edmanson; 148 AA/M Chaplow; 149 AA/M Chaplow; 150 AA/M Chaplow; 151 AA/J Edmanson; 155l AA/M Chaplow; 155c AA/P Wilson; 155r AA/J Edmanson; 156 AA/D Robertson; 157 AA/P Wilson; 158 AA/P Wilson; 159 AA/M Chaplow; 160/161 AA/J Edmanson; 162 AA/P Wilson; 164 AA/M Chaplow; 166/167 AA/D Robertson; 168 AA/D Robertson; 169 AA/D Robertson; 170 AA/J Poulsen; 171 AA/P Wilson; 177l AA/M Jourdan; 177c AA/M Bonnet; 177r AA/P Wilson; 178 AA/M Jourdan; 180 AA/S Watkins; 181 AA/S Watkins; 184 © Ken Wilson; 186 AA/M Chaplow; 188 AA/J Poulsen; 189l AA/S Watkins; 189c AA/M Bonnet; 189r AA/M Bonnet

Every effort has been made to trace the copyright holders, and we apologise in advance for any accidental errors. We would be happy to apply any corrections in the following edition of this publication.

SPIRAL GUIDES

Questionnaire

Dear Traveler

Your comments, opinions and recommendations are very important to us. So please help us to improve our travel guides by taking a few minutes to complete this simple questionnaire. Thank you.

Your recommendations...

We always encourage readers' recommendations for restaurants, nightlife or shopping – if your recommendation is added to the next edition of the guide, we will send you a FREE AAA Spiral Guide of your choice. Please state below the establishment name, location and your reasons for recommending it.

Send to: Spiral Guides, MailStop 64, 1000 AAA Drive, Heathrow, FL 32746–5063

About this guide...

Which title did you buy?

Where did you buy it?

When? m m / y y

Why did you choose a AAA Spiral Guide?

Did this guide meet your expectations?
Please give your reasons.

Exceeded ☐ Met all ☐ Met most ☐
Fell below ☐

Were there any aspects of this guide that you particularly liked or thought could have been done better.

About you...
Name (Mr/Mrs/Ms)

Address

Zip

Daytime tel nos

Which age group are you in?

Under 25 ☐ 25-34 ☐ 35-44 ☐ 45-54 ☐
55-64 ☐ 65+ ☐

How many trips do you make a year?
Less than one ☐ One ☐ Two ☐ Three or more ☐
Are you a AAA member? Yes ☐ No ☐
Name of AAA club

About your trip...

When did you book? m m / y y
When did you travel? m m / y y
How long did you stay?
Was it for business or leisure?
Did you buy any other travel guides for your trip?
Yes ☐ No ☐
If yes, which ones?

All information is for AAA internal use only and will NOT be distributed outside the organization to any third parties.

Please send me AAA Spiral
(see list of titles inside the back cover)

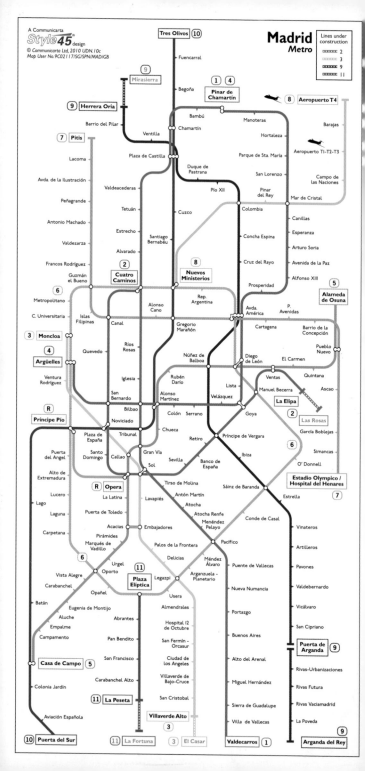